SIGNPOST BIOGRAPHY

James Welwood

SIGNPOST BIOGRAPHY

James Welwood

Physician to the Glorious Revolution

Elizabeth Lane Furdell

COMBINED PUBLISHING
Pennsylvania

PUBLISHER'S NOTE

The headquarters of Combined Publishing are located midway between Valley Forge and the Germantown battlefield, on the outskirts of Philadelphia. From its beginnings, our company has been steeped in the oldest traditions of American history and publishing. Our historic surroundings help maintain our focus on history and our books strive to uphold the standards of style, quality and durability first established by the earliest bookmakers of Germantown and Philadelphia so many years ago. Our famous monk-and-console logo reflects our commitment to the modern and yet historic enterprise of publishing.

We call ourselves Combined Publishing because we have always felt that our goals could only be achieved through a "combined" effort by authors, publishers and readers. We have always tried to maintain maximum communication between these three key players in the reading experience.

We are always interested in hearing from prospective authors about new books in our field. We also like to hear from our readers and invite you to contact us at our offices in Pennsylvania with any questions, comments or suggestions, or if you have difficulty finding our books at a local bookseller.

For information, address:
Combined Publishing
P.O. Box 307
Conshohocken, PA 19428
E-mail: combined@dca.net
Web: www.dca.net/combinedbooks
Orders: 1-800-418-6065

Library of Congress Cataloging-in-Publication Data available

ISBN 1-58097-005-2

Printed in the United States of America.

For Lizzie and in memory of my mother and father

Contents

Preface to the Series

BIOGRAPHY IS THE SOUL OF HISTORY—THE STORIES OF INDIVIDUAL lives that give meaning and life to the past, and allow the reader to share vicariously in the drama of other times and places. It the classic form of historical narrative, for it is through the lives of individual men and women that we can best come to comprehend the complexities of other ages. At the same time, good biography does not reduce the past to "Great Men"—and occasionally women. Rather, it appreciates the limits we all face in defining our lives, whether imposed by social forces beyond our control, the framework in which we interpret reality and opportunity, or our own limited experience and knowledge. Biography reflects the human condition: our actions, our decisions, our thinking have consequences. Biography also reflects and illuminates the world in which its subjects lived, an expression of another time and place.

Signpost Biographies are designed to bring the past alive through the stories of individuals whose lives have helped make their world, and whose lives provide the modern reader with an opportunity to be part of that world. Biographies in the series reflect the best in contemporary historical scholarship while never forgetting that the essence of history is storytelling, and that good history is also good literature. The subjects of Signpost Biographies are men and women whose lives were inherently interesting, often spanning a broad range of endeavors, and whose stories provide insight into their world. They include men and women from different cultures and social positions, those who protested their age as well as those who guided it. Among our authors are both professional historians and compelling writers with a love of historical scholarship.

James Welwood participated fully in the complex, dynamic world of seventeenth-century England as physician, publicist, scholar, courtier. His life reflects the opportunities and possibilities of that age: raised in remote Scotland of a family of modest means, he skillfully combined innate intelligence, professional credentials, and carefully-cultivated connections into a formidable career as a "gentleman-scholar" and "man of affairs." On one level Welwood reflects modernity: the opinion-maker on the edge of power, never quite in charge but always present, impossible to ignore. At the same time, Welwood embodied the very particular qualities and contradictions of his own age, from his almost fanatical hatred of Catholicism to his craving for tolerance and reasonableness, the latter inspired, no doubt, by his own youthful memories of witch hunts. Like his contemporaries, Welwood recognized no separation between his profession and politics. His was a time of universal interests, not narrow specialization. Politics, broadly defined, was the arena for discourse among educated elites, and professional credentials provided entree into that world.

Elizabeth Furdell brings to this compelling biography a lifetime bringing the past to life as a teacher and scholar of seventeenth-century England. She engages us in Welwood's own story while at the same time immersing us in his world in such a way that Welwood becomes our escort and our metaphor for his own life and times. Indeed, it is precisely the broad range of experiences and activities that make Welwood so appropriate a guide for that dramatic period of English history that still captures our imagination today.

James Welwood was an important participant in the England of religious persecution, civil wars, and constitutional formation, of ill-fated Stuarts and Glorious Revolution. Furdell's biography makes available Welwood's story and that of his age for the contemporary reader.

Author's Preface

MY "DISCOVERY" OF JAMES WELWOOD, M.D., WAS SERENDIPITOUS. Over the past several years, I have been engaged in developing a prosopography, a collective biography, of the physicians, surgeons, and apothecaries who provided health care for the Tudor-Stuart era monarchs (1485-1714). However, some of the individuals, not all of them giants in the medical world, resist amalgamation; some of their lives merit specific recall. As a result, biographies of British royal doctors like Thomas Linacre, William Harvey, John Arbuthnot, and Hans Sloane line many a library shelf. There are far more medicos below those celebrated physicians whom contemporaries counted as noted men of their age, professional successes whose life stories warrant better attention than short entries in the *Dictionary of National Biography*.

While doing archival research on these royal doctors, I accumulated some routine biographical information on Welwood, but his involvement late in life as a go-between in a Georgian triangle compelled me to study him further. That rather salacious aspect of an otherwise upright career lured me into examining all of his writings and all of those done about him. An extraordinary man emerged, a man of prodigious courage and philosophical consistency, who combined professional success with political activity during dangerous times. Though becoming an advocate for one's subject is a pitfall for biographers, I found my admiration for James Welwood growing the more I perused his works. Several episodes in Welwood's long life intrigued me further and I composed a short article about him for the

Royal Society of Medicine. Nevertheless, for a number of reasons, not the least of which is his principled courage, I believe he deserves much more attention; I continue to marvel that no biographer before me has found his life not only intrinsically interesting but illuminating to an era. Luckily, Michael Burke of Combined Publishing's Signpost series shared my enthusiasm for Welwood as a touchstone for Britain's Augustan Age (1680-1730) and agreed to serve as the project editor. His encouragement and advice shaped the direction of this work from start to finish. Senior Editor Kenneth S. Gallagher improved the clarity of the final copy.

Like most works of scholarship, this effort resulted from a combination of research in public and private archives with further exploration of published primary and secondary sources via my home institution. Today's historian faces the dizzying challenge of working with fragile, original manuscripts, with sturdier microfilmed records available through inter-library loan, and at institutional websites in cyberspace on the internet. More helpful hands than ever before are needed to make the researcher's task possible amidst the many varieties of documents. Part of my work was done in London repositories over several summers. While there, I resided at Crosby Hall in Chelsea, a historical haven for female academics that no longer exists. Shortly after my last stay, the British Federation of University Women sold the building to a wealthy stockbroker who transformed it from a dormitory into a private riverside mansion. I miss the place and the intellectual camaraderie it provided for distaff scholars far from home. Nevertheless, thanks must be tendered to BFUW for maintaining the residence for as long as possible.

I owe a measure of gratitude to the staffs of several London libraries and archives including the Manuscripts Room at the British Library, the Manuscripts Division of the National Library of Scotland, the Royal College of Surgeons, the Wellcome Institute, Tyne and Wear Archives Service, the Herald College, the Society of Antiquaries of London, the Corporate Affairs Archives at the Royal Bank of Scotland, and the Public Record Office, Chancery Lane and Kew. The author is grateful to Librarian Geoffrey Davenport and the Royal College of Physicians for permission to quote from the appropriate volumes of its *Annals*. Norman Reid, Keeper of the Manuscripts at the University of

St. Andrews, provided me with invaluable information. The University of North Florida has a fine group of librarians who aided me in my quest for microfilm and arcane books. Express mention needs to be made of Barbara Tuck, who gave me resource leads and encouragement along the way, and Alisa Craddock, inter-library loan specialist. Jennifer Weisflog Kastensmidt tracked down miscellaneous information for me from the University of Florida whenever I needed help.

I am indebted to a number of scholars who generously shared bibliographic and personal findings with me. Working as the only British historian on my campus is no longer a severe handicap, thanks to electronic networks like H-Albion. I am particularly beholden to Harold Cook, Anita Guerrini, Mordechai Feingold, Daniel Szechi, Robert Palmer, Michael Landon, Mark Goldie, J. D. Alsop, Barney Cochran, Sara Mendelson, James Carrier, Sharon Arnoult, Paul J. Voss, Beryl Diamond, Edward Furgol, and Robert Frank for their miscellaneous suggestions and cautions. My good fortune extends to supportive departmental colleagues, especially to my husband and fellow Europeanist, Theophilus Prousis, always ready with challenges and questions to make the material better. I must also thank my sons: James, for his technological expertise, and Andrew, for enduring a writer's eccentricities. Whatever errors or omissions that remain are my doing, but I hope that Dr. Welwood would appreciate the finished product.

A few caveats need be mentioned before I urge you to turn the pages of this first biography of Dr. Welwood. First, English money in the Augustan Age was calculated in terms of pounds, shillings, and pence; twenty shillings to the pound, twelve pence to the shilling. Actual currency was more complex, and included coins of various metals and mints with many names and nicknames. It is difficult to figure what a pound or shilling from 1700 would be worth in American dollars today, because Augustan Britons bought different things than we do, and estimates from economic historians vary from $20 to $200. The changes in relative monetary values have been great, but according to the Bank of England multiplying late seventeenth-century money by a hundred will give a crude approximation to amounts understandable at the end of the twentieth century; one Augustan pound would therefore equal $160. Second, most of the dates in the book are English and therefore given in the Old Style, based on the Julian calendar used in Britain until 1752. During Welwood's lifetime there was an eleven day lag in England from the rest of Europe. For dates between January 1 and March 25, from which latter day the new year was still reckoned, I have employed the New Style or Gregorian calendar year; in the New Style, which was the practice in Scotland, January 1 inaugurates a new year. Third, translations from the French are mine unless otherwise indicated. And finally, Ralph Waldo Emerson in 1849 admonished writers with: "I hate quotations. Tell me what you know." Nevertheless, because the formal complexity and erudite flavor of impassioned debate in the Augustan Age would be lost without some direct echo of those words, I have included numerous quotations. Most but not all spellings have been modernized for clarity.

As I have thought about his life and the intricacy of his times over the past few years, James Welwood became my constant companion. I came to appreciate his political passion, his seriousness of purpose, his stable family and professional life, and his commitment to his friends and associates. Not all of his opinions are attractive today, but on balance James Welwood was an honorable man. I tell my students that just as we of the present try to imagine the men and women of past centuries, they tried to foresee us, their future. Janus-faced, we can picture our offspring stretching into the next centuries. Historical imagination connects us all on a very human continuum, and so perhaps some three hundred years ago, Welwood imagined me. I invite the reader to trace with me the life and times of Dr. James Welwood, a noted man of his day relegated by the weight of passing centuries to near obscurity. Let this rediscovery of the good doctor serve as a reminder to historians and biographers looking for fresh subject matter in oft-plowed scholarly fields that there are still many fascinating people who rest, as George Eliot wrote, in unvisited tombs.

Introduction

Dr. James Welwood, physician and classicist, wrote extensively on politics at the time of England's Glorious Revolution, keeping up a consistent demand for personal and religious freedom even after his preferred faction triumphed. In the years following the accession of William and Mary to the throne, partisan rancor became particularly vicious, creating a political climate made even more dangerous by vague group boundaries. Given the constantly shifting parameters of party and the varying degrees of commitment its adherents felt to any party program, defining these factional differences is as fraught with peril for the historian as it was for Augustan Age Englishmen. The origins of these divisions will be explored in a later chapter, but three fragmentary political blocs need identification. The Glorious Revolution was largely accomplished by the Whigs, men dissatisfied with the foreign and domestic policies of the Stuart kings Charles II and James II, in particular with their pro-French and pro-Catholic schemes. Some Whigs subscribed to belief in a contractual basis for a government bottomed on the legislative branch, while others simply wanted a different king than the one they had and thought Providence had been their deliverance. A group of Whig leaders called the junto, as miscellaneous as the party they represented, held institutional power during the reign of the joint sovereigns and for several years after. They were opposed by the more traditional Tories, who had complied with the revolution that overthrew James, but who nevertheless disdained many of the views advocated by the Whigs. A Tory could not for long abide a relaxation of traditional religious requirements in the Church of England or prolonged continental warfare against Louis XIV, just to suit their foreign-born King William. A splinter of the Tory party, the Jacobites, would not accept the revolution at all and actively continued to demonstrate their loyalty to James II and his heirs.

James Welwood was a feisty but principled Whig and devoted Williamite, whose pen was infrequently at rest. His outspoken opposition to any imposed philosophical orthodoxy, even from his own party, occasionally got him into official trouble in Scotland and in England. For Welwood a life combining medicine and partisan activity must have seemed instinctive, encapsulating care for the body natural and the body politic. His contemporaries envisioned the constitution of society as sick, infected by popish monarchy or radical republicanism and in need of strong medicine, perhaps even surgery to rid the country of a political cancer. By Welwood's time the doctor had become a man of science, dignified by the assumption that his analytical skills might be useful to the state. An enlightened medical man like Welwood could be physician to the nation.[1]

Overcoming a childhood beset with political and economic woes, Welwood became something of a celebrity in the Augustan Age, that brilliant era of English letters, self-confidence, and material well-being.[2] An educational sojourn on the continent in the 1680s brought Welwood into direct contact with disaffected refugees who extended the future writer valuable insights and with Prince William of Orange, symbol of Protestant virtue and resistance to tyranny. Besides establishing himself in the British medical profession, Welwood came to stand among his contemporaries for courageous dedication to principle and uncommon erudition. An unrepentant enthusiast for the Glorious Revolution and its goals, Welwood first took up his quill in Newcastle upon Tyne in a series of letters with a Jacobite vicar.

Shortly after moving to London in 1689, the new doctor began to write a complete history of the seventeenth century at the behest of Queen Mary, tracing events from the death in 1603 of the last Tudor monarch, Elizabeth I, and the accession of Scotland's Stuart dynast James VI to the throne of England as James I. Welwood carefully followed the evolving struggle between the Stuart kings and a coalition of Parliamentary and Puritan opponents during the reign of James' son, Charles I, a struggle that culminated in civil war, regicide, and the equivocal, mid-century Commonwealth of Oliver Cromwell. Welwood concluded his history with the optimistic restoration of Charles II and the Stuarts in 1660, his explanations for their inability to rule wisely and justly, and a narrative of the disastrous three-year reign of James II ending with the triumphant arrival via Holland of William and Mary in 1688.

Simultaneously with his history writing, Dr. Welwood started a lively and important newspaper in the City. His broadly-informed, twice-weekly *Mercurius Reformatus* provided London readers with the latest information from the continent and demonstrated his continued support of King William. Having seen the deleterious effects of fanaticism and forced uniformity of conscience at close range, Welwood developed a marked aversion to imposed religious conformity. Like many of his era, Welwood disdained the Roman Catholic Church as an institution because he associated it with absolutism, but he opposed any power used arbitrarily. Louis XIV of France personified the forces Welwood feared would crush individual freedom of the spirit and force a rigid orthodoxy upon free thinkers like himself. Nonetheless, Welwood was no fanatic; his positions were always moderate and he strove to establish consensus. Unlike John Locke and other more radical Whigs, Welwood eschewed the right of deposition based on the natural law case for resistance in favor of a contractual resistance to tyranny. Moreover, despite the role of key Whigs in precipitating the Glorious Revolution, Welwood refused to buckle to the Parliamentary majority upon the souring of its honeymoon with William. When personally chastised by the House of Commons for criticizing in *Mercurius Reformatus* its stingy appropriations for war with France, Welwood abandoned his newspaper rather than repudiate his position or his king. Nevertheless, his well-articulated enthusiasm for William and Mary was appreciated by the monarchs' ministers and they solicited Welwood's stylus to reply to unfavorable Jacobite broadsides and declarations. A physician and a wordsmith, James Welwood may have been the first true "spin doctor!"

But there is more to Welwood than his politics. He turned his attention after 1700 to the pursuit of the classics and history, writing valuable memoirs and translations. He also subsequently became more active in the most eminent professional organization for medical men in England, the Royal College of Physicians.[3] In the final years of his long life he continued to be involved in medicine, government, and court life. With the Whigs firmly back in power upon the coronation of George I in 1714, Welwood once again enjoyed access to the highest circles of power, acting as an intermediary in a messy romantic triangle.

James Welwood crossed back and forth between work in medicine and politics, often mixing the two. He used his cachet as an opponent of James II to win medical appointments in the government of William and Mary. Those appointments gave him access to an influential circle of men, ministers and intelligentsia, who valued his skill as a Whig propagandist. Even in the most searing polemic, Welwood usually identified himself as a physician although his acknowledged accomplishments as a medico were few. His writing energies were exceptional and his output prolific. When not lambasting those with whom he disagreed, Welwood turned to scholarly pursuits including translations and explications of ancient texts. Moreover, he epitomized for many of his contemporaries the ideal physician whose dignity of character was maintained by literature. Although *The Cambridge Bibliography of English Literature* dismisses James Welwood as a "minor historical writer" for his book on England in the seventeenth century, it includes reference to his bi-weekly London newspaper, two political tracts, and translations of some classical works.[4] No mention is made of his other publications of letters, commentary, or medical papers. Indeed, many of Welwood's works, written anonymously to avoid the unpleasantness of partisan notoriety, may still be unidentified, including his heretofore uncredited authorship of one 1692 pamphlet that stirred up trouble among King William's ministers. The abundant diversity of Dr. Welwood's writings even in the extraordinary Augustan Age hampers further authorial confirmation.

James Welwood rose from humble beginnings as a Scottish minister's son, using native ability and educational opportunity to create a place for himself among the leaders of his profession and to secure financial comfort for his family. In many ways he epitomizes the Augustan Age in England, the era identified with pride by Englishmen as comparable to the glory days of the Roman Empire. Welwood was effusive, energetic, partisan, fiercely loyal, and eager to find parallels in classical literature to his own time. In his newspaper he acknowledged that "there are few characters I am more in love with than that of Augustus, and there was never a court where learning and virtue was more triumphant."[5] Welwood was a man of paradoxes, the scion of a family enmeshed in religious controversy who believed that only William of Orange offered freedom for Britain. An advocate for a free press, and a victim of Parliamentary meddling with his own newspaper, Welwood nonetheless scripted attacks for William's government on Jacobite publications. He did so because he was convinced that sectarian toleration would only be possible under true Protestant leadership and that even Catholics would be freer under a Williamite monarchy than if subjected to the regime of a papist. From Welwood's perspective, religious forbearance and political freedom ought to be the primary goals of government.

He grew up in Scotland at a time of religious and political upheaval, witch-hunts, and war. That his father was a minister during those spiritually treacherous years only increased the family's involvement in contemporary affairs. Welwood's own rhetoric propelled him to the forefront of political activity in Britain and to a prominent place among the apologists for liberty. The rise of James Welwood from poor cleric's son to Augustan Age fame makes clear the possibility of dramatic social mobility and the benefits of financial aid to the education of bright juveniles. Welwood, who relished the medley of curricular and insti-tutional challenges to becoming a physician, attended universities in Scotland and on the continent at the very moment when the profession was experiencing change. After the Glorious Revolution he practiced medicine in London, the most vibrant city of the century, and lived in the midst of uncommon urban development as the face of the capital altered. In the 1690s he participated in the partisan pamphlet wars that kept a generation politically aquiver; for his contributions to the printed broadside, he was castigated by Parliament but hardly stilled his pen.

James Welwood witnessed war, revolution, persecution, and the beginnings of Britain's empire; he rubbed shoulders with monarchs, minions, scientists, and collectors. Welwood had a wide circle of friends in Britain and on the continent that ranged from the founder of the British Museum to renowned diplomats at most of the major royal courts to an aging courtesan and her salon. In his later years, he invested in the South Sea Bubble, socialized with England's literati, and enjoyed an industrious retirement from medicine. Walking in James Welwood's shoes as he progressed through a long life gives us a panoramic opportunity to view the past as if we were present, to move from the seventeenth to the eighteenth centuries just as he did.

Because he is a second-tier figure in an age of titans, no biography of James Welwood has been written until now, nor has there been an attempt to place him in the context of any of his worlds — medicine, publishing, politics — all of which were in various stages of transition. Perhaps that is due to the complexity of Augustan Age problems as much as to the complexity of the man. He was certainly more than just a partisan hack for the Whigs; yet he was less than an ideologue. He was against arbitrary Catholic monarchy and forced orthodoxy, but he was no convert to republicanism. A year before John Locke published his musings on the social contract, Welwood argued for constitutional limitations on power based on a contractual theory of the origins of government; however, he sometimes overlooked the excesses of the government he supported. Welwood personifies the dilemmas faced by Britons seeking to balance newly-articulated liberties with age-old traditions, the need for peaceful commercial trade with the control of foreign aggression, and the desire for religious orthodoxy with the Protestant principle of individual conscience. He embodies the typical contradictions manifested by many Whig revolutionaries.

Additionally, Welwood's life demonstrates an ideal in British history and one that he relished, the gentleman-scholar. Although never considered the best doctor in London or the best commentator on current events, Welwood is an archetype, the Briton who loved scholarship, classical and scientific, and applied its lessons to the world in which he dwelled. He lived a life of the mind, but remained active in his profession and served his government when called. A physician by training, and an active one in his professional organization, Welwood became an inveterate reader and scribe, writing about everything from the classics to current incidents. Welwood's value as a touchstone for an age merits an investigation of his life that both rewards and humbles his biographer. Because he was mobile, versatile, and long-lived, Welwood's years provide us with myriad subjects for consideration. Knowing Welwood's life, more than most others, enables us to know the intricacies of Augustan Britain. It is true that "history is biography writ large."[6]

The work of a historian is like that of a detective. One must assemble all the evidence and construct both a life and a milieu, asserting when possible, suggesting when necessary. No portraits of James Welwood exist, he never referred to the way he looked, and in none of the commentary written to and about him is there mention of his appearance. Many recorded witnessing his industry, honesty, and seriousness of purpose but no one described his features. In an age when few bodily flaws escaped the catty observation of friends, even Welwood's enemies omit any mention of his looks. No one wrote that he was handsome or ugly, short or tall, malformed, lame, myopic, obese, pockmarked, bearded, swarthy, or bald. The inescapable conclusion is that he was of average dimensions and had few, if any, distinguishing physical characteristics. Although James Welwood wrote a number of political columns and personal letters that allude to his development, there is little surviving information about his youth and schooling. Here the historian must try to recreate the collage of events that informed his opinions and made the man. Similarly, Welwood's supporting actor status in Augustan England has kept anyone from heretofore connecting all the dots of his associations and friendships, but he was an intrinsic part of a small network of puissant men. Dr. Welwood was an indispensable polemicist for William and Mary, so much so that he was called upon by the government to parry thrusts from the Jacobite end of Grub Street.

A puzzling aspect of Welwood's life is his apparent gradual transformation from ardent Scottish presbyterian to moderate English episcopalian. Did he change because the political culture of the London establishment implicitly required him to do so or because Welwood himself deliberately chose a more irenic public posture? Did Welwood become "British" even before the official Act of Union in 1707, embracing both the religious and national implications inherent in that descriptive? How did he justify his apparent and ultimate rejection of the irreconcilable Calvinism of his younger days for participation in the Church of England? Indisputable answers to these questions remain elusive.

Organizing this biography has been a challenge, given the concurrent activity of Dr. Welwood in so many aspects of Augustan Age society. Finding one's way through a maze as challenging as Welwood's life requires investigating such disparate topics as Scottish history, witchcraft, university culture, medical training in Britain and abroad, French institutional history, monetary exchange, partisan politics, publishing, professional medical organizations and their jurisdictional squabbles, the city of London and its development, governmental appointments, the South Sea Bubble, royal mistresses, and the dysfunctional Hanoverians. The path of the early chapters is generally chronological with obligatory topical detours to give meaning to Welwood's choices and texture to his times. Because of his concomitant work in several fields after 1688, the later chapters by necessity focus on specific avenues of Welwood enterprise.

Chapter One deals with Welwood's childhood and schooling in Scotland, the zealous presbyterian background from which he sprang, and the polarizing incidents which stained the Stuart restoration and impelled him to study medicine abroad. The second chapter assays Welwood's medical education on the continent, the state of the French institution from which he obtained a degree, and his political maturation as a result of his time in France and Holland in the early 1680s. Chapter Three addresses Welwood's return home to escalating sectarian trouble, his move to England at the time of the so-called Glorious Revolution and the enemies he made, and the beginnings of his career as a Whig polemicist in London. Chapter Four evaluates Welwood's significant newspaper, *Mercurius Reformatus*, and the trouble it caused him, as well as his continued role as a Whig corrective to the Jacobites. Chapter Five examines Welwood, the gentleman-scholar, whose extensive post-*Mercurius* writing included an effectual popular history and translations of the classics. Chapter Six deals with the medical world of Dr. James Welwood, his exemplary efforts on the Commission for the Sick and Wounded along with other governmental appointments, his energetic fellowship in the Royal College of Physicians, and the state of his profession in transition. Welwood's most intriguing service to Britain may have been in his role as aged royal go-between for the

House of Hanover in the 1720s, the subject of the seventh chapter. An epilogue evaluates Welwood's legacies, material and otherwise.

Caveats abound, nonetheless, for detours into the Augustan Age are fraught with the twin dangers of oversimplification and obscurantism. Historians continue to debate the origins and composition of party in England, so that attempts to summarize partisan developments risk error. Similar pitfalls threaten explanation of Scottish society, educational institutions, political theory, and medicine, yet explanatory sketches may cause the reader to want to see more. Conversely, research invariably produces detail too minute for some. The ideal is a readable contextual balance between synopsis and minutia, keeping Welwood in the foreground where personal particulars are necessary.

Luckily for anyone interested in the Augustan Age, a magnificent number of published works from the late seventeenth and early eighteenth centuries survive in their original format. Dr. Welwood was not the only physician of the era to compose a book, in fact many of his colleagues in the medical profession were, like himself, aspiring authorities in fields outside medicine. The British Library, as well as distinguished university repositories in the United States, has a vast collection of these valuable antique books written by doctors on all manner of subjects, and it is a treat to examine the very text owned by one of Welwood's colleagues. Though a significant number of the tomes are of peripheral value on those subjects, they demonstrate a breadth of interest and enthusiasm for learning that is endearing whatever the content. Like Welwood, some of the other royal doctors translated and commented on the classics, some expounded on natural history, and some wrote about politics. A few even ventured to write about science and medicine, often appending some of their treasured prescriptions and therapies.

Most of the books published by physicians in early modern Britain are pocket-sized. They were carried to and read in coffee houses, and not displayed, as we do now, on coffee tables. Welwood's books are often only six inches tall, yet bound solidly enough to withstand three centuries of readers. *Mercurius Reformatus*, Welwood's weekly two-page political broadsheet, measured about twelve by six inches. Some of Welwood's medical fellows kept handwritten journals, recipe books, and other notations in book format but did not have them published.

A few of Welwood's personal letters are scattered amongst the Additional Manuscripts and the Sloane Manuscripts in the British Library. These, too, are a revelation for the modern researcher because they add much humanity to a historical quest.

Notwithstanding, for the convenience of students of the period who cannot read the originals on site, a collection of microfilmed early English books and newspapers is widely available at libraries everywhere. Therein, photographed for posterity, can be found all of Welwood's published oeuvre including every issue of *Mercurius Reformatus*. Given that he was also deemed by his peers to be a major memoirist and chronicler, and that his writing provided inspiration for the Whig interpretation of history, the absence of a biography on James Welwood needs remedy.

Welwood inhabited a rather dangerous world on the cusp of modernity. The doctor's insistence on liberty, freedom of religion, and toleration for all brought him both honor and trouble: honor when it served the purposes of the king and the Whig leadership, trouble when he continued to press for openmindedness after his faction attained power and became established. Welwood's ostensible championing of diversity of opinion seems especially courageous in light of what he had suffered growing up in Scotland in the midst of official chaos. Given that Welwood's family was linked to religious extremism, James Welwood's ultimate embrace of relative moderation is all the more remarkable.

The modern reader may be somewhat shocked at the obsessive preoccupation with Roman Catholicism that colors the work of Welwood and other Augustan Era writers. After a remarkable exodus caused by excessive government harassment in the late 1670s, only about 50,000 to 60,000 Roman Catholics, about one per cent of the population, lived in later Stuart England; most of them were politically docile and rurally based, constantly tormented by the penal laws.[7] Nonetheless, anti-popery was the *idée fixe*, the most portentous impulse, and the most consistent motif of politics throughout seventeenth-century Britain. Bombarded by propaganda from the pulpit and taught that the modern nation was born of Protestantism, Welwood and his contemporaries equated Rome with tyranny and slavery. They recoiled from secret treaties with France and they suspected most foreigners; fear of plots and conspiracies abounded throughout the Augustan Age. When Catholic James II fathered a male heir in 1688, visions of a long line of crowned papists spurred revolution, a revolution with lasting impact and far-ranging implications.

James Welwood came to detest France, the "eldest daughter of the Church," and its king, Louis XIV. The French monarch represented everything that Welwood feared: absolute kingship, dedicated Catholicism, and international power which might be used to undermine Great Britain. While a medical student in France, Welwood had experienced the erosion of religious toleration when Louis XIV abrogated that long-held policy. As a resident of London, Welwood could measure the stream of Huguenot refugees seeking asylum there from repression in France. Catholicism and France intertwined in Welwood's mind to create a monstrous threat to all Britons. He pledged to fight that threat with his considerable writing skills.

Yet Welwood and his kind were equally worried about Puritan extremism, having known firsthand the horrors of fratricidal civil war. Scots and Englishmen alike wanted to avoid the religious and political excesses of Protestant fanaticism for they still had respect for lawful government and legitimate hierarchy. The trick was to find the balance, the *via media* of England's glorious Elizabeth I. For Scotsman James Welwood the reign of Good Queen Bess had been an ideal one, and he referred to her as a model for both Stuart queens, Mary II and Anne. Elizabeth had not only repulsed the Spanish armada; she had made possible the official establishment of Protestantism in Scotland.

However, James Welwood repeatedly asserted that even Catholics should enjoy religious tolerance under a government committed to rights and liberties. He had nothing against them personally, he wrote, only disdain for the historical oppression that their church had sanctioned. Frankly, there is an element of condescension rather than respect in Welwood's patience with Catholics and other outsiders; nonetheless, in his histories, almanacs, newspapers, and letters, he stressed the importance of remaining vigilant against any excess. Witness to three generations of tension and tumult, Welwood understandably sought peace from institutional interference in men's lives. He found that peace through his writing, in his profession, and from his doting family.

JAMES WELWOOD

Dr. James Welwood led a fascinating, multi-faceted life that carried him to the pinnacle of success in medicine and to some degree of celebrity in Augustan Britain. Welwood was sufficiently respected as a medical doctor to earn a place as an officer in the Royal College of Physicians. He also came to be appreciated as a stylish writer and a serious intellect, who produced an impressive amount of political tracts, classical translations, and influential chronicles, most of which are still available and useful to those interested in seventeenth and eighteenth-century Europe. He won appointment to lucrative government posts and the friendship of the joint monarchs, William and Mary. At the end of his long career, he maintained his connections among the powerful, serving as go-between in a Hanoverian triangle. In short, Welwood's life is of intrinsic interest for who he was and what he did.

More importantly, Welwood's life can be useful as a window on his complex times. Like those fictional heroes whose luck makes them witness to the crucial occurrences of their age, James Welwood participated in an uncommon variety of experiences which defined both him and his era. His observations and opinions on those experiences, which he described directly and indirectly in his twice-weekly newspaper, are used throughout this biography to provide the reader both with Welwood's perspective on events and the impact of those events on Welwood.

CHRONOLOGY

1637	Scottish rebellion against English religious reforms.
1638	Scottish National Covenant.
1640	The Long Parliament opens.
1641	Irish Rebellion.
1643	Solemn League and Covenant with Scotland.
1649	Charles I is executed in London; Puritan Commonwealth.
1651	Final defeat of the Royalists; flight of Prince Charles.
1652	James Welwood is born in Scotland. First Anglo-Dutch War.
1654	Oliver Cromwell made Lord Protector.
1658	Cromwell's death.
1659	The Welwoods move to Dumfriesshire; Welwood's mother dies.
1660	Restoration of Charles II.
1661	Witch-craze begins in Dumfries.
1663	Rev. Welwood is dismissed from his parish.
1664	Second Anglo-Dutch War begins.
1665	Plague in London.
1666	The Great Fire in London.
1668	James Welwood enrolls at St. Andrews.
1670	Secret Treaty of Dover between Charles II and Louis XIV.
1671	James Welwood graduates Master of Arts.
1672	Louis XIV's attack on the Netherlands; William of Orange becomes Stadtholder; Third Anglo-Dutch War.
1673	Test Act.
1677	Marriage of William to Charles II's niece, Mary.
1678	"Popish Plot" is exposed.
1679	Archbishop Sharp's murder in Fifeshire; Monmouth suppresses Covenanters. Exclusion Crisis in England. Welwood on the continent to study medicine.
1682	Welwood visits Paris.

1683 Rye House Plot against the Crown; John Locke goes to
      Holland.

1684 Welwood receives his M.D. from Reims; returns to Scotland.

1685 Death of Charles II; accession of James II. Monmouth's
      Rebellion. Revocation of the Edict of Nantes.

1686 Welwood's first daughter born in Edinburgh.

1687 James II repeals Test and Penal Acts; expulsion of Protestant
      fellows from Magdalen College, Oxford; Dr. Welwood
      moves to Newcastle.

1688 Birth of male Catholic heir to James II. William lands at
      Torbay. James flees to France.

1689 William and Mary crowned: Bill of Rights. England joins the
      Dutch in war against France. James lands in Ireland with
      French help. Welwood settles in London and starts
      Mercurius Reformatus.

1690 James defeated by William at the Battle of the Boyne.
      Welwood named a royal physician and joins the Royal
      College of Physicians in London.

1691 Welwood appointed to Commission for the Sick and
      Wounded; starts to write *Memoirs* and publishes *Weekly
      Remarks.* Parliament castigates him for published criticism.

1692 Defeat of Jacobites with French invasion fleet at La Hogue.

1694 Death of Queen Mary from smallpox; Anderton trial and
      execution.

1695 Licensing Act lapses; Dispensary founded.

1697 Treaty of Ryswick forces Louis to return post-1678 conquests.

1698 Darien scheme.

1700 Publication of Welwood's *Memoirs.*

1701 Death of James II; his son proclaimed "James III" by Louis
      XIV; Act of Settlement. Spanish succession crisis provokes
      new war against France.

1702 Death of William III; Anne succeeds to the throne.

1703 James Welwood marries Elizabeth Seymour.

1704 *Rose Case* decided in favor of apothecaries.

1705 Welwood publishes his almanac.

1707 Act of Union with Scotland.

1710   Sacheverell riots in London; Whigs toppled. Welwood's translation of Xenophon is published.

1713   Treaty of Utrecht concludes War of the Spanish Succession; Tories dominate politics.

1714   Death of Anne; George I crowned; Whigs ascendant.

1715   Death of Louis XIV and Bishop Burnet. Jacobite rising.

1720   South Sea Bubble; Mrs. Howard becomes Prince George's mistress.

1721   Robert Walpole is named chief minister.

1726   Dr. Welwood acts as go-between for the Howards and the Prince.

1727   Death of Dr. James Welwood in April in London. George I dies in June and is succeeded by George II.

CHAPTER ONE

Tumultuous Beginnings

*D*ramatic and sometimes frightening events colored the Scottish youth of James Welwood. Three powerful phenomena in Scotland dominated the lives of all who grew up in the isolated northern kingdom in the seventeenth century. First was the perpetual, often violent struggle with England for sovereignty over national politics and culture, a struggle complicated by an English civil war and regicide. Second was the pernicious religious division among Scots themselves that pitted Protestants against one another and both against Catholics. Third was a terrifying witch-hunt, especially horrific in the region where Welwood grew up, which produced community fear and division. If we all are the products of our childhood environments, public and private, James Welwood had many soul-shaping influences with which to cope. To understand Welwood as an archetype one must understand the tumult of the Scottish seventeenth century at the national, regional, and local levels.

James Welwood was the third son of the Reverend James Welwood and Margaret Dury. He was born in 1652 in Dunfermline, Fifeshire, former capital of Scotland and burial site of Scotland's first king, Robert the Bruce. Standing above the town like sentinels, Dunfermline's abbey and ruined palace recall Benedictine monks and the sainted Queen Margaret, as well as frequent sackings and burnings. It is in a region of Scotland long beset with strong religious dissent and the desire for political autonomy, an area associated with the Scottish Reformation of the sixteenth century. The Church of Scotland, the National Kirk, was a Calvinist product of the Reformation, governed not by a hierarchy of bishops and archbishops, but at first by Kirk Sessions of lay elders and later by distinct presbyteries, meetings of elected elders and ministers. The General Assembly of the Kirk, which met biannually to decide questions for the whole Church, grew into a forum for Scottish opinion on secular and ecclesiastical matters. Under the influence of John Knox and his disciples, the early Kirk was austere in character: Christmas and Easter were no longer observed, spontaneous prayer supplanted the liturgy, singing was unaccompanied, even Holy Communion was celebrated infrequently. Throughout Scotland the influence of parish ministers became paramount in lay and kirk business, although a strong body of Scottish Protestants including the king demurred from this philosophy. James VI was no Presbyterian. He grasped the implications of the radicals' challenge to episcopal authority when he made his oft-quoted remark: "No bishop, no King."[1]

Though a single Stuart monarch ruled over all the British Isles after Scotland's James VI was crowned James I of England in 1603, the kingdoms were not united. Religious differences between the majority of Scots with their militant devotion to the presbytery and the English, who favored episcopacy, were in fact exacerbated upon James' accession to the English throne. The extreme Calvinist reformation in Scotland meant that the northern kingdom associated itself with national distinction, anti-papism, and a more severe daily spiritual life. To maintain his position atop the political hierarchy in Scotland while he ruled in England, James appointed a few Scottish bishops, later consecrated in London by Anglicans, as prelude to superseding the presbytery altogether. By 1618 some Catholic rites had even been reinstated at the instigation of the king, and since neither James I nor his son, Charles I, chose to summon the General Assemby of the Church of Scotland after that date, the collective voice of the presbytery had been stilled.

But the imposition in Scotland of an Anglican-dictated *Scottish Book of Common Prayer* by Charles I in 1637 infuriated national and religious sensibilities, provoking defiance and violence. Receiving no response to their demands against mandatory use of the book, Scottish ministers and elders met in Edinburgh in 1638 and composed the National Covenant, a bond of alliance signed by those opposed to the king's

religious policies in Scotland. The Covenant was enthusiastically accepted in the Scottish Lowlands, but not in the predominantly Gaelic Highlands still controlled by semi-autonomous clans. The Covenant repeated the anti-Catholic language of the General Assembly of 1581, listed all the acts of the Scottish Parliament condemning Catholicism, and bound its adherents (called Covenanters) to remain united to each other and to God in upholding the true religion. Supporters of the Covenant dominated Scotland from 1638 to 1651, the year before James Welwood's birth. In the words of Robert Baillie, one of the participating ministers, Scotland's "Second Reformation" had begun.[2]

Differentiating among the various Protestant factions in seventeenth-century Britain can be a daunting task. The term "Puritan" covers a myriad of doctrines and attitudes, but Puritan theology was basically Calvinist. Puritans demanded purification of the Church of England by eliminating components that they regarded as Roman Catholic, superstitious, or not based in scriptural authority. The Puritan group identified with Parliamentary opposition to the monarchy, and the more extreme Puritan sects were well-represented in the New Model Army of Puritan leader Oliver Cromwell. Nonconformists, dissenting Protestants who did not conform to the practices of the Anglican Church, included Presbyterians, Baptists, and Congregationalists, as well as numerous small sects. Quakers, Unitarians, and Methodists were later added to that list. In Scotland, where Presbyterianism was the established religion, Episcopalians were among the nonconformists.

Mid-century Great Britain was a perilous place. By the time James Welwood was born, Cromwell and his allies in the English Parliament had defeated Charles I on the field of battle, tried the king on charges of treason, and executed him. The Scots initially had played a significant part as Cromwell's early ally in challenging Charles I, even invading England after the prayer book incident. In September 1643, an agreement was reached between the Scottish Covenanters and the English Long Parliament, known as the Solemn League and Covenant. In return for a formal Parliamentary endorsement of Presbyterianism in England and Ireland (and £30,000 a month), Scotland joined the allied opposition to the king, sending 21,000 troops into England, attacking Royalist forces in the north. For their part, the English summoned the Westminster Assembly, charged with the task of

establishing uniformity of worship in the three kingdoms. Eventually, however, the Scots' own divergence and the undisguised enmity they perceived toward their Covenant emanating from London resulted in a scuttling of the bargain with Parliament and a practical settlement with the monarch. King Charles himself preferred an entente with the Scots to negotiating with an insolent legislature, and in 1647 he promised to establish Scottish Presbyterianism in England for three years. This pledge radicalized the already anti-Scot Houses of Lords and Commons in England; no future compromise with the king seemed possible and the final phase of the civil war commenced.

Any hopes Scotsmen had of winning some guarantee of political autonomy and religious freedom for themselves were dashed with the ultimate triumph of the Roundheads and the killing of the king that followed. Nevertheless, just a few months after Charles I's execution in 1649, the dominant Presbyterian party in Scotland obtained approval of their Covenant at Dunfermline by Charles Stuart, the late king's son and heir. Scottish accommodation with the Stuart dynasty threatened the new English republic and provided a launching pad for a monarchical restoration. Displaying brilliant military prowess against the northerners' numerical strength and political savvy to exploit their divisions, Cromwell attacked, defeated, and quickly subdued the Scots. After 1651 England was more firmly established in Scotland under the Commonwealth of Lord Protector Cromwell than ever before. James Welwood, although himself raised a Presbyterian, would later contemptuously describe the Lord Protector as a usurper.[3]

Cromwell's regime could not survive his death in 1658, and the Stuart family was restored to both thrones with the coronation of Charles II in 1660. Scotsmen who had prayed for the prince's safety throughout the Cromwellian years were to be disappointed. One of the new king's first acts was to renege on his subscription to the Solemn League and Covenant and to impose episcopacy on Scotland by fiat. Charles estimated that "Presbytery was not a religion for gentlemen." Moreover, never during his twenty-five year reign did Charles II set foot again on Scottish soil. He governed his northern kingdom through a Privy Council situated in Edinburgh and a Secretary based in London. He packed the Scottish Parliament with reliable minions who strength-

ened the monarch's position in the system. James Welwood was eight years old at the time of the Stuart restoration.

Welwood always considered Fifeshire his homeland, even in later life after decades of residence in London as a successful physician. The Fife peninsula is carved out by the Firths of Forth and Tay and is barricaded from the interior by the Ochil hills, creating a land physically apart and a people fiercely self-reliant. The few roads between the principal towns were of poor quality. A stagecoach from London arrived in Edinburgh every three weeks, but horseback was the mode of transport anywhere north of that city. Traditionally Fife has been called a kingdom, perhaps because of its association with the ancient Pictish domain, certainly because of the spirited independence of its inhabitants. The University of St. Andrews, the first Scottish university, was a Fifeshire center in the late sixteenth-century for reformist doctrines, thus involving the institution in struggles with both the established Church and the Crown. Leading Covenanters came from Fifeshire, and key seventeenth-century events including the assassination of a Caroline archbishop happened within Fife. As recently as 1975 citizens in Fifeshire showed their continued resistance to outside interference when they successfully opposed the splitting of Fife in a British local government organization scheme.

James Welwood came from a family well-known for its outspoken opinions about religious and political matters. Many Welwoods (or Wellwood as it was sometimes spelled in inconsistent seventeenth-century records) lived in the vicinity of rural Falkland, a favorite hunting seat of the Stuarts; others were associated with coastal Fifeshire and St. Andrews. One celebrated ancestor, maritime law specialist William Welwood, supported Church reformers in late sixteenth-century Scotland, incurring the disapproval of King James VI. Even though the University of St. Andrews was notorious for its rebellious personnel, William Welwood was removed in 1597 by royal agents from a professorship there for his pronounced published views on ecclesiastical prerogatives. John Welwood, William's brother, had already been banished by then from the city of St. Andrews for his part in a lethal skirmish in the High Street that involved some of William's political enemies. St. Andrews was a dangerous academy in various ways.

Though the financial background of James Welwood's parents seems modest, some of the Welwood family were important residents of Fife. Seventeenth-century Welwoods owned estates at Touch, Garvock, and Pitliver; Robert Wellwood, born 1649, acquired Garvock Wood and inherited Touch. His son, born 1690, is listed in Robert Sibbald's famed local history of the region as a "principal heritor of the shire of Fife whose valued rent is known to entitle them to vote for the representative of the county in Parliament." Nonetheless, Sibbald notes that "from the present possessors being minors or females, [Robert Wellwood is] not on the roll of freeholders." Another Robert Wellwood is described as a heritor of Pitliver, and his house is recommended by Sibbald as "uncommonly elegant with plantations and pleasure grounds." This Robert Wellwood, a cousin of James Welwood, was a subscriber to Sibbald's antiquarian literary effort. According to the 1695 valuation of the shire recorded in a revised edition of Sibbald, Garvock was assessed at £169 and Pitliver at £868, the latter a notable sum.[4] A family contemporary of James Welwood, Thomas Welwood, was a physician, and Welwoods were prosperous merchants, burgesses, and kirk-treasurers of Edinburgh.

Education ranked at the top among the Welwood family goals, helping to create strong individuals with tenacious wills and a sense of righteousness emanating from their belief in predestination. A good education made for an independent spirit less likely to succumb to the superstitions and lies of an autocratic Church. The senior James Welwood earned a Master's degree at St. Andrews University in 1623, and served as a schoolmaster in Errol from 1630 until 1651. Very often young men took up an instructor's post while they were undertaking theological study, or on trial for the ministry, or waiting for a charge. In 1643 Mr. Welwood was nominated at a St. Andrews presbytery meeting to preach on a rota basis in Leuchars parish church, only a few miles from St. Andrews, during a vacancy of that charge. His name also appears for the same day at an exercise organized by the Kirk Session to discuss theological topics and to examine candidates for the ministry before licensing by the presbytery.[5] Having established himself as a preacher, James Welwood continued as an educator until shortly before the birth of his third son, when he turned for full-time employment to the Scottish Church. Education and Protestantism, specifically Presbyterianism, became synonymous for young James Welwood.

The moral and religious instruction of their sons and daughters occupied much of the Welwoods' attention. The minister and his wife told young James edifying stories with moral lessons to shape his conscience and spiritual commitment. Contemporary events were explicable when seen through the prism of religious faith. In a Calvinist family like the Welwoods, the Bible was the main source for finding deeper meaning in everyday occurrences, and those ordinary events resonated with a Biblical interpretation. Spiritual instruction and intellectual preparation went hand in hand. School life began for the Scottish child in the seventeenth century at the age of five, though many did not arrive until they were seven and had finished a sort of kindergarten or dame-school. The Covenanters and the General Assembly had emphasized an education program, and by 1646 heritors without exception financed parish schools. By the eve of the Restoration and the beginning of James Welwood's education, all the parishes in Dunfermline Presbytery had a schoolmaster as did most in Fife. There were numerous private schools outside of Church control which greatly increased literacy among the Scots. After five years the child could go on to a larger burgher school, but parents of poor children could seldom afford to let their offspring stay much beyond the age of eight without a bursary. While he attended, the child worked hard. The school day lasted eight to twelve hours, generally starting at 6:00 a.m. in the summer and allowing two breaks of an hour each for breakfast and lunch. Since small children could not possibly be kept at their books for that length of time six days a week, two or three playdays were instituted each week to allow for physical exercise. There were no official holidays during the year, but as it was impossible to keep country children from being withdrawn at harvest time, some schools closed for a month in late summer.

The curriculum varied according to the knowledge of the teacher, but everywhere religious instruction and good behavior were accentuated. Everyone learned reading and writing, but many schools taught Latin and arithmetic to more able children. The main emphasis was on piety, and the Bible was the only English reading text. The system judged corporal punishment as necessary within reason. School teachers reported that they taught catechism, prayers and grace for meals, and chastised the profane and disobedient.[6] Of course, the best teachers believed education to be more than rote learning, to be an intellectual process, requiring understanding and explanation. Monday discussion of the Sunday sermon followed compulsory attendance at services, and the Church authorities made sure the schoolmaster held orthodox convictions. Little James Welwood probably began his lifelong affinity for learning and his pattern of written expression about 1657 at a Fifeshire school. One day he would use his education to leave Scotland and its traditions behind.

Not all of James Welwood's childhood was spent in Fifeshire. From 1659 to 1664, Welwood's father was minister at Tundergarth in Annandale, Dumfriesshire in lowland Scotland. Annandale is a fertile river valley, known for grain production, little markets, horse and cattle fairs, that stretches southward from the spa at Moffat to the Solway Firth. Just a couple of miles east of the midpoint in the strath is Lockerbie, remembered before terrorist bombs on airplanes for its sheep sales and lamb fairs; Dumfries is about five miles to the west, itself a harbor with bustling quays and steeples of sandstone as rust-red as the stone and soil of the surrounding countryside. At the mouth of the river Annan is the village of the same name. Daniel Defoe described Annan as "a town of note and a sea-port...having a good river and harbor." However, he noted, the English have taken and plundered the town so often in war that it never recovered its economic footing, even with a thriving salmon fishery and trade to the Isle of Man.[7] The area abounds with architectural reminders of the more violent aspects of Scottish history and of Scotland's devotion to Christianity. Young Welwood would have been impressed with nearby Drumlanrig and Caerlaverock castles, fourteenth-century strongholds against Edward I of England, and with thirteenth-century Sweetheart Abbey, the last Cistercian foundation in Scotland. He may have heard from his father about the Ruthwell Cross, a seventh-century example of early Christian art depicting the life and passion of Christ, but he would not have seen it. The General Assembly had ordered it destroyed in 1642. Certainly James Welwood's childhood years in this landscape were crucial.

During this impressionable stage in his young life, a witch-craze blazed up in Dumfriesshire, consuming the lives of many in the region who were accused of witchcraft. Throughout the sixteenth and seventeenth centuries in Europe, thousands of people, most of them women, were tried for the crime of witchcraft and about half of those tried were executed.[8] Scotland saw more than its share of trials and executions, principally during its two major witch-hunts in 1590-92 and 1661-62. Periodic panics ensued between the primary outbreaks including one in Dumfriesshire in 1628. Of the 5,000 documented witch trials in the British Isles, over half were in Scotland.

Witch-hunts occur where belief in witches prevails, where religious heterogeneity creates confusion, and where authorities permit and encourage public anxiety. In the sixteenth and seventeenth centuries, Scotland was such a place. Dating from 1563, Scottish law on witchcraft prescribed death by burning for all witches, good or bad, and for those who consulted them. Despite the severity of the punishment, conviction rates were high because Scottish juries required only a majority to convict. Although punishment by death was not necessarily imposed by the court, execution rates in the northern kingdom were unusually high compared to Europe in general and the British Isles in particular. Scottish witch cases were often handled ad hoc by local magistrates without judicial supervision. Ninety-one per cent of those persons tried by local commissions in Scotland were executed as compared to only 16% tried in the circuit courts. No wonder that prosecutions in Scotland were so much more intense than in the rest of Britain. England's population was four times that of Scotland, but three Scottish witches were put to death for each English execution. Yet, even in enlightened England, witch-hunts were supported as a necessity by some learned physicians.

In 1640, having gotten rid of bishops, the Scottish General Assembly ordered ministers to find and punish witches. Among the places which experienced long-term, self-perpetuating witch-hunting were two counties associated with James Welwood: Fife and Dumfriesshire. According to William McDowall, author of a history of Dumfries, while witchcraft in the mid-seventeenth century was "an article of almost universal belief in Scotland, the southern part of the [Dumfries] Presbytery was especially in thrall" to the witch-craze.[9] Fear of the witches' sabbath, an essential component in the development of witch-hunts, consumed Dumfriesshire with rumors that Locharbridge

Hill was the favorite trysting place of the weird women of the burgh, a town of about one thousand souls.

Alleged witches, generally married and poor, usually manifested the Scottish female quality called "smeddum," a feisty querulousness and disrespectful tongue. They were often midwives and healers sought out by commonfolk seeking help for medical problems, so even though they were in a position of socio-economic dependence, accused witches failed to act with deference and subservience to authority. Therefore, witches were viewed as dangerously deviant and anti-social. Physicians may have felt their own business threatened by witches' remedies. Some witches were Catholic, and in parts of Dumfriesshire, popery had survived to become a focal point for persecution by Calvinists who believed that Catholics followed the anti-Christ. Friends and relatives of the accused were suspect as well, certainly their mothers and daughters. Even consulting such a wise woman could be problematical, such as it was for a man in 1656 who went to a "witch-wife" for salve and was rebuked by the presbytery. The Kirk Session of Dumfries subsequently required ministers to announce from their pulpits that all persons with information about witches or their customers should furnish it to the session. Some informants must have done so, for in 1657 two convicted witches were publicly burnt to death on a peat fire.

The Privy Council in Scotland forbade the use of torture without its approval, but because central control of justice was sporadic, inflicting pain was a frequent feature of the pre-trial investigation of witches. Confessions were extorted from the accused by judicial torture, creating and multiplying both victims and evidence. Among the various devices used in Scotland during its sixteenth and seventeenth century witch-crazes was the pennywinkis, a vise which crushed the tips of fingers and toes. The "Spanish boot," a sort of leg screw which squeezed the calf and broke the shin bone into pieces, is mentioned in reports of Scottish witch trials. It is possible that the Scots invented sleep deprivation as a means of extracting information when a backlash developed against conventional torture.[10] Conservative estimates number 1500 executions for witchcraft in Scotland from 1590 to 1680 in part because of the widespread use of torture. England by contrast convicted a few witches and hanged even less. In England judges handled the witchcraft cases, torture was rarely employed on the accused, and conviction required unanimity. In addition, English law did not demand the death penalty.

The Reverend James Welwood and his family arrived in Dumfriesshire in 1659; Mrs. Welwood died that same year, leaving her youngest son only seven years old. According to one history of the Scottish Kirk, the senior Welwood told an elder of his parish that he spent the entire night following his wife's death in prayer, with "not...one thought concerning the death of my spouse, [but in] meditation of heavenly things...upon the banks of Ulai, plucking an apple here and there." Surely the offspring of Reverend Welwood were impressed by their father's words and deeds. Hagiographers have attributed the spirituality of his older sons to the pious example of the Welwood patriarch.[11]

Besides having to cope with the loss of his mother and adjust to a new community, young James was witness to the start of the greatest witch-hunt in the county. Defoe characterized Dumfries as a "good town, full of merchants...who trade to foreign parts." He wrote of a fine fifteenth-century red-stone bridge over the River Nith, a castle, merchant exchange and town hall.[12] But tourist attractions in the "Queen of the South" hardly interested the devout Welwoods. Ministers played an active part in the witch-craze, acting with the lay elders of their parishes in the Kirk Sessions, conducting the initial examination of persons arrested for witchcraft, and interrogating witnesses. Ministers sometimes administered torture and supervised searches for the Devil's Mark, blemishes on the bodies of the accused that were insensitive to pain.[13] Some professional witch hunters, operating for profit, specialized in pricking suspects in order to find the marks; others were content to extort money from those who sought to prove their innocence. Whatever their motives, "prickers" were certainly active in the Great Scottish Hunt which was already gathering momentum as the Welwoods arrived to take up their new ministry.

In 1659 the Dumfries Presbytery appointed eight men "to attend to nine witches...on the day of their execution," which took place on April 5 between two and four in the afternoon. The women were first strangled and then burned at the stake; their moveable goods were confiscated by the presbytery. The hunt throughout Scotland intensified two years later, when James Welwood was nine years old. Scholars have proffered a variety of explanations for the Great Hunt including a backlog of witch cases, economic distress, and clergy eager to prove their enthusiasm by driving the roundup of witches. Whatever the cause, never before in Scottish history were so many people accused of witchcraft within such a short period of time.

Reverend Welwood may have played a role in the witch-hunts, given the involvement of Covenanting ministers while he led a congregation in Annandale. Although no documentation is extant, there was ample opportunity for him to direct his parishioners in the early 1660s to root out evil among their neighbors, no matter what form it took. Between April of 1661 and the autumn of 1662 there were over 600 cases (89% female) and approximately 300 executions in Scotland.[14] During that time, eight women were charged with witchcraft in the town of Dumfries alone. A jury of fifteen brought together to consider the evidence was composed of small laird and grand tenants from within a ten-mile radius of the town, indicating a wide communications network and widespread rumors. Five of the accused witches were eventually sent for trial before a circuit judge in Kirkcudbright, but the other three were found guilty and executed summarily in Dumfries. Subsequently, the Privy Council of Scotland became concerned about the use of torture and reduced the rights of local authorities in obtaining confessions, thus inhibiting the pretrial stages of pursuing a suspect. Nevertheless, even pretending to be a witch could still cause trouble in southern Scotland. In 1664, the Welwoods' final year in the shire, the Dumfries Church Courts exiled an imposter witch from the community. Although the great hunt was over by then in most of the northern kingdom, there were still more cases in Dumfries in the 1670s. Young Welwood carried with him throughout life an aversion to any religious extremism, doubtlessly forged in those terrible years.

As if the witch-hunt in Dumfriesshire were not enough to disturb the peace of Welwood's childhood days, after the Stuart restoration the area was rife with religious dissent and unrest, which resulted in initial fines for non-conformity followed by imprisonment and even trans-portation abroad. The county already rated among the most harshly fined in 1662, but Dumfries' authorities feared more serious trouble. In July of that year seventy-three citizens were armed with firelock guns to help keep the peace. Three months later, the Reverend James Welwood was deprived of his parish at Tundergarth by acts of Parliament and the Privy Council. He was not the only cleric so affected. Under new regulations restoring episcopacy, the nine hundred or so ministers appointed since 1649 were required to resign their charges and receive them again from their bishops and patrons. No significant changes were made in doctrine or in the order of worship, so most ministers agreed to the new procedure. But about three hundred implacable churchmen refused and left their chapels rather than submit. Especially in the southwest of Scotland, these ministers had the support of their congregations, and soon secret services or conventicles were being held in houses, in barns, and on bare hillsides. Troops were sent to collect fines from people attending these illegal conventicles, and armed clashes ensued. In spite of the punishments inflicted on them, Covenanter resistance continued unabated.

Peasants throughout the Lowlands sympathized with clergy ejected from their livings, but Dumfriesshire was one of the few localities where excluded ministers could gather a following to keep a secret church functioning. For instance, when a new curate was appointed that year in Irongray, six miles from Dumfries, parishioners attacked him with rocks. The Privy Council in Scotland named an investigative committee composed of the Earls of Linlithgow, Galloway, and Annandale, Lord Drumlanrig, and Sir John Wauchope of Niddry to bring the offenders to justice. Certain culprits were charged with conspiracy and assault, including a man sent to Edinburgh under guard and a woman, Margaret Smith, ordered transported to Barbados. The entire parish had to pay the expenses of the commissioners and their retinue.[15]

James Welwood was eleven years old when the Reverend Welwood's tenure in Annandale ended with official dismissal from his parish. His father was replaced by a man acquiescent to the government's preference for hierarchy. Like other ousted ministers, Rev. James Welwood took up field preaching and did not go quietly. In a letter written in 1665 to his brother, the Welwood paterfamilias revealed his anger at the destruction of Presbyterian principles. Calling for glorious victory over their enemies, he wrote that he expected "terrible judgments...and...monstrous troubles." He did not call for violence himself, but believed that Jesus Christ would vanquish those who destroyed the Church.

> Let us enter into our chambers and shut the doors about us, until the indignation be over-passed that is to be upon this land. Great is the indignation, dreadful are the judgments that are coming upon this land; I tremble to think upon them, and yet I cannot tell you; for as feared as I am for them, I am not deprecating them, but desiring rather that they may come and convince the land of the horridness of these sins now reigning in it, which are counted but light sins by some, and no sins by other some, and gloried in as high virtues and duties by many.

The Reverend Welwood envisioned a fiery demise for the iniquitous, and shrugged off the activities of the High Commission as a hot, but little furnace around which many were then warming themselves. The senior Welwood himself may have felt some heat, for he cautioned his brother not to let anyone see his letter, "because of some things in it that may seem hard." The letter is like a sermon, full of fearful images, but promising heavenly reward for all true believers.[16]

Shortly after the dismissal of their ministers, Covenanters in Dumfriesshire rose up against what they gauged was governmental tyranny and took prisoner Sir James Turner, the man assigned control of Ayrshire, Dumfriesshire, and Galloway by the Privy Council. The insurgents were eventually beaten at Pentlands and sentenced to death at Dumfries, county town for sixteen of the rebels. In 1668, the year James Welwood enrolled at the University of St. Andrews, all residents of Dumfries were required by the authorities to sign an anti-rebel statement, but the area remained a center of religious and political discontent. Welwood would always associate the imposition of religious uniformity by any group with misery and tyranny.

While the Reverend Welwood may have been somewhat circumspect outside his immediate family about his opposition to governmental interference in parish matters, his older sons Andrew and John were not.[17] Both enrolled at St. Andrews University in 1663, just as their father was losing his Annandale congregation. In some ways, the town epitomized the Christian schism: much of the pale grey and golden stone used to build the houses in St. Andrews was taken from what was once the largest cathedral in Scotland. Crosses in the cobbled streets mark the spots where martyrs were burnt at the stake. That legacy of religious division permeated the activities of the Welwood men. After receiving the M.A. two years later, Andrew began a career in the ministry that encompassed the writing of meditations and hymns. He railed against episcopates and lectured those who would tolerate ecclesiastical pollution:

> I am fully persuaded that this Prelacy is abominable Antichristian-
> ism; and that Prelates and Curates are the Ministers, not of Christ,
> but of Antichrist and Satan; and that it is utterly unlawful to hear
> them or do anything that may show you esteem them ministers or
> any Way strengthen their Hands.[18]

He is best remembered for "The Dying Saint's Song," a lugubrious spiritual in which many of the lines begin with "No more shall...." Dying himself from tuberculosis in 1688, Andrew wrote sermonizing final letters to his step-mother, sister Helen, cousin Thomas, and brother James.

The farewell letter to James admonished him to be about the business of his salvation, since death might assault him at any moment. Andrew urged James to be holy, "for without holiness no man shall see the Lord." He suggested that James read William Guthrie's "Trial of a Saving Interest in Christ" and eschew all other temporal business.[19] Andrew reasoned that although "this whole half-year of my life has been a continual winter," his sickness was actually a blessing, since God "hath weaned my heart from the world." The five-page missive chastised James, warning him that "you have never rightly sought God, until it be your chief delight to seek him....I take to writing against you...that if you continue in any vain imagination, living without God in the world, neglecting so great a Salvation, you are a Trampler under foot of the Blood of the Covenant."

Andrew's dour last message to James ended without any particular references to family, friends, or memories of their younger days. None of the other relatives to whom Andrew wrote in the last weeks of his life was treated quite so impersonally, hinting that the writer may have disapproved of his brother's more secular ways. Andrew Welwood's letter to his step-mother reminisced about the "sweet days" he enjoyed with his father and counseled her to see that Mary, his half-sister, did not neglect prayer or reading of the Scriptures and did not frequent bad companions. The valedictory epistle to cousin Thomas Welwood begins with a recollection of their "sweet friendship" and concludes with regards to the recipient's mother-in-law, wife, and children. In his letter to sister Helen, Andrew Welwood evinced signs of tenderness: "I would be glad to spend my last breath upon you [and] cannot forget you [because] you are precious to me." However, in the same letter he criticized their "old man" for desiring "still to be swimming in the ease and vanities of the world," rather a severe judgment for a minister deprived of his congregation because he defended his faith.[20] Andrew Welwood died in London, lambasting sinners and their bishops to the end.

John Welwood was for a time the best known of the Reverend Welwood's three sons. Presbyterian hagiographers commemorate his piety and zeal.[21] He finished his Master's requirements in 1666, and entered the Church although he was not ordained to any particular incumbency. John returned to Annandale and held field meetings to inspire Christians whom he felt had lost their fervor when religious doctrines were imposed on them from the throne. The curate who had succeeded John's father at Tundergarth sent letters to several gentry seeking their help in silencing John Welwood. Such exhortation may have been due to jealousy, for the young preacher delivered sermons in that very parish. Admiring Scots later collected several of his sermons. John Welwood also preached against episcopacy in the early 1670s near the Borders on both the Scottish and English sides and in Fife, where he took a strong stand against bishops in general as a disguise for popery. He became a model conventicler: absolutely certain about the righteousness of his position, monkishly acetic in his habits, and perpetually anxious about the state of his countrymen.

When Charles II began to appoint moderate Presbyterians to Church positions in Scotland under a so-called Declaration of Indulgence, radical conventiclers like John Welwood became more easily discernible to the government. The fulminations and illegal field preaching of John Welwood and other young, irreconcilable Covenanters continued; attempts made by their older brethren to dissuade them from dangerous defiance of authority and to forge a compromise with the ministers who had accepted the Indulgence failed. In 1677 Welwood and his friend Richard Cameron, an equally tendentious Calvinist, were summoned to a meeting in Edinburgh and faced with removal from the Church by the delegates for their rhetoric. Welwood and Cameron denied the legitimacy of the meeting, and refused to accept its admonitions. Later that year, John Welwood intruded into the kirk at the weaving village of Tarbolton in Ayr, causing the Council to order his apprehension.

Besides berating the indulged clergy, John Welwood focused his exclusive ire on the Archbishop of St. Andrews, James Sharp. According to an anecdote related by antiquarian Peter Chalmers about the young preacher, after delivering a stirring sermon outside of St. Andrews, John Welwood sent a message to Sharp via the archbishop's servant warning of damnation and death.

> When ye go home, ye'll tell your master from me that his treachery, tyranny and wicked life is now nearan end, and his death shall be both sudden, surprising, and bloody; as he has thirsted for and shed the blood of many saints, he shall not go to his grave in peace, and that shall be in the beginning of May next.[22]

Although Sharp downplayed the threat, the archbishop's wife cautioned of the danger that such ominous predictions might become self-fulfilling prophecies. John Welwood departed soon after for Perth, maybe on the archbishop's orders, but Mrs. Sharp's fears proved justified. Welwood's harangues against Sharp did arouse indignation among inconsolable Presbyterians and foreshadowed more religious violence. He had surely made a name for himself in Scotland. According to one authority, John Welwood had emerged by the late 1670s along with Richard Cameron as one of the leaders of the "progressive party of the Covenanters."[23]

John Welwood's health began to suffer and his friends noticed growing melancholy and frailty. Never a robust man, in early 1679 he had to abandon preaching altogether, but quietly visited like-minded brethren in Perth. During his time of sickness, many friends came to see him, and he continued to prophesy perdition for the apostates but glorious reformation in the future. In April 1679 John Welwood died of consumption in Perth at the age of thirty, labeled a saint by his

Presbyterian followers. Though his friends were permitted to bury him outside of town, those who attended the funeral were imprisoned by the local magistrates. Authorities were on their guard against potential trouble inspired by Welwood's demise. Even in death, John Welwood's name was anathema to the government. A few weeks later, Archbishop Sharp was murdered in Fifeshire by a small band of frenzied conventiclers.

Young James Welwood did not follow in the vocational footsteps of his father and brothers. Given the dangers inherent for those with any religious calling in the 1660s and 1670s, and the parlous, near fanatical radicalism of the Welwoods, a career in the healing arts must have appealed to one who saw directly the effects of his country's murderous spiritual rift. It is probable that he was inspired to contemplate the profession of medicine by contact with ministers who knew something about doctoring, given the sparseness of medical practitioners in rural districts.[24] Clergymen in parishes with no trained doctors needed to know the rudiments of physic, and Welwood's father probably picked up some information during his college course. Young Welwood would have been exposed to itinerant mountebanks like John Ponthus, who practiced chiefly in Fifeshire. Ponthus built a public stage and sold drugs to the people who enjoyed the variety acts that accompanied his sales pitch. Similarly, Cornelius Tilborg traveled the medicine show circuit to Edinburgh, selling a poison antidote, orvietan, which he was licensed to do by the king himself. Charles II gave Tilborg, who titled himself "Doctor," a gold medal and made him physician-in-ordinary, a doctor to the king. Nonetheless, there were few opportunities for medical schooling for the son of a poor vicar and none in Scotland. Given the insecurity of the times and the precariousness of his father's living, young Welwood opted to stay relatively close to home.

In 1668, at the age of sixteen, James Welwood enrolled at the University of St. Andrews, alma mater of his father and brothers. The town of St. Andrews that greeted his arrival spread out above a wide bay and was open to chilly North Sea breezes. It was medieval in plan: three main streets converging on the cathedral. The university, third oldest in Britain, consisted of three colleges at the time of Welwood's matriculation: St. Salvator's, founded in 1450; St. Leonard's, established in 1512; and St. Mary's, created in 1537 as a seminary of

Protestant theology. The university had experienced hard times during and after the Interregnum, and the importance of the town had declined. In Welwood's era some Scotsmen even proposed transferring the university to Perth because the town of St. Andrews had shrunk to only a noisome hamlet inhabited by rustics. Nevertheless, Scottish nobles and landed gentry continued to consider St. Andrews the fashionable place to send their sons for education, so that leading Scotsmen of the seventeenth century were often Andreapolitan graduates.[24] The University of St. Andrews continued to exercise profound social and political influence through its alumni on the life of Scotland into the eighteenth century.

James Welwood matriculated at St. Salvator's College, attended by his father, when there were notably fewer nobility and gentry enrolled than in previous decades. According to the bursar's book for the period, Welwood paid fees at the rate usually associated with the sons of tenant farmers and artisans, a step below most sons of clerics, suggesting his father's parish was a poor one or that the Reverend Welwood was still deprived of a living by the government. Though young James could have applied for a competitive scholarship or bursary, there were no special funds set aside for the sons of the cloth. While there are no records about Welwood's actual performance, he did take the standard arts course for the period. Sessions at St. Andrews lasted from mid-fall to July 20 with few holidays during which to travel home. Dressed for all college activities in the traditional red gown of St. Salvator's, Welwood studied Latin, ancient Greek, mathematics, logic, ethics, and natural philosophy, subjects that continued to fascinate him throughout life. He spent the first year conquering Greek grammar and language, and the opening weeks of the second year translating Greek into Latin and vice versa. Besides attending his classes, Welwood's presence was expected at other college functions. Welwood would have been summoned by a college bell (named "Katharina") to attend prayers each morning and weekday evening, and on Sundays he proceeded with his college to church. Traditionally following the Sunday services, he and his fellow students, colorful in their bright red attire, would walk the grey harbor wall.

The center of St. Salvator's was the splendid collegiate church, its tall tower still the principal ecclesiastical landmark visible from the

Royal and Ancient Golf Club of St. Andrews. The college kirk, originally a seminary for the training of priests and a basilica for daily worship, opened onto the public road, North Street, and into St. Salvator's quadrangle. The church was splendidly furnished and enriched with altars and chaplainries by benefactors. Access to the quadrangle was possible through the archway of a tall entrance tower; classrooms and a great hall occupied the west side with dormitories on the north and east of the square. Every Monday morning discipline was meted out at a solemn meeting called "common schools" in the great hall of the entire college.[26]

The town of St. Andrews derived its name from its magnificent cathedral, according to legend a repository of the martyr's bones and site of pilgrimages made by the devout. As center of the Scottish Church, it was the burial place of famous clergy and nobility, a sort of Scottish pantheon. However, Welwood knew that the cathedral had been plundered by supporters of John Knox in the sixteenth century, its sacred books set on fire and its altars smashed. He was aware that townspeople afterwards had used the cathedral as a quarry, taking stone away in carts to build themselves houses. Consequently, for Welwood the cathedral shell was a constant reminder of the immoderate Calvinist ideals of the Scottish Reformation and the destructive legacy of zealotry and fanaticism in his homeland.

Regardless of the iconoclasm of his disciples, Knox had proposed a needed re-organization of Scottish education that included establishment of medical teaching at St. Andrews. The scheme never came into operation in part because a complete medical school requires a fairly substantial basis of population in which to flourish. Nevertheless, the curriculum could contain required medical courses even without leading to a medical degree. A university commission appointed by King James VI recommended that the principal of St. Salvator's should be a professor of medicine, and should read this subject four times a week. Among the readings suggested were the aphorisms of Hippocrates. Additionally, the faculty prescribed certain books and lectures about anatomy for general education at St. Salvator's. Notwithstanding these efforts, whatever medicine was taught was merely a small part of the arts curriculum deemed part of an educated man's knowledge.[27]

The town of St. Andrews continued to suffer physical and emotional humiliation in the 1650s at the hands of Cromwellian soldiers quartered on its inhabitants. English troopers amused themselves in the parish kirk by ridiculing Scottish practices and by debating local ministers. During the Interregnum the commissary court convened in St. Salvator's church; meanwhile, in order to eliminate all vestiges of resistance to the Lord Protector's government, thousands of Scots Covenanters and other prisoners of war were sent overseas to toil on plantations. Furthermore, the efficiency and order of Cromwell's regime in Scotland notwithstanding, many wealthy residents then voluntarily left St. Andrews for good, trying to escape high taxes and quarterings costs.

However, the Stuart Restoration and the revival of episcopacy returned prosperity to St. Andrews and its university, since the town again became the ecclesiastical capital of Scotland. Further, the Archbishop of St. Andrews, James Sharp, was after 1661 ex officio Chancellor of the university where he had been both a regent and a professor of divinity. As a result, he actively sought financial support from the government for the institution. Sharp certainly demonstrated that a break with the Calvinist pattern at St. Andrews could usher in new ideas and academic excitement, however belated. Sharp, though avowedly Presbyterian, had developed into a more pragmatic leader of the Scottish Kirk than many Covenanters could tolerate. He had supported the Stuart Restoration and with it the re-imposition of episcopacy, earning the enmity of his Presbyterian brethren and the reputation of religious traitor. Hatred for Sharp had hardened after he accepted nomination as archbishop and publicly endorsed elimination of Covenanting principles.

It seems ironic that Archbishop Sharp, to whose later murder Welwood's family was unjustly connected by unsubstantiated rumor, revivified St. Andrews at the moment of Welwood's matriculation. Though Sharp was a patron of St. Leonard's College, under his auspices in 1668 St. Mary's added a chair in Hebrew. That same year, the year of James Welwood's enrollment, Sharp persuaded Charles II to found a Regius Professorship in mathematics. James Gregory was selected for this university-wide position, bringing with him discoveries in differential and integral calculus and association with the famous Royal Society in London. He had just learned of a new method for expanding a logarithm by an infinite series and was anxious to try it out on his students.

Gregory arrived at St. Andrews at the height of his creative powers, already having written several books of remarkable originality. For six years he brought palpable excitement to the university, all the while keeping in touch with his friends in England and abroad. From his learned contacts he received news that a young man at Cambridge, Isaac Newton, was performing wonders in analytics; he learned of Newton's telescope and entered into a friendly correspondence with him. On one occasion, separate statements of the same discovery by Gregory and Newton crossed in the mail.[28] Gregory designed equipment for an astronomical observatory to be installed atop St. Leonard's. He worked in a long upper room of the University library, seeking advice from Robert Hooke, a great innovator in the field of scientific instruments, and from John Flamsteed, then a young astronomer in Derby and later the first Astronomer Royal. Armed with their suggestions, Gregory planned to erect a third story above the upper hall with six tall windows facing north, south, and east in pairs. However, Gregory's scheme was not carried out and there are few traces at St. Andrews of his astronomical instruments.

For the six years he taught at St. Andrews, James Gregory had a significant impact in the classroom, too. Enlivened by Gregory's informed views on Kepler, Galileo and Descartes, St. Salvator's students, Welwood among them, were inspired by his revolutionary teaching and they ridiculed the mediocre pedantry of other preceptors. Students may have been encouraged in this attitude by Gregory, who felt stifled by the failure of his observatory project and by the overt jealousy of his colleagues. When his pay was withheld and his laboratory assistants refused to serve him, in 1674 he accepted another position as Chair of Mathematics at the University of Edinburgh at double the salary.

Whatever their inspiration, Gregory's students were right to recognize the legato pace of curricular change at St. Andrews until well after the Restoration. Throughout the Augustan Age, conflict raged among the erudite over the superiority of ancient versus modern scholars and whether history was science or literature.[29] Ordinarily, religious reformers and political dissenters took the side of the moderns and demanded a course of linguistic and historical studies which reflected the latest scholarship. Methods of instruction could also be "modern," even encouraging the student to use his own initiative. However, due to its small town setting, fewer progressive demands had been made on St. Andrews by local bourgeoisie than on any other university in Scotland.[30] Archbishop Sharp was understandably pleased with the impression Gregory made on his colleagues and students, and therefore continued to press for more funds for the university. He was rewarded with the Act of 1672 which allocated vacant stipends for university purposes. How ironic that the Archbishop, promoter of intellectual change at St. Andrews, was regarded as a conservative tyrant by Presbyterian patriots; ironic, too, that a Welwood directly benefitted from Sharp's championing more vigorous instruction at the university. Though young James could not have known it, his studies coincided with the beginnings of a Scottish Enlightenment.[31]

By reason of the Calvinist domination of Scottish university education in the seventeenth century, some historians have dismissed the notion of an early Scottish Enlightenment as an oxymoron. However, persuasive findings exist that new ideas did enter university courses in general after the Stuart Restoration and in particular at St. Andrews with the advocacy of Archbishop Sharp. Student notebooks and graduation theses from the last half of the seventeenth century contain proof that university professors taught a transitional mixture of old and new philosophy, exposing their classes to educational controversy of the best sort. James Welwood would have been introduced to this critical spirit expressly in his courses in natural philosophy and physics. Although modern pedagogues may shudder at their methods, professors in the 1660s and 1670s dictated lectures which students faithfully recorded. Student notebooks, a few of which survive from seventeenth-century St. Andrews, show a definite shift from Aristotelian to Cartesian to Newtonian physics. Although the University of Edinburgh led the way by incorporating modern trends in philosophy and science, the faculty at St. Andrews recognized and disseminated the fruits of the Scientific Revolution, probably owing to the influence of James Gregory and his successors. The printed graduation theses of the period, produced at the end of the four-year arts course such as Welwood took, relate to the student's subject matter and were defended by the candidates for graduation. Only a handful from the late seventeenth century survive for St. Andrews, Welwood's not among them, but these demonstrate an awareness of theoretical frictions among published authorities with the resultant widening of philosophical horizons. Scottish university library catalogs at about the time of Welwood's enrollment likewise suggest a healthy broadening of intellectual inquiry and foretell the flowering of learning to come in eighteenth-century Scotland.

In Welwood's time, the baccalaureate degree implied fitness to go further, and the license granted at the end of the fourth year was a permit to lecture anywhere in the world. Welwood chose to study more at St. Andrews, and continued there until he received a graduate degree, an academic feat accomplished by a minute portion of the educated elite. Therefore, the ceremony accompanying the awarding of Master of Arts was suitably impressive; the magistrand received a beret, a ring, and a book. The graduate was expected to give a dinner attended by town and gown alike, and to present berets and gloves to his guests. Eventually the faculty recommended limiting promotion expenses except if the graduate were very wealthy. Once made Master of Arts, the new M.A. was obligated to lecture for two years, unless cash payments were made to dispense with the requirement.

James Welwood graduated Master of Arts on July 25, 1671, still not yet twenty years old.[32] Upon completing his teaching requirements at St. Andrews, he may have been a tutor for a time, perhaps in Fifeshire. Welwood displayed a lifelong, fond association for his birthplace, known for its quaint houses with curved red pantiles. For several years his quiet life is shrouded in obscurity, but parallel political events in Britain were far from quiet or obscure.

Shortly after Welwood's graduation from St. Andrews, public fury over Charles II's religious duplicity and connivance with France's Louis XIV exploded in 1672 with revelations about the Treaty of Dover, a secret agreement signed two years earlier which gave Charles fiscal freedom from Parliament in return for compliance with French policy goals. Besides coordinating England's foreign plans with France, Charles covertly assented to re-establishing the Roman Catholic Church in Britain. Suspicious of any religious nonconformists, Parliament responded with the famous Test Act of 1673, designed to ban all non-Anglicans from holding any civil or military office. Office holders had to receive communion in the Church of England and to repudiate the Catholic doctrine of transubstantiation. Although dissenting Protestants frequently evaded its requirements, the English Test Act branded Catholics untrustworthy citizens, perceived as lackeys of France and the Papacy.[33]

Anti-popery, already the dominating motif in English culture, became an obsession in Scotland. James Welwood discerned another impulse for general outrage among his fellow Scots, later regarding the animosities between Presbyterians and Episcopalians as the product of wholesale mismanagement by English governmental agents in Scotland. In his history of that troubled period written twenty years afterward, James Welwood blamed the severity of all Caroline administrative policy in Scotland, specifically that directed by John Maitland, Duke of Lauderdale, for occasioning full insurrection in the northern kingdom. Most contemporaries, however, viewed the strife as almost entirely religious in nature. Many Scottish preachers argued to their Calvinist congregations in the 1670s that bishops and other Anglican Church hierarchy constituted a dangerous remnant of Catholic tradition. Moreover, bishops personified a return to religious authority beyond the reach of the individual believer. Hence, for religious and political reasons, bishops became the target of the dissatisfied in Scotland; the activity of Archbishop Sharp made him uncommonly vulnerable to vigilante assaults. An attempt on his life had been foiled in 1668, but the perpetrator remained at large until 1678. The execution that year of the would-be assassin, coupled with a new round of Covenanter persecution in Fifeshire, aroused passionate hatred for Sharp among the locals. At least one nineteenth-century writer, John Wilson Croker, avers that the Welwood family conspired in the death in 1679 of the archbishop. However, other than the sermons delivered against the prelate by John Welwood, there is no evidence of their doing so. Croker provides no proof whatsoever of the Welwoods' culpability in Sharp's death and no basis for his inferences.

Despite his beneficial reforms at the university, Sharp became the focus for those in Scotland enraged by Charles II's perfidy. In May 1679, the archbishop and his daughter were trapped in his carriage on a Fifeshire road between St. Andrews and Cupar by local Covenanters.

Claiming they had a call from God and believing that providence had delivered the archbishop to them, the attackers shot and beat Sharp to death. Since Sharp had once himself been a staunch Presbyterian, many Scots deemed his murder divine retribution for betraying Covenanting principles. The moment for decisive military action had come at last. Not long after the assassination, three troops of government horse under Graham of Claverhouse were utterly routed on a boggy moor at Drumclog by a much smaller group of armed Covenanters. Thereafter, Charles II's government reacted even more vigorously than before, sending an army under the King's illegitimate son, James, Duke of Monmouth, to deal with the rebels. At Bothwell Brig the Covenanters were soundly defeated and 1400 prisoners were herded into Greyfriars churchyard in Edinburgh to await their various unpleasant ends. The years immediately following the Sharp homicide became known as the Killing Time to the Scots.

Croker asserted in an 1824 edition of the letters of Henrietta Howard that the older Welwoods conspired in the assault on Sharp and thereafter had to flee to the continent following his murder. According to Croker, because of his family's flight, James Welwood, then twenty-seven years old, received his medical education among other Protestant exiles at Leiden. In fact, Sharp's assassins, known local lairds and farmers led by John Balfour of Burleigh, fled to the west of Scotland and fomented an abortive revolt there, as narrated in Sir Walter Scott's 1816 novel, *The Old Mortality*. Nowhere is there any mention of the Welwoods as conspirators in either the assassination or the subsequent insurrection. Nevertheless, James Welwood remarked in 1692 that he "was ruined in the two last reigns."[34]

Even so shocking an event as the Sharp murder and the savagery that followed did not end the preoccupation of the common man with erstwhile papists. One can hardly overestimate how much that fear of Catholicism colored both popular culture and educated discourse. Even more problematic for those who associated anti-popery with patriotism was the acknowledged conversion of the king's brother and heir, James, to Roman Catholicism. In spite of producing a profusion of bastards with several mistresses, the "Merry Monarch" had no children by his wife, the Portuguese princess, Catherine of Braganza. Therefore, James, Duke of York in England and Duke of Albany in Scotland, would become king of both realms upon Charles' death, bringing the feared doctrines of Romanism with him to the throne. Amidst a swirl of plots and counter-plots, opposition to James' succession crystallized in 1679 under the direction of the Earl of Shaftesbury. The political nation split on the question of excluding James and passing the crown on to the next Protestant in line.

Supporters and opponents of exclusion became better organized than political groups had been heretofore. Even before the Exclusion Crisis, a so-called Country Party had begun to coalesce around landed Members of Parliament, men free from royal patronage who were for individual liberty and against Catholics. They had an inherent distrust of the Crown and its Court. The Whigs, as Country Party supporters of exclusion soon came to be named, held a majority in the House of Commons as Shaftesbury developed sound political organization and pamphlet propaganda. They were opposed by a Court Party, royalist and Anglican sympathizers in Parliament who supported Charles II, and from both interest and principle sought to maintain the orderly functioning of his government. Later known as the Tories, they effectively opposed exclusion by relying on their own political strengths including the king and the public's recurring fear of renewed civil war.[35] From 1679 to 1681 the gulf between the two factions seemed deep enough to warrant those fears. Even during long periods of parliamentary prorogation, the Whigs sustained a campaign of petitions to the king and of popular demonstrations. But, however united on excluding James from the succession they may have been, the Whigs disagreed on who should succeed. Some wanted Charles' illegitimate son, James, Duke of Monmouth, but others espoused the cause of James' older daughter, Mary. She seemed more suitable except for her marriage to the Dutch prince, William of Orange, and the threat of involving England in an expensive continental war against the French. Even Shaftesbury was ambivalent about an alternate to James.

The Tories were able to exploit the Whigs' failure to agree on a successor in their exclusion demands. The Tory leadership shrewdly connected the barring of a legitimate claimant to inherit the throne with the potential restriction of any legitimate claim to inherit property. The revolutionary implications of exclusion repelled many who still had vivid memories of Oliver Cromwell. Furthermore, the king and the Tories had allies in the judiciary who disdained radical rhetoric and on the treasury commission, which gave the king some measure of financial independence from Parliament during the crisis. Therefore, in retrospect the king's position was really quite solid, but in 1679 the hostility in England between political factions over exclusion appeared grievous.

Fearing that his brother's presence would exacerbate an already delicate situation, the king dispatched James to Scotland in late 1679, ostensibly to provide liaison, but practically to remove James from center stage. Charles may have hoped that out-of-sight his brother would be less likely to provoke hasty action by the legislature in London. James could serve the king's purpose in the north, demonstrating a personal royal insistence on obedience to the crown and a demand that religious resistance cease. From 1663 to 1679 Charles' chief minister for Scotland was the Duke of Lauderdale. James seems usually to have supported his policies, but by the time James reached Scotland Lauderdale's enemies had capitalized on his failing health, and Monmouth had to be called on to put down the rebellion at Bothwell Brig. James felt there was need to brace the powers of the crown and to identify the inimical.

James Stuart appeared in Edinburgh at a dangerous moment in Scottish affairs, but settled in to make a success of his stay at the recently rebuilt palace of Holyroodhouse. It was he who suggested creating a classical New Town of Edinburgh, and granted the city powers not only to extend its jurisdiction, but the right to levy "cellarage," a tax on basements and property at the end of and under the King's Highway. James' court in Edinburgh included his second wife, Mary of Modena, and his younger daughter, Anne. A minor revival took place as the palace became the scene of musical recitals, theatrical plays, and balls.[36]

Despite his successes in Edinburgh, James Stuart faced supplementary challenges to his authority in Scotland. Objections to religious conformity and episcopacy had hardened into open defiance as uncompromising Covenanters, some of them ministers ordained in Holland, formed into armed groups. Donald Cargill and John Welwood's friend, Richard Cameron, led one such group, the Society People, and after Cameron was killed in 1680, Cargill "excommunicated" the Stuarts.[37] Using market crosses for bulletin boards, the

Society People posted their complaints and threats for communities to see. Later captured by government forces, Cargill was hanged for treason in 1681, about the same time that James Stuart appeared as a Royal Commissioner. Irrespective of the deaths of their leaders, the Society People continued to castigate the Stuarts and their agents in Scotland.

James Stuart summoned the feeble Scottish Parliament in the summer of 1681 and pushed through the measures he wanted. Besides securing additional taxation to support the army and obtaining an act guaranteeing his succession to the Scottish crown, in 1683 James procured a Test Act of his own, an oath of non-resistance, to be taken by all office holders, clergymen and Parliamentary representatives. His energetic work done in Scotland, James Stuart returned to England.

James Welwood left Scotland to study medicine on the continent even before the antagonism between strict Covenanters and the Stuarts had reached a fever pitch. Welwood's medical doctorate obtained in 1684 from the faculty at University of Reims is not at all mysterious or politically suspect; he probably did not have the option of studying in Britain. No Scottish university by 1680 had established an adequate medical faculty or program leading to the degree, and both Oxford and Cambridge universities required its doctoral candidates to obtain a bachelor's degree in medicine before admittance to the higher program. Oxford University statutes mandated that a medical curriculum would normally follow the arts curriculum. The sequence of degrees would be Bachelor of Arts, Master of Arts, Bachelor of Medicine three years later, and finally Doctor of Medicine four years after that. If a total of seven years or more had elapsed since the M.A., then candidates could take both medical degrees "by accumulation," paying two sets of graduation fees and getting both degrees simultaneously.

Besides the time and prerequisite degree involved in obtaining an M.D. from Oxford or Cambridge, Welwood would have been discomfited and perhaps even disqualified by the religious requirements of the institutions during the 1670s and 1680s. If he could not swear allegiance to the Thirty-nine Articles of the Anglican Church, then a student could not matriculate or get a degree at either Oxford or Cambridge. Given his family's history, Welwood would probably have disapproved of such enforced conformity; given his family's history, the universities would certainly have disapproved of him.

Many Scotsmen as well as Englishmen chose to study medicine on the continent, some because they preferred a less traditional curriculum than offered at Oxford or Cambridge. Indeed, disagreement over medical theory and pedagogy had already disrupted the Royal College of Physicians in London, and by Welwood's time nearly half of its licensed fellows had studied abroad in order to acquire a more progressive education.[38] The Royal College of Physicians in Edinburgh, established in 1681, also numbered fellows with foreign training. The University of Reims, however, was not noted in the 1680s for its advanced course of studies or for the excellence of its medical faculty; it was regarded as a convenient vehicle through which foreigners could procure acceptable credentials enabling them to practice medicine outside France. Whatever his reasons, James Welwood sometime in the mid-1670s departed Scotland for the continent and schooling in medicine.

CHAPTER TWO

Educational Controversies

*J*ames Welwood received a medical degree in January 1684 from the University of Reims in the Champagne country of northeastern France. With its cathedral school, Reims was one of the most important educational centers in the Middle Ages and during the early sixteenth century successive Cardinals of Lorraine intervened to establish a facility of higher learning there. Founded in 1548 by Pope Paul III, the University of Reims and the city in which it was located were flourishing in the 1680s when Welwood arrived. Reims had long been an important hinterland entrepôt for wines, surrounded by well-tended vineyards amidst gentle, rolling hills and ancient chalk caves, where merchants stored thousands of bottles of champagne. However, Reims' chief source of wealth was its woolen textile industry, and wealthy manufacturers and bankers competed with royal patrons to embellish the city, still surrounded by its medieval walls and dotted with remnants of its Roman past. Home to about 30,000 Rémois at the time of Welwood's matriculation, the city had an air of prosperity noted by travelers, who found the river Vesle pretty, the streets broad, the inns large, and the gates of the town superb.[1] Although most civic celebrations were religious in nature, the University bustled with young students, and sometimes their bibitory celebrations got out of hand. Ribald secular fêtes in the Fourth Quarter of the city occasionally disturbed the peace of those who worshipped in the area's many churches. Roads passed through Reims from Burgundy and Lorraine to Flanders and the Channel ports, bringing strangers constantly into town and creating even more commotion. The presence of many nobles and a puissant church organization enlivened Reims society, but high culture remained essentially clerical and marginal.

James Welwood certainly knew some of the erudite clergy in Reims, especially those who were interested in history and the classics, such as the famed Benedictine monk Jean Mabillon, archivist and historiographer. More likely, Welwood would have been cognizant of the Rémois historian and canon, Francois de Maucroix, biographer of St. John Chrysostom, and expert on the works of Lactantius, Demosthenes, and Cicero, all favorites of Welwood. Among those contemporaries of Welwood who hailed from Reims was Jean Baptiste Colbert, Louis XIV's great financial minister and himself the son of a draper.

Though it may seem odd that Welwood chose a French school at which to study medicine, many Scotsmen obtained medical education in that country. There were no medical schools in Scotland in the early 1680s; even a decade later when John Arbuthnot, physician to Queen Anne and Tory essayist, obtained a medical degree from Aberdeen, he did so after examination by a group of doctors rather than by taking classes. French medical schools may have had many Scottish students because of the Auld Alliance, the special relationship between France and Scotland; historically Scottish Protestants had access to legal and medical studies to universities anywhere in France.[2]

French provincial schools were easier to get into and had fewer prerequisites for admission. Attending Oxford or Cambridge for a graduate medical degree first required completion of their undergraduate course of studies, but continental universities expected their students to matriculate at several institutions. A degree from Reims may have been easier to finish, too. At the behest of University Rector Thomas Mercier, the statutes of the university were remodeled in 1660. A four-man committee of medical faculty from the University of Paris, headed by physician Guy Patin, introduced fifty new measures aimed at boosting the reputation of Reims to that of a premier school equal to Paris or Montpellier. Despite these efforts, the belief persisted for another century throughout Europe that degrees were too easily obtained from the Reims faculty.[3]

The University of Paris may have offered the dedicated student more medical facilities, but the universities at Reims and at Angers were particularly popular with Scotsmen. Language presented no problem, since Latin functioned as the lingua franca in Europe well into the eighteenth century, encouraging the possibility of a cosmopolitan realm of learning in which national identities were obscured. Archibald Pitcairne, Scottish physician and poet, received his M.D. in 1680 from Reims, as did James Douglas, a 1675 Reims M.D., who like Welwood would later seek his fortune as a London physician. The Dutch medical schools at Utrecht and Leiden drew significant numbers of Scottish students, including Fifeshire historian Robert Sibbald in 1661 and Robert Wellwood (or Walewood), who at age twenty-two obtained an M.D. from Leiden in 1675.[4] Archibald Pitcairne taught at Leiden from 1691-94 before returning to Scotland. Of the founding members (including Pitcairne and Sibbald) of the Royal College of Physicians in Edinburgh in 1681, nearly all had degrees from either France or the Netherlands.[5] However, religious differences did not appear to factor into a Scotsman's decision to attend a continental university for medical education. During most of the seventeenth century, as long as the Edict of Nantes enforced religious toleration in France, Scotsmen often chose to study medicine at French institutions. Because of its affirmative effect on all of Europe, James Welwood later referred to the Edict of Nantes as the French Magna Carta.[6]

Catholicism and Reformed French Protestantism had co-existed since 1589, when Henri IV's decree compelled mutual restraint under the law. But despite the apparent legal immunity of the Huguenots from persecution, the Catholic clergy lobbied ceaselessly for conversion campaigns, thereby limiting real toleration to certain regions of the country for certain periods of time. Nevertheless, until 1661 while Cardinal Mazarin exercised authority during the minority of Louis XIV, pragmatism triumphed over orthodoxy.[7] Even after Louis' personal assumption of power, strategy dictated that in order to defeat France's natural enemy, the powerful Hapsburg family of the Holy Roman Empire and Spain, the king needed the alliances of Europe's Protestant princes. Within the borders of France, common sense and Minister Colbert's commercialism required continued fair treatment of the Huguenots, whose considerable wealth helped stabilize the country. At least until the late 1670s, Louis took a somewhat temperate approach to the religious issue and maintained France's official policy of toleration. Apparently to monarchs and to ordinary men of Welwood's time, the concept of toleration came wrapped with the indulgence of condescension rather than with respect.

Regardless, studying in Reims must have provoked some response in Welwood, for the town was as closely associated with Catholicism and kings as it was with sparkling wine and woolens. Most of the French monarchs since Clovis had been crowned there in the great Gothic cathedral of Notre Dame, including Charles VII in 1429 after his rescue by Joan of Arc in the Hundred Years War against the English. Successive kings had lavished many favors on the city to show their thankfulness. Moreover, the archbishop of Reims was made a peer of the realm. Rue d'Université still runs right behind the church to the southeast, a constant reminder of the connection between Roman Catholicism and college life in the city.[8] Shortly before Welwood's arrival, the elegant archiepiscopal palace, built between 1498 and 1509, was restored; its famed salle du Tau displayed medallions of the archbishops of Reims who consecrated France's rulers. For over a century before Welwood's time at Reims, many Catholic Irish and Scottish students had sought scholarly refuge at the Jesuit college from religious harassment at home, and the chapters of the monastic orders in the city were among the richest and most powerful in the country. The mere presence there of a university faculty, most of whom were priests, augmented the Reims church's scholarly standing and its title to political as well as moral superiority in the district.

Welwood's curriculum at Reims would have differed only somewhat from the course of studies he might have gotten in England. Although many continental universities pursued the more experimental medical theories of the Swiss professor of medicine Paracelsus and his followers, Oxford and Cambridge still deemed appropriate the traditional Galenic theories of sickness and health dating from second-century Rome.[9] Galen was the Greek-born court physician to Emperor Marcus Aurelius who wrote over 500 treatises on medicine and philosophy. He postulated that four "humors" or bodily fluids govern the body's health: blood, phlegm, yellow bile, and black bile. According to established Galenism, personality is also affected by the humors: people with too much blood are sanguine, or ardent and hopeful; those with an excess of phlegm are phlegmatic, or dull and apathetic; melancholiacs, the depressed and unhappy among us, suffer from immoderate black bile, and the peevish and cross are understandably bilious, burdened with superfluous yellow bile.

Galenism embraced the notion of balance and moderation, postulating that human beings are a balance of warm, cold, dry and moist, and viewed disease as a product of humoral instability. Too much or too little of any these humors led to more than personality quirks: it ended in dangerous imbalance and illness. According to the Galenic method, a physician must prescribe ways of redressing humoral equilibrium, either by removing a surfeit or adding to a deficit. If a person was feverish, flushed, or hot, he had an overabundance of blood. Too much blood required bleeding, sometimes preceded by applying a vacuum cup to the skin and producing a welt which could then be pierced, or by scarifying the area before attaching the cup. On other occasions a vein was simply opened and kept open with a crudely inserted shunt. Purging via vomitories, laxatives, or emmenagogues eliminated other excessive humors. Medications or other recipes promised restoration and rejuvenation, albeit usually taken by a patient denied fresh air or sunlight.

Even food was considered medicinal if prepared properly, reflecting the ancient conviction that internal medicine was a specialized construct of dietetics and that preparing food was akin to preparing medicines. Cooking must reflect the Galenic ideal of balance: wet, dry, cold, and hot. A tempered diet must include food from each category; beans were considered cold, so they should be supplemented by hot spices to balance them. Febrile patients should eat predominantly cold foods. John Archer, an advertising empiric who treated Charles II, categorized hare as "a melancholy meat, and therefore not good for those who have dry bodies."[10] Auxiliary to these theories was the idea that each person had a unique constitution and therefore needed to be treated individually; particular treatments in one case might not be good for someone else. Since disease could change over time as the physiology of the patient changed, treatment needed to be varied according to the current state of the illness. Galen's theories went virtually unchallenged until the sixteenth century, thus inhibiting much medical investigation and experimentation.

Paracelsus, born Theophrastus Bombastus von Hohenheim, challenged Galenic teaching and the authority of the medical establishment in ways parallel to Martin Luther's defiance of the Roman Catholic church. Paracelsus ridiculed humoral speculations, instead advocating chemical and metallurgical experiments combined with a sort of mysticism to attack disease. He upset the medical profession with his unorthodox ideas, monumental ego, and insistence on writing in German rather than Latin. He was exiled from his post at the University of Basel and led an itinerant life, practicing medicine, writing books, and studying diseases of miners. Nevertheless, his influence was profound, revolutionizing medical training on the continent through a more empirically-based course of study tied to the observation of patient symptoms and the insistence on better nutrition. Myriad diseases, his followers held, revealed themselves through fairly constant symptoms easily recognized by the patient and easily diagnosed by any observer. Once diagnosed, exact countermeasures could be prescribed, rather than the protean regimen required by the learned Galenics. Many of Paracelsus' Calvinist followers believed that iatrochemistry had a "religious vision" lacking in stock medicine.

The universities of Oxford and Cambridge continued to embrace a Galenic curriculum in medicine until the mid-to-late seventeenth century when empiricism became the fashion in London. Prompted by an enthusiastic Charles II and by a changed Royal College of Physicians in London, English medical degrees began to reflect a new emphasis on finding specific cures for specific diseases. Followers of the new medicine stressed familiarity with human anatomy and observation of patient symptoms. Since the Royal College of Physicians licensed men to practice in the London metropolitan area, and since nearly half of its membership by 1670 was continentally-trained, it is not surprising that the English universities started to reshape their curricula to reflect the new medicine.[11]

At Reims, however, Welwood would have found a faculty and a course of study tardy in its awareness of the new medicine. Unlike the Italian or Dutch universities, French colleges, especially those in the provinces, had not made much progress in the study of medicine. Instead, the French were still devoted to a slavish reading of texts and to the medical wisdom of bleeding and purging. Moreover, of the "eighty-seven doctors, officers, members, and their henchmen of the four faculties" at the University around Welwood's time, most were priests.[12] Although the Roman Catholic church had become less directly absolute in seventeenth-century Gallic education, the teaching of conventional medical doctrines predominated in the *ancien régime* for another century and a half. A few faculty mavericks, often Huguenot as well as Paracelsian, preferred the new metallic drugs like mercury and antimony over historic methods of bleeding and purging. For the most part, however, there is little novelty evident in the extant medical theses of Scotsmen who studied in France and none at Reims.[13]

Then why did Welwood go to Reims? Historian Charles Coury suggests that the Reims faculty was reputable, while decidedly inferior to Paris, Montpellier, Toulouse and Strasbourg.[15] The medical faculty was made up of "regent" doctors headed by a Dean who was also the primary examiner. The Reims medical faculty was founded in 1545, preceding the university itself by two years and inheriting the medieval episcopal schools of Champagne. Its revised statutes date from 1660 and were similar to those of the faculty of Paris. The activity of the medical school at Reims, based on the number of students and degrees awarded, placed it among the three or four most important of the old French faculties.

Like physicians in Britain challenged by charlatans and irregulars, French doctors wanted to maintain control over licensed health care; they were able to do so through the faculties of medicine in France, through the teaching of medicine, and through the conferral of degrees. At Reims students studied medicine in three categories as described in the statutes. For "natural subjects," there were courses in anatomy and physiology; "unnatural subjects" included hygiene and diet; and "subjects against nature" meant courses in pathology, medicine, and therapy. Chairs of botany and pharmacy were added at Reims when Welwood was a student there. Lectures on required subjects were delivered to regular students in Latin with special emphasis and commentary on Hippocrates, Galen, and the sixteenth-century French court physician, Jean Fernel. Fernel had criticized established medicine without completely rejecting it. His ideas, including denunciation of establishment physicians for lacking chemical knowledge, were popularized in England by herbalist Nicholas Culpeper's 1652 book, *The Practice of*

Physick. During Welwood's time at Reims, lectures were additionally given in French on surgery for apprentice barber-surgeons.

There were three levels of recognized accomplishment regulated by French medical faculties. The baccalaureate degree gave only a restricted right to practice medicine and to lecture; a license gave freer reign to practice, although usually outside the university city, where competition from faculty physicians rendered a license less respected than a doctorate. The doctoral degree conferred broader rights: to "teach, lecture, interpret, and freely exercise all medical activities, ...here and in all other places." Ever competitive, universities often refused to recognize degrees granted by other faculties and required supplementary examinations for practice in their jurisdictions. Paris did not give the right to practice to provincial doctors, not even those nominated from Montpellier. Kings and princes, however, occasionally overrode the professional prerogatives of physicians by accrediting numerous foreign "doctors" who treated monarchs, but were little more than mountebanks or crackpots.[15]

Moreover, there were three kinds of degrees in medicine available at seventeenth-century Reims. The most prestigious, the *grand ordinaire*, guaranteed that the recipient had studied a rigorous curriculum for four years (only three years were asked of sons of Rémois) and had passed difficult examinations in Latin. For the Bachelor of Medicine degree, the candidate was interrogated on all his medical studies and asked to comment extemporaneously on an aphorism of Hippocrates. Those students receiving a Medical License took tests after receiving the bachelor's degree, prescribed sequentially over several months.

First, in February the student underwent an anatomy exam of four hours duration that included oral tests and dissection. A physiology thesis was defended sometime in May during a six-hour disputation. In late May or early June, planned for the blossoming of springtime in Reims, the candidate demonstrated his competence in botany. December brought both a three-hour oral dissertation on some unspecified illness and dissection of a cadaver. During the following May the candidate presented a thesis on physiology or pathology and submitted to a four-hour debate on his thesis. In June came the required discourse on Hippocrates and finally in September a practical consultation.

To receive the diploma of the *grand ordinaire*, one had to develop a cardinal thesis on a pathology or hygiene question, and then deliver and debate that thesis in great solemnity in front of a number of invited guests during a five-hour morning examination. The ability to speak on one's feet and the stamina to endure the rituals of the process were evidently as crucial to a successful graduation in the seventeenth century as medical and scientific prowess. At noon, upon victorious completion of the presentation, the candidate received a doctoral hat and took an oath. A few words of thanks from the candidate were expected, especially by the dignitaries there to receive him into the profession. A great feast followed for masters and students at the expense of their new colleague. At the climax of the festivities, the candidate was awarded the title "Doctor Regent" and the right to practice in Reims as well as in the rest of the kingdom. Few could surmount the hurdles of time and money required for the *grand ordinaire*, especially foreigners, and so the number of these degrees granted was somewhat limited.

A second variety of degree, the *petit ordinaire*, was awarded to those who had studied medicine elsewhere for at least three years and had resided for six months in Reims. Candidates for this doctorate defended two theses in public and received a diploma that gave them the title "Doctor Regnicole." With the diploma came permission to practice anywhere in France except in Reims and in the other hometowns of its faculty.[16]

Lastly was the *doctorat étranger*, reserved for foreigners who were not subject to any residence requirements. They needed only to pass a single exam, but since it was assumed they would return to their native lands, they were licensed to practice outside France as "Doctor of Reims." Because the *doctorat étranger* was acquired so easily, it was not respected. Certain prestigious faculties, such as Paris and Montpellier, refused to award it at all, but nine Gallic universities including Reims did confer the degree. These institutions were ridiculed for the ease with which they awarded successive degrees in a few weeks, sometimes even without examinations. It was said that one went to sleep in Reims and woke up a doctor![17]

Thus, despite the fact that Reims required years of study for its baccalaureate degree in medicine and was among the better-endowed provincial universities in France with eight professors and seven professorial chairs, its reputation was sullied by the *doctorat étranger*. Nevertheless, as a degree-granting institution Reims remained attractive to foreign students like Welwood. Although the influx of foreign scholars began to wane in the seventeenth century, once inside French frontiers students could move from one university to another, studying in one place and being examined elsewhere. Foreign students could then take an examination for the *petit ordinaire* at the end of a scholarly Grand Tour after finding a professor willing to serve as faculty sponsor. The individual student's ability to solicit instruction was not dependent on any institution. For instance, Archibald Pitcairne spent five years in France, taking courses in chemistry and anatomy in Paris open to anyone, before getting his degree at Reims. Since at Reims no residency requirement existed for the *doctorat étranger* and was inconsistently enforced for the *petit ordinaire*, one only had to present a thesis, sometimes only four folio pages in length and usually of marginal scientific interest, in order to get the degree.[18] From the fees it assessed for the *petit ordinaire* and the *doctorat étranger*, a university like Reims could find the awarding of such degrees a convenient way to increase its income. Final ceremonies were less spectacular for the awarding of a "foreign" doctorate than for a French one, but for the serious student they marked the end of what might have been a peripatetic process.

Additionally, Reims could offer practical experience in hospital care, and its faculty was dispersed in a variety of specialized local hospitals. At the 225-bed Hôtel-Dieu, just a short distance from the medical college, 4,000-5,000 cases were admitted annually. The university staffed the Hôtel-Dieu with four doctors, two surgeons, and a number of adjuncts faculty. St. Mark's Hospital catered to patients who suffered from "cold humors, collapse, and cancer;" St. Eloy's dealt with lepers. There were auxiliary hospitals in Reims for the aged, for orphaned children, and for undiagnosed ailments.

For some foreign students less interested in curricula and practica, the costs of a French medical education may have been appealing. Formal university training in England in the 1680s required a substantial monetary outlay, perhaps as much as £1000 from matriculation to final degree, at a time when a successful London shopkeeper could count on an income of only £150 per year. Costs could run nearly as high at Leiden or Paris, although the final tally depended upon how much schooling the student entering a Dutch or French university already had. In 1697, several years after Welwood's schooling, physician-turned-playwright Thomas Browne tallied the price of a regular physician's education at £1000. Generalizing about money equivalents over a prolonged period of time is always risky, but it is necessary for our purposes. The French *livres tournois* was the standard used during the seventeenth century, not a coin but fictive money of account. The exchange rate during Welwood's era was fairly stable at about fourteen *livres* to the English pound.[19] When traveling student John Ward contemplated his choices for schooling in medicine, he noted that "Angiers in ffrance [was] not above nine livres and [feasting the professors] not necessarie neither."[20] By any calculation, for less than an English pound Ward thought he had found a bargain.

In practice, however, obtaining a *petit ordinaire* or *doctorat étranger* could have been much more expensive than Ward anticipated. Even discounting whatever scholarly peregrinations and costs preceded the final steps in the process, there were fees for examination and for the degree itself, as well as expenses for tips and presents. By the time that James Welwood received his degree from Reims, hundreds of *livres* would have been required in various fees; he had also paid registration charges and other living expenses. Coury puts the cost of a baccalaureate in medicine around 1700 at 3500 *livres*, nearly £300, and notes that by 1750 the degree of doctor of medicine cost 5614 *livres*, over £430. By contrast a Parisian professor in 1700 received 200 *livres* salary (slightly over £15), and the incomes of provincial faculty were considerably less.[21] Though there were a few prizes and scholarships provided by rich benefactors, Welwood would hardly have qualified for aid as a thirty year-old foreigner. The source of his financial support, whatever his expenditures, remains an intriguing concern.[22] Nevertheless, a Reims doctorate cost less than its English counterpart and many Britons availed themselves of the "cheaper fares on the [continental] physic line," significantly diluting the social exclusiveness of English physicians.[23]

The University of Reims produced a significant crop of doctoral degrees during Welwood's era, averaging thirteen per year. Oxford University, by comparison, awarded only five doctorates in medicine per year over a fifty year span. Despite the relative ease with which it granted doctoral degrees, contemporary statements in English medical literature probably exaggerate the disrespect afforded a Reims diploma. Moreover, Oxford University itself often incorporated foreign degrees and licensed unincorporated foreign degree-holders. During the last half of the seventeenth century seventy-eight foreign medical degrees were incorporated at Oxford; at the same time 223 degrees were awarded to Oxonians. In addition, nearly one-third of the licenses granted by the Oxford faculty to practice medicine went to unincorporated foreign degree-holders.[24]

Furthermore, while there were Reims M.D.s with dubious academic backgrounds, some of its alumni rate highly among the medical and scientific community of the day and were not just the shabby products of a disreputable diploma mill. Though the original records are lost, most of the British degree recipients at Reims (classified as Angli, Scoti, and Hiberni) had matriculated first at Leiden, and after graduating from Reims had gone on to Paris for more study.[25] However, the Irish Rémois, who outnumbered their English and Scottish counterparts four to one, offer an exception to this pattern. Few of them attended Protestant Leiden, a university founded by William the Silent in 1575 as a center for Calvinist theology.

Did James Welwood matriculate first at Leiden or other medical schools before moving to Reims for the degree? There were surely advantages to the medical student at canal-ringed Leiden, advantages born of the sophisticated teaching accomplished there. Clinical and chemical training, taught by the professors themselves, added to orthodox lecturing and debating made for an outstanding integrated curriculum. The medical faculty at Leiden was among the most innovative and distinguished in late seventeenth-century Europe. Public anatomical demonstrations in the anatomy theater complemented skeletal studies; the oldest botanical garden in Europe provided lessons about plants and nature. Medical teaching was integrated into one of the city hospitals, giving students the opportunity to observe sickness and its relief. Leiden's emphasis on anatomy, botany, chemistry, and the clinic differed substantially from the emphasis on medical philosophy still pursued at ancient universities like Paris, Oxford, and Cambridge.[26]

It is impossible to say for certain, but it is a reasonable assumption that James Welwood had a Leiden link of some sort. There was the twenty-two year old Scot named Wellwood (listed as Robert) on the Leiden books in 1675; that would be the approximate age of James Welwood, although we know of at least two Robert Wellwoods in Fifeshire who would have been his contemporaries. He had a cousin about the same age named Thomas Welwood who may have been a Glasgow graduate; perhaps James accompanied a wealthier relative abroad, earning his own expenses in the fashion of tutor or factotum. If James Welwood were in Leiden as early as 1675, he went there four years before Archbishop Sharp's murder, putting the lie to one persistent rumor about him. Most medical degrees took seven years of study beyond the master's, making 1677 a good estimate for the beginning of Welwood's medical instruction. Although there is no existing evidence that conclusively places Welwood in Leiden for any medical training, it is probable that Welwood studied at least for a time at Leiden. If Welwood did acquire some schooling at Leiden, he may have found it prudent to leave for another institution when French forces attacked the Spanish Netherlands and Luxembourg in 1683. How many years did James Welwood spend in the pursuit of a medical degree and was he traveling from one university to another? Where was James Welwood after 1677 and what was he doing until his 1684 graduation from Reims?

During Welwood's continental years, doubtlessly he did accumulate more medical schooling in the typical peripatetic fashion of the time, presumably in Paris, a more traditional school than Leiden. Welwood recorded meeting a Gallic author in Paris in 1682, not long before his enrollment at Reims, and claimed having been in the French king's library in Paris. There were a number of benefits that could accrue to a medical student stopping even briefly at the university in the French capital: the facilities were good, the professorate was large, and the chairs properly filled.[27] Paris was one of only two French institutions which demanded that their graduates have some experience observing and treating patients, and it had an amphitheater for dissections to augment its course in practical medicine. In 1682 Welwood would have been exposed to a faculty enamored of iatrochemistry and no longer completely acquiescing to the Galenic rationale behind phlebotomy. As a Protestant, he might prefer to affiliate with one of the lay and independent extra-university institutions in Paris, such as the Collège Royal, where research and teaching were promoted. The college had chairs of medicine, botany, surgery, and pharmacy during Welwood's time in Paris; teaching was free and consisted of seventy to eighty lectures a year by each professor. He surely would have benefitted from the widely available medical literature printed in Paris. Throughout the Latin Quarter and in the small streets neighboring the Hôtel-Dieu were bookshops filled with both classical works and recent papers from the Parisian medical community. And, as Welwood remembered, there was the royal bibliothèque, housed after Mazarin's death in the Cardinal's mansion, the repository by law of a copy of every French book published after 1537.

A stay in Paris must have certainly impressed the Scotsman; some authorities label it the largest city in Europe with a population growing to around 500,000 during the reign of Louis XIV.[28] Though the French king did not reside in Paris after 1671, and permanently moved his whole entourage to Versailles the year of Welwood's visit, Paris was central to everything identified with him. All the institutions of various hierarchies were there: five sovereign courts, the lesser courts, thirteen abbeys, the university, and four hospitals including Invalides, a new military hospital opened in 1677 for 7000 disabled veterans.[29] James Welwood would have noticed a remarkable amount of construction going on in Paris on either side of the Seine. The city walls were demolished in 1670, and Parisians pushed out into the countryside through two triumphal arches built to commemorate Louis' victories in the Dutch wars. Although the university district retained its Gothic architecture intact during Welwood's time, other buildings were being remodeled as befitted the capital of the Sun King's empire. New edifices included St.-Sulpice on the Left Bank and St. Nicholas du Chardonnet, just east of the university. The Champs-Elysées and the Place Vendôme were likewise recently established.

Since the university still lacked its own herbarium in the 1680s, James Welwood doubtlessly strolled through the famed Left Bank botanical *Jardin du Roi*, conveniently adjoining La Salpêtrière Hospital. "It is a very great piece of ground, [with] woods, ponds, meadows, mounts, besides a vast level, well furnished with plants and open also to walk in, to all people of note," wrote Dr. Martin Lister a few years later. He reported that the Botanic Reader there "showed 100 plants every lesson for 30 different lessons." Impressed by the king's generous endowment of £2500 for the garden and its supervisory physician, Lister described the fascinating exotica in the greenhouses.[30] No mere garden, the activities of this academy extended to all the natural and biological sciences. The first three chairs there were devoted to botany, chemistry, and anatomy with surgery. All were held by renowned men, and after 1673 the faculty at the *Jardin du Roi* was guaranteed by royal declaration the right to carry out surgical operations and anatomical demonstrations; additionally, they had priority obtaining the bodies of executed criminals. The *Jardin du Roi* faculty waxed superior to the university's in botany and chemistry during Welwood's era.[31]

In 1656 Louis XIV had established the adjacent hospital, an immense edifice in the style of the Grand Siècle for the poor of Paris on the site of an old arsenal where gunpowder was made from saltpetre. Charity was not the king's sole motive; he intended to clear the capital's streets of paupers, the mad, and the infirm. La Salpêtriére had to be significantly enlarged in the 1670s, after the government ousted miscreants from the notorious Court of Miracles, that maze of passages and blind alleys in the Sentier Quarter inhabited by beggars, prostitutes, and rogues who feigned disabilities on the streets of Paris during the day. Described vividly by Victor Hugo in *The Hunchback of Notre-Dame*, the neighborhood got its name from the "miracles" that enabled residents to shed wooden legs, bandages, and other props when they returned to their warrens at night. Many of the legitimately feeble ended up at La Salpêtriére. By the time of Welwood's French sojourn, the hospital housed over 10,000 pensioners and others with debilities, plenty of patients for the faculty next-door and their informed guests to observe and treat.[32] As a student of the sciences, Welwood would have been similarly fascinated by an observatory not too far from the Latin Quarter. Located two degrees east of Greenwich, the observatory became the longitudinal norm for all French maps. Even if he did not attend classes at the university or partake of the city's many educational opportunities, there was much for a foreign medical student to notice in Paris. Among the new *hôtels* in the western part of the city was one housing the Dutch Embassy.[33]

But Paris was not the only locus of government in which James Welwood tarried during his continental circuit in the early 1680s. He made written reference to several conversations during the same time frame with foreign dignitaries in The Hague, one of the chief diplomatic and intellectual centers of Europe in the seventeenth century.[34] The Hague was the capital of the Dutch Republic and residence of its chief executive, the stadtholder. After 1593 the States General met in The Hague, birthplace of Welwood's hero, William of Orange. Simply strolling through the Binnenhof, the central palace courtyard of the Counts of Holland, or gossiping with visitors at the nearby summer lodge of the House of Nassau, Welwood became acquainted with famous men and their intentions. Among those whom Welwood met at the court of the Prince of Orange was Charles II's bastard son, James, Duke of Monmouth. From 1683 to 1689, John Locke resided among the Dutch, under an assumed name for part of that time; he came to the attention of William and Mary as a member of a circle of distinguished men of letters and often visited their court. Locke, who was twenty years Welwood's senior, wrote "On Tolerance" in 1685 and published it anonymously in Holland. It is quite likely that if James Welwood was based at The Hague or studying in Leiden, he came to know Locke and his work. More importantly, as Sir Henry Imbert-Terry, an early twentieth-century antiquarian, remarked, Welwood spent "a considerable portion of his early life in Holland" as part of a large contingent of Protestant foreigners in the Netherlands, a place which had become in the 1680s a haven for disaffected Scotsmen.[35]

The exodus of her citizens is one of the intermittent themes in Scottish history. The impetus to leave Scotland in the sixteenth and seventeenth centuries was intensified by many factors: the general poverty and discomfort of the native land, lost wars in the Lowlands, fruitless uprisings in the hills, religious molestation as Episcopalians and Presbyterians vied for preeminence, sudden and terrible famines. By the time of the Stuart Restoration there were tens of thousands of Scots in England, Ulster, Germany, Poland, Sweden, and Holland.[36]

Scotland had a long and significant bond with like-minded Calvinists of the Dutch Republic; many Scots had served in the three Scottish regiments of the Anglo-Dutch brigade and their prime allegiance was to the Princes of Orange from the House of Nassau. Besides Scottish soldiers, a steady stream of religious refugees filled Scottish churches in Holland, refugees with direct experience of severe religious repression. The Scottish colony in Rotterdam, Locke's address in 1687, had about 1,000 names in its church registers then. These emigrant churches provided bases for exiles constantly on the move. Additionally, they sheltered a secret society of Covenanters. Prince William drew the best and brightest of the Scotsmen into his service, men who had spent many years on the continent. Among those Scottish exiles whom he employed were John Hutton, a future royal physician in Britain and Member of Parliament, William Carstares, later Principal of Edinburgh University, and the Episcopalian cleric, Gilbert Burnet.[37] Burnet's Covenanting cousin, James Johnston, an exile from Scotland for over twenty years, became William's principal agent in London in the months before the revolution.

Although Imbert-Terry called the Netherlands "an asylum for all discontented politicians," he did not categorize Welwood as such and argued instead that the Scotsman's time there imbued him with a sense of impartiality borne witnessing the follies of each faction. After his Reims graduation and return to Scotland, Welwood was accused in 1684 of corresponding with Scottish expatriates in Holland, which seems plausible, and even later of accompanying William of Orange from Holland to England in 1688, which does not.

So much had happened and so many things had changed during the several years of James Welwood's European sojourn. Surely, he felt mounting anxiety and excitement about unfolding events at home and their implications internationally, which he knew of from correspondence with his friends and acquaintances throughout Europe. During his first years away, plots and conspiracies in England, most tied to Catholics, had absorbed the attention of Englishmen and Scotsmen to the point of distraction. Welwood followed the escalating political hostilities from his vantage point on the continent, informed of every crisis in the Caroline government by his fellow Protestant expatriates. Fears of popery, always pronounced, reached epic proportions during the final years of Charles II's reign, even raising doubts about the loyalty of his brother, James, the Duke of York, who had converted to Roman Catholicism in the late 1660s. As an ardent anti-papist, Welwood subscribed to the assumption that Roman Catholicism and despotism were intrinsically coupled; as an amateur historian Welwood was familiar with the horrible treatment Protestant heretics received at the hands of the Church. He could have recounted such outrages against Protestants as the Massacre on St. Bartholomew's Day in France, the Inquisition in Spain, and the Gunpowder Plot in England as examples of Catholic terror. Instinctively then, James Welwood believed in the veracity of the Popish plot, one of the most remarkable outbreaks of mass hysteria in English history.

In the fall of 1678 Titus Oates and a group of unscrupulous perjurers convinced both Parliament and the public that a Jesuit-led Catholic conspiracy threatened to destroy the Protestant establishment. According to what Oates, an Anglican priest and one-time Roman Catholic, told the Privy Council, the plan had several phases. First, Jesuits posing as Presbyterians would travel to Scotland and foment insurrection there. Next, with the help of French troops and money extorted by Jesuits from penitent Catholics, a rebellion in Ireland would be initiated. The murder of James Butler, the king's liaison to the Anglo-Irish nobility was already arranged. Finally, the conspirators would assassinate Charles II himself to hurry the succession of his Catholic brother James. Protestants were to be exterminated, Oates said, and James would then rule over a Catholic country. Albeit totally fabricated, in an age of widespread religious oppression the plot captured the apprehensions of Protestants ready to believe Catholics capable of anything.

The obsession with religious conspiracy might have blown over had not some treasonous letters been discovered from the secretary of the Duchess of York to a French Jesuit. And when the London judge to whom Oates had told his story died under mysterious circumstances, public fear turned to frenzy. In the wake of the Popish plot, hundreds of Catholics were imprisoned and twenty-four were executed, prompting a crisis in the succession and producing attempts in Parliament to deny James the crown.[38] Rudimentary political parties coalesced over exclusion from the throne of the legitimate, although Catholic, heir. In short, the Popish plot is a watershed in British history.

Although the Popish plot was felt chiefly in London, it also had repercussions in Scotland; Welwood would have learned of those repercussions from his friends at home and in Holland. Passions about

Romish conspiracies may have played a part in Archbishop Sharp's murder in Fifeshire in 1679. Anti-Catholic exclusionists in 1679 used their advantage to nominate James, Duke of Monmouth, to command royal troops against the Covenanter uprising in the northern kingdom. Monmouth was the king's illegitimate son, a Protestant, and an attractive alternative to James. On Christmas Day, 1679, students in Edinburgh participated in the burning in effigy of the pope. Welwood certainly knew of the crisis brewing in his native land.

But Charles II wielded his own weapons of persuasion and beginning in 1681 started to retaliate by proroguing Parliament, not summoning one again during his reign. Buttressed by financial support from Louis XIV, the king bought time for his beleaguered brother. The Rye House Plot, another assassination conspiracy, this one aimed at both Charles and James, gave the king cause to execute several key Exclusionists or Whigs. Not insignificantly, the leader of the Whigs in 1682 fled to Holland when Welwood was there. The emergency in England was averted; Charles had secured the succession for James.

The Popish plot provided proof to Welwood that his association of Catholicism with enslavement and foreign domination was correct, underscored by the news he received from friends and family at home. He became more convinced than ever that only Protestantism, any sort of Protestantism, provided real spiritual and political liberty. As if to offer Welwood superfluous proof of the twin dangers posed by Catholicism and absolutism, the vise of religious uniformity had been tightening in France right before his eyes.

James Welwood was among the last contingent of British students at Reims before the government of Louis XIV revoked the Edict of Nantes, officially ending religious toleration in France and non-Catholic enrollments at Reims. Even before the revocation, however, the king had started to alter France's domestic and religious policies. Between 1661 and 1679 there was a steady erosion of the privileges granted by the Edict of Nantes; synods ceased, ministers were forbidden from wearing clerical garb outside their churches, and Protestants found it harder to enter the craft guilds. After securing the Peace of Nijmegen with the Dutch in 1678, Louis pushed for Huguenot conversions to Catholicism, offering financial incentives to new converts. Welwood reflected later on the end of religious toleration in France, purporting to be flabbergasted by any attempt to vindicate the anti-Nantes policy of coerced conversions. Louis XIV undoubtedly had his reasons. His motives included repairing relations with the Papacy, strained because of Gallic reluctance to take up arms against the Turkish invasion of the Holy Roman Empire. Therefore, the Huguenots felt the heat when quarrels between France and the Papacy intensified. Ironically, Pope Innocent XI challenged Louis' malevolent persecution of the Huguenots, widening their rift even more.[39]

Between 1679 and 1682 Louis XIV issued over eighty decrees relentlessly eroding the rights of Huguenots. French Protestants were excluded from all offices of justice and finance, prohibited from inter-marriage with Catholics, and restricted in selling their lands and houses. One proclamation commanded the conversion of children aged seven without parental consent. When French armies failed to participate in the Christian victory over the Turks near Vienna in 1683, Louis counterbalanced that absence by approving dragonnades, a form of suppression, against the Huguenots. By then, Colbert was dead and his temperance as the king's foremost minister had been replaced by the brutality of François Le Tellier, the Marquis de Louvois. The dragonnades were Louvois' idea. Unruly troops were quartered in the homes of opinionated French Protestants to speed up the conversion process, forcing thousands to submit to the will of the state. Of course, attacks on Protestants by the military stimulated Catholic civilians to do the same while the government closed its eyes to the violence until the heretics abjured. The Archbishop of Reims during Welwood's time at the university, Charles Maurice Le Tellier, was Louvois' brother. Archbishop Le Tellier, although not a supporter of physical brutality as a means to religious metamorphosis, had to worry about Sedan, an area of ardent Protestantism within his diocese. Autonomous for a century, the principality remained faithful to Protestantism even after re-annexation to France thirty years before Le Tellier's elevation to the see. As a result, the Archbishop often intervened in troublesome cases, adopting a strictly legal attitude, and tightening restrictions on the Reformed Church and its pastors to the limits that he was permitted by royal law. Le Tellier increased the presence of Catholic institutions in Sedan, establishing convents and schools there, and gradually winning a number of conversions. He believed he could produce a change of heart in Protestants through discussion of controversial points of doctrine; he was convinced that some of the more dubious Catholic superstitions could be cleared up through open dialogue. Therefore, though religious interference did occur in the archdiocese under Le Tellier, it resulted from the Archbishop's belief in the chance of rapprochement between Protestants and Catholics. Revocation of the Edict of Nantes delivered a blow to his strategy of gradual reconversion.[40]

With the onset of the dragonnades in 1683, many more Huguenots fled France, enabling the king to pronounce the nation Catholic, and finally in 1685 to revoke a century of official toleration. Signed at Fontainebleau, the act of revocation permitted the demolition of Protestant churches, the forcible dispersal of Huguenot assemblies, and exclusion but not exile of Protestants.[41] According to official records from Reims and the surrounding archdiocese, Le Tellier personally received the conversion of thousands of abjuring Protestants whereas two hundred families chose to emigrate.

James Welwood at Reims personally experienced Catholic hostility towards his own pronounced Protestantism. He focused his understandable animus on Archbishop Le Tellier, convinced that the metropolitan was complicitous in his brother's plots against prominent Protestant leaders throughout France. Later, in his London newspaper, Welwood referred with horror to the "dragoon-reformation" and to Louis' "booted missioners," who for years tried to obliterate Huguenot enclaves in Poitou, Languedoc, and the principality of Orange. He long remembered his friends in various parts of France, "subject to unparalleled cruelties," like the Reverend Roussel of Montpellier, who was hounded from his home. He railed against Louis XIV's personal insistence that pregnant Protestant women must be treated by Catholic midwives. One auxiliary provision of the revocation that would have particularly enraged Welwood prohibited burial in Protestant cemeteries, reminding him surely of his brother's final indignity at the hands of episcopates. Welwood drew from his own time in France a determination forever to foreswear religious persecution and to disdain governments based on ecclesiastical despotism.

Louis XIV's actions caused widespread reverberations, appalling Protestants everywhere and galvanizing William of Orange. Furthermore, the French king inadvertently undermined the new Catholic king of England, James II, who succeeded his brother in 1685, inauspiciously the same year as the revocation of the Edict of Nantes. Of the Huguenots who left France during Louis' reign, 40,000 to 50,000 settled in Britain, their most common choice of refuge after the Netherlands; they also settled in Switzerland, Brandenburg and other parts of Germany, Ireland, Scandinavia, America and Russia.[42] After 1685 Louis XIV never acquired another Protestant ally. Communities of Huguenot refugees in England made a substantial contribution to James' downfall, actively promoted the cause of the Prince of Orange, and by their very presence confirmed the existing English belief that Catholicism, absolutism, and cruelty were indissolubly bound together.

Welwood empathized with the Huguenot exiles as a fellow Calvinist and religious expatriate. More personally for Welwood, the Edict of Fontainebleau made Protestant students unwelcome at French institutions of higher learning including Reims. The removal of Gallic universities, however temporary, as a viable option for British Protestants, was yet another reminder to him of the myopic wickedness of intolerance and the tyranny of its icon. James Welwood had already seen too much fanaticism in his time. After Reims he dedicated himself to curing the sick and writing about injustices. In the City Library at Reims there is a list of *étrangers* who graduated from the university between 1680 and 1700, each of whom signed the list. Among the autographs is that of James Welwood.

CHAPTER THREE

Welwood and the "Glorious Revolution"

Doctor James Welwood, newly credentialed, returned to Scotland shortly after his Reims graduation in early 1684 and took up residence in Edinburgh. While Welwood had been studying on the continent, political opinion in England had crystallized during the last half of Charles II's reign into opposing but still-fluid masses. The Tories, conjuring up frightening memories of the Civil War, supported kingly prerogatives, a hierarchical church, and the succession of James Stuart to the throne. The Whigs strongly objected to Caroline policy, foreign and domestic, demanded greater Parliamentary rights, and abhorred the Catholicism of the king's brother and heir, whom they wanted to exclude from the throne. Although historians differ on when these factions became political parties and how coherent the groups were, the Tories and the Whigs provided fundamental philosophical and practical ideas for public discussion.[1]

The political fortunes of the two groups seesawed up and down. The Whigs reaped the benefits in 1678 when a fictitious Popish Plot for Jesuits to kill the king, massacre Protestants, and put the Catholic Duke of York on the throne caused widespread panic in England. Invented by an irrational clergyman and fueled by unscrupulous perjury, the plot gained credibility when a secretary to the Duchess of York was implicated in treasonable correspondence. Hundreds of Catholics were imprisoned and two dozen were subsequently executed including Oliver Plunket, primate of Ireland.[2]

The Tories' political principles embraced loyalty to the king and to their Church, institutions they believed were indivisible. They viewed Whiggery and dissent as threats to their own self-interest. The Rye House Plot (1683) gave them a chance to recoup their position as defenders of the status quo and to return as the majority faction. Several prominent Whigs and the Duke of Monmouth were implicated in a conspiracy to murder both royal brothers as they traveled from the Newmarket races to London. During the four years (1681-85) of "Tory reaction," the Whigs were demoralized and ineffective.

Political maven that he was, Dr. Welwood knew about the unfolding of events in England and recognized that Scotland was directly and adversely affected by the decline of the Whigs. First, however, he needed to situate himself in Edinburgh. The city had originated as a tiny "burgh" on the impregnable castle rock overlooking the Firth of Forth to the north, and had great strategic value in commanding the coastal route. In the sixteenth century, Edinburgh survived English occupation and periodic maulings, protected from the south by the hastily-built Flodden Wall, and reached out to the nearby port of Leith for trade. After Scotland's king acceded to the throne of England in 1603 and moved with his court to London, Edinburgh became a deserted capital of secondary importance. During Welwood's few years in the Scottish capital, Edinburgh remained a small, enclosed town, but a revived one, where princes, magnates, and other nobles were in frequent concourse.

True to his family's tradition of public nonconformity, Welwood soon caught the disapproving attention of the Stuart government which suspected him of corresponding with discontented Scottish exiles in Holland. Maybe the authorities had been waiting for the return of the new physician, given the Welwoods' rumored association with the murder of Archbishop Sharp and James Welwood's own opposition to the succession of the Duke of York. There was talk of a more dangerous Dutch connection with William of Orange himself, as the government was well-aware that a network of the Prince's agents plotted against it. Because of Welwood's sojourn in the Hague in the early 1680s and his outspoken admiration for the Calvinist prince, official suspicions about his loyalties were well-founded.

What next happened captured the interest of Sir John Lauder, inveterate diarist and chronicler of Scottish affairs. Through Lauder's journal, we know that on August 6, 1684, James Welwood was detained and interrogated in the Edinburgh tolbooth, the city jail, by order of the Earl of Balcarres, Sheriff of Fife and a staunch supporter of the Duke of York. According to Lauder, who was sympathetic to Welwood's political views, Balcarres was determined to root out any Covenanters in his jurisdiction. The sheriff found Welwood guilty of nonconformity in religion, and three weeks later Welwood was transferred to the Cupar town prison to serve his sentence. However, Doctor Welwood was evidently able to make some sort of payment in lieu of jailtime to secure his release. The quarrel between Welwood and the sheriff may have been personal; it was certainly political. Later, fellow Scot Bishop Gilbert Burnet would write that Welwood had been "ruined in the last reign by a most signal injustice, which was one of the most crying oppression that was in Scotland."[3]

It was not easy for a newly-minted M.D. to establish himself in a good general practice, even in Edinburgh, so James Welwood could be expected to affiliate with the Royal College of Physicians in Edinburgh, an institution which combined the functions of a professional guild with some educational purposes. He could have joined upon his return to Scotland, but since he never identified himself as a member, he likely did not. The college's minutes from December 1684 to March 1693 are missing.[4] Although he would not have approved of its corporate ties to the Stuart monarchy, Welwood surely saw the need for such an institution in the Scottish capital. He may have disagreed with the strong support of one of its founders, Archibald Pitcairne, for the succession of the Duke of York, but Welwood apparently submerged his disdain for the erstwhile Catholicism of another, Robert Sibbald. One founding fellow who was a lifelong friend to Welwood was Sir Thomas Burnet, physician-brother of the famous bishop, and a medical graduate of Montpellier.[5]

The Royal College of Physicians of Edinburgh grew out of a medical club that met fortnightly in Sibbald's lodgings to discuss letters from learned friends abroad, rare medical cases, and books in natural history and science. Sibbald and his coterie established a physic garden which the town council financed before the College received its charter from

Charles II in 1681. It was no coincidence that the college in Edinburgh came into its own at the same time as a retrenchment of the domination by university-educated physicians in London. The foundation of the Edinburgh college is clearly tied up in the politics of medicine at court and was mutually advantageous to monarch and Scottish medicos alike. With the Royal College of Physicians in London on the verge of losing its charter in the government's wholesale challenge to established corporations, the king's doctors in Scotland could serve his purposes by winning royal favor as compliant professionals while achieving their goal of providing a Scottish licensing organization.

Charles II died in February 1685, having smoothed the way for the accession of his Catholic brother to the throne. But not all of the monarch's subjects were sanguine about the succession. A sizable contingent, especially in the west of England, rose in support of Charles' bastard Protestant son, the Duke of Monmouth. Having won a good name for himself as captain general of the army, Monmouth had been dispatched by his father in 1679 to put down the Covenanter revolt. His victory and subsequent clemency toward those Protestants earned him high praise, but he fell out of favor with his father over reckless intrigues and insubordinate behavior. Charles even twice denied Monmouth's paternity before the Privy Council, so fearful was the king that the young man had become a nucleus for governmental opposition and a threat to the legitimate succession. Monmouth retired to the Netherlands, cultivating the support of other exiles there until Charles' death in February 1685.

Welwood had met Monmouth in Holland and later described him as "brave, generous, affable, and extremely handsome, constant in his friendships, just to his word and an utter enemy to all sort of cruelty." Welwood likewise observed the young Duke's weaknesses, including ambition and a fondness for popular applause, concluding these led him to all his misfortunes despite noble and patriotic aspirations. Monmouth recognized his educational shortcomings, studying constantly and making considerable progress, which according to Welwood was remarkable given the excesses of his father's luxurious court.[6]

Among Monmouth's allies was Scotsman Archibald Campbell, Earl of Argyll, a staunch Protestant, Rye House plotter, and fellow resident in Holland. Argyll mounted an expedition against James II (James VII in Scotland) in favor of Monmouth in May 1685 which rendezvoused with Covenanters in Scotland, but even his own clan failed him. Few Scots rallied to Argyll's call. He was captured and beheaded along with a few other conspirators in Edinburgh. In his history of those terrible times, James Welwood later recorded his own attendance at the Argyll execution. Monmouth's landing in the south of England failed to arouse the gentry, according to Welwood because the Duke delayed claiming the crown, and his ill-equipped army was routed at Sedgemoor in early July. Despite humbly submitting for his life, the Duke of Monmouth was beheaded on Tower Hill. Welwood wrote that he died "with the greatest constancy and tranquility of mind, and such as became a Christian, a philosopher, and a soldier." Therefore, despite several crises during the kingship of Charles II and the final indignity of Monmouth's rebellion, James Stuart sat on the throne in 1685. But his crown was only secure for the moment. James II's pro-Catholic policies almost immediately antagonized English Whigs, many Tories, and most of Scotland.

Though aware of these momentous political developments, Dr. James Welwood had only recently re-established himself in a peaceful existence. He could hardly jeopardize his professional standing in Scotland with foolhardy associations. Besides, he was by then more interested in personal matters. Sometime in 1685, James Welwood took a bride, Barbara Armor, and was in Edinburgh in October 1686 for the birth of his daughter, Mary. The delivery was witnessed by an illustrious quartet: Sir Robert Sibbald; Sir Thomas Burnet; Welwood's wealthy merchant cousin, Robert; and surgeon William Borthwick. Probably because of his quarrel with Sheriff Balcarres or as a result of political conditions in Scotland, Welwood left the country in 1687. He later admitted being forced to flee his native land, but defiantly gloried "in having chosen to be overwhelmed in the ruins of my country, rather than to have any share in the causes of them."[7]

Welwood resettled across the English border in Newcastle upon Tyne, a provincial capital, money-market, and thriving port at the eastern terminus of Hadrian's Wall. Newcastle was said to resemble London; its streets were broad and handsome, dotted with fresh water fountains and lined with good shops.[8] Residents and visitors alike bought groceries, wine, haberdashery, and other commodities often transported to Newcastle from London by sea in returning empty colliers. The bustling city became the door to London, to the continent, and to the world for the north of England. Newcastle, which with its suburb on the south bank had a combined population of about 25,000 in the late 1680s, needed physicians. Dr. Welwood brought his young family with him.

Welwood ensconced himself with relative ease in his new place of residence, part of a substantial Scottish migration to northern England in the late seventeenth century. Newcastle, experiencing periodic food emergencies and plagues brought on by growth and economic change, had a high death rate that made it more dependent on immigrants than a smaller town. The municipality drew young men and women from all four northern counties as well as from Scotland. Locals who welcomed the Scots thought of them as religious brothers-in-arms, opposed to popish plots and the heavy hand of the established church there. Many Scotsmen worked in the fabled coal trade, keeping Newcastle England's hearth; the descendants of early Huguenot refugees plied the traditional glassmaking craft around Newcastle. The city's experience in the Civil War had made it accepting of different Protestant religious perspectives, and a place of lively debate on the merits of James Stuart.

When Welwood came to Newcastle as a still-fledgling doctor, he had the opportunity to develop his skills and his clientele free of the distractions that colored his Fifeshire years. Although the town customarily had a permanent physician named by the corporation, during Welwood's time no City Physician as such was employed by the Common Council.[9] While Newcastle lacked an organization of physicians, the city had a longstanding, incorporated Barber-Surgeon's Company with whom physicians mingled. In the hierarchy of British medical care-givers, the barber-surgeons ranked significantly below university-trained doctors. Since physicians rarely undertook "hands on" medicine, they worked with surgeons who administered the purges and did the bleeding which Galenic theories required. Surgeons (whose origins go back to cutting hair and shaving) also set bones and pulled teeth. Their Newcastle company was housed at a site called the Manors in a handsome stone structure made from dismantled pieces of the Austin friars' priory. Arranged in the gardens surrounding the hall were statues of Hippocrates, Galen, and Paracelsus. Anatomical study took place there along with dissections and specimen maintenance, offering Welwood additional professional growth.

In Newcastle, Welwood could both practice medicine and observe the increasingly nervous reactions of Englishmen and Scottish expatriates to their Catholic king. Having endured the trials of the anti-Catholic Test Act, Exclusion Bills, and Monmouth's rebellion, and having elicited sympathetic allegiance from his people, the new King James foolishly squandered the public's overt goodwill upon his coronation. What did James II do to engender such a reaction among certain subjects? His steadfast adherence to Roman Catholicism continued to produce real fear among obsessive anti-papists, and like many converts James was zealous about his chosen faith. As a Catholic he had good reason to grieve over his co-religionists' protracted loss of rights ever since the 1605 Gunpowder Plot, attributed by most Englishmen to the machinations of the Jesuits. Among the far-reaching and long-lasting effects of that farcical conspiracy was the banning of Catholics from practicing law or serving as officers in the army or navy. They were not permitted to possess weapons, receive a university degree, or vote in English elections.[10] They were forced to be married in Anglican churches and to have their children christened in them, and finally to be interred in Anglican burial grounds. Just as Protestants recited their litanies of religious injustices done to them, so did their Catholic counterparts. Understandably then, James II intended to improve the lot of his fellow Catholics, hoping eventually to reconvert the country to Rome. After Monmouth's rebellion James concluded that his army should be officered by Catholics in whom he had confidence. When Parliament objected, the king prorogued the legislature, which never met again in his reign. King James began to replace civilian office holders with his own nominees, naming Catholics as lord lieutenant of Ireland, as commander of the navy, and relying on a Jesuit, Father Edward Petre, for advice as a member of the king's inner council. Anticipating the king's need for a more compliant Parliament, Petre helped to Catholicize municipal corporations. Additionally, he worked to place Catholic fellows at Magdalen College, Oxford University, and ejected Protestants who would not acquiesce.[11] Catholic schools, chapels, and friaries reappeared in London, and the king sought the support of Protestant non-conformists by issuing a Declaration of Indulgence.

Toleration of dissent is the product of political rather than religious belief. Most Anglicans evinced the conviction that other denominations, even Catholics, might reasonably be treated as fellow Christians and be allowed to worship at peace. Except during times of acute political anxiety, dissenters were normally left undisturbed in local communities. In the winter of 1687-88, James' government canvassed the country for its opinion on whether Englishmen could live in harmony with their neighbors of all religious persuasions. All but a meager minority answered "yes," even though the proposition allowed for toleration of non-Christians, as well as of Catholic and Protestant dissenters. However, these same respondents voiced negative replies to questions about repeal of laws which discriminated against these groups.[12] Catholics and Protestant non-conformists were perceived as separate threats to the constitution; together they might bring down the nation. James' attempt to ally these subversive outcasts confirmed the fears of Anglicans that something ominous was afoot. Ironically, many Protestant dissenters refused to accept James' somewhat transparent largesse because toleration came at the expense of constitutional propriety. They felt they were being used by a monarch whose own faith denigrated spiritual compassion. Given the dislocation caused in France by the revocation of the Edict of Nantes, suspicious non-conformists might well distrust James' motives. The king used his prerogative powers in lieu of legislative action and manipulated the judiciary so that it might repeal the penal laws against Catholics. Not surprisingly then, James himself pushed the Church of England into open opposition without having constructed a firm alliance with non-Anglicans. When in September 1688 the king belatedly understood what defiance he had provoked, he tried to restore his position by making concessions and reversing his fiats. James' political epiphany came too late; he had already lost the hearts of even his Tory English followers.

James Stuart was not well-liked in Scotland either, where as James VII he ruled as the first Roman Catholic king in a hundred and twenty years. Fearing eventual establishment of the king's faith in Scotland, his subjects there objected to James' use of the royal prerogative to grant religious toleration to all. Opposition to James II coalesced around James' Dutch son-in-law and nephew, William of Orange, who was both a hereditary Protestant Prince and the elected Stadtholder of the United Provinces of the Netherlands. Moreover, he had the cachet of being the principal opponent on the continent of the Catholic Sun King, Louis XIV of France. William had long been involved in English affairs, foreign and domestic, certainly since his marriage to James' elder Protestant daughter, Mary, in 1677. William's mother was another Mary Stuart, sister of James II, making the bride and groom first-cousins and William fourth in the line of succession for the English crown. The Prince of Orange was interested in England from a strategic point-of-view, since one of his chief policy goals was to prevent an alliance between the English and the French like the one which had been so disastrous for the Netherlands in the early 1670s. William supposed that the English king and Louis were conspiring to destroy the Dutch Republic. His determination to prevent such destruction seemed reasonable since the royal cousins would likely succeed to the throne of England upon the death of the aging James II, who had no male heirs.

In Newcastle as elsewhere in England, local grievances intertwined with national policies. A new charter for Newcastle, delivered at the time of James II's accession, reserved to the king control over the mayor and aldermen. Uneasiness over the charter was exacerbated when the king sent a mandate to the corporation in March 1686 instructing them to admit a Catholic, Sir William Creagh; he was admitted, but not without an address from the mayor to James which expressed deep concern about interference in Newcastle's liberties and privileges. However, James still had his adherents in Newcastle, some of whom felt obedience to the king was as necessary as obedience to one's own father. The patriarchal theory of kingship had buttressed the Stuarts during the crisis to exclude James and still exerted power over their subjects. One local politician, Ambrose Barnes, organized support in the municipal election of 1687 for the king in hopes of earning a Parliamentary seat for himself, but as local rivals bickered over the prudence of erecting a statue of James II in Newcastle, Barnes failed to sway the electors. In retaliation for the victory of his critics in Newcastle, the king tried to reconstruct the corporation into a more pliant instrument of his will by dismissing the elected officers and installing the recently intruded Creagh as mayor. Even Barnes deserted James by the spring of 1688; royal policy in Newcastle was in shambles.[13]

Then, in June 1688 the unexpected happened. The birth of a healthy son to the fifty-five year-old James and his second wife, after fifteen childless years of marriage, conjured up the specter of an endless line of Catholic Stuarts and stimulated conspiracy against the king. Many Protestants, not to mention James' own daughters who were displaced in the line of succession, surmised the blessed event was a hoax, that the baby had been smuggled into the queen's bed in a warming pan.[14] Dr. James Welwood was too wise in the ways of medicine to swallow the rumor of a suppositious birth, and later in his newspaper and history he distanced himself from the idea, even acknowledging a later pregnancy of the queen. What really terrified opponents of James was the certainty that the delivery of a Stuart heir was legitimate. Three weeks after the birth, seven major English conspirators sent a letter to the Dutch prince inviting him to come to England with a force and promising him support; the letter was written at William's insistence. He thought of an invasion as a "pre-emptive strike" directed against an Anglo-French alliance.[15] Subsequently, the Prince of Orange responded to growing hopes for his intervention by issuing a moderate declaration which called for a free Parliament and by demanding an explanation from the king about his government's policies and about the truthfulness of the nativity of the latest Stuart. The proclamation was designed to appeal to the widest possible spectrum of English opinion, while agitating few partisan hostilities. Printed in Dutch, German, and French, as well as in English, it was intended to justify William's conduct in the eyes of the European public.[16]

Finally, in November 1688, his arrival anticipated with widespread enthusiasm, thirty-eight year old William of Orange landed at Torbay with a polyglot force carried by a fleet much larger than the Spanish Armada. Much of the peerage rallied to William, and even James' younger Protestant daughter, Anne, defected from the king. Rather than engage the invaders in a military showdown as his forces disintegrated, James II, suffering from unstanchable nosebleeds, threw the Great Seal of his office in the Thames and fled to France. His departure enabled his enemies to claim that he had abdicated the throne, leaving it vacant.

With James somewhat unexpectedly in France, the Convention Parliament, a sort of constitutional convention, met to decide what to do. After considerable debate during which the Tories complied with the reality that a revolution of sorts had taken place, the throne was offered to William and Mary in February 1689 with sole administrative authority vested in William alone. They were crowned King and Queen of England and Ireland in April ceremonies, having agreed to accept a Declaration of Rights. Following some initial confusion in the northern kingdom, the Scots soon ratified the English proclamation, when a Convention of Estates met and echoed the English example.

The citizens of Newcastle upon Tyne had anticipated this outcome. When the Dutch prince landed in southwest England in November 1688 and claimed the throne, Newcastle forsook James II. Mobs in the city in early December sacked a "Mass house" there and turned it into a playhouse. Throughout the month depredations there continued. The town declared for William, and the commander of the Newcastle garrison supported that decision. Nearly six months after James had fled his kingdom, the brass equestrian statue of James II was pulled from its location on Sandhill, dragged to the quay and into the river without any interference from government troops or civil authorities.[17] Dr. James Welwood quickly entered the verbal fray, exchanging barbs with a Newcastle vicar over the righteousness of opposing the king and supporting William and Mary. Though no longer in his beloved Fifeshire, Welwood felt he had found a comfortable philosophical home among the triumphant English Whigs. The bloodless ousting of James II, called the "Glorious Revolution" by the victorious Whigs, changed James Welwood's life. The man whom he supported, at whose court he had visited, and the ideas he espoused had won out, enabling Welwood to move from the dangerous political fringe and the margins of professional success to the vibrant center.

Like many Scotsmen, Welwood rejoiced at the Glorious Revolution and its promise of religious liberty, which he associated with Protestantism and the House of Orange. Like most Whigs, Welwood was committed to a balance between independence and order, fearful of both absolute monarchy and a democratic republic. If there is a consistency in Welwood's politics, it is his firm belief that moderation in spiritual matters assured mutual goodwill and freedom from tyranny. He presumed that the essence of Protestantism, with its promotion of individual conscience and religious literacy, ought to buttress the rights of men against absolute government. But Welwood was no republican proponent of popular sovereignty. He believed in the monarchy of King William, who as ruler of the principality of Orange in France, had left Catholics there free to exercise their religion. By the standards of a generally bigoted age, William III practiced religious toleration and showed no eagerness for leading a denominational war.[18] Therefore, James Welwood came to equate true Protestantism with compassion and autonomy, but he was wary of the radicalism of some dissenters. His horror of Roman Catholicism was based in part on that church's intolerance and an assumption about international popish conspiracies. Protestants like Welwood judged Roman Catholics to be a subversive force because they owed allegiance to a foreign power, the Pope, and it was widely believed in England that Catholics condoned regicide if this would promote the reconversion of the country. Dr. James Welwood wanted domestic peace. Despite his Calvinist upbringing, Welwood did not object to episcopacy as an institution. Indeed, Welwood would come to number Anglican bishops and their associates among his closest friends. Welwood's disapproval of James II included the king's courting of radical Protestant dissenters and abandonment of Anglicanism in Ireland, the care of which had been solemnly entrusted to the monarch.[19]

Instead of stability, however, the leitmotif of the reign of William and Mary from its inception is partisan rivalry and political instability. There were men in Newcastle and elsewhere who resolutely refused to accept the legitimacy of the Prince of Orange as King of England. An ardent Williamite, Dr. James Welwood could hardly keep silent, as he saw it, in the face of such stupidity. In the early months of 1689, he commenced a vitriolic war of words with the Reverend John March, Vicar of St. Nicholas in Newcastle, a High Church cleric long concerned about the activities and agitation of dissenters there. For over a decade March had excoriated in print and from the pulpit those "false prophets" who sought to destroy the relationship between the magistrates of Newcastle and the monarchy. When James II alienated the older governing elite of the town by interfering with its charter and simultaneously estranged himself from nonconformists by his papist policies, the corporation revolted.

Vicar March, however, refused to concede the righteousness of the Glorious Revolution. The spirited letters he and Dr. Welwood exchanged provide the modern reader with a primer on the allegiance controversy that was at the heart of the revolutionary debate.[20] Vicar March had preached a sermon at St. Nicholas before the mayor and aldermen in late January 1689 on the anniversary of Charles I's 1649 execution, since the Stuart Restoration a practice in Anglican churches commemorating the royal martyrdom.[21] In his sermon, the Vicar condemned all unlawful resistance to sovereign princes. March extolled passive obedience and unequivocally described recent events in Newcastle as rebellion, all of which provoked a written rejoinder from Welwood, who had been in the congregation. Welwood fired the first shot in a truculent epistle of February 1, mainly berating March for scurrilous remarks in the sermon directed at the influential Whiggish cleric, Gilbert Burnet, and Burnet's *Enquiry into the Measures of Obedience*. Burnet's lifework had been aimed at rapprochement among Protestants, and his sympathetic understanding of true religious faith came to encompass all Christian persuasions. He was an outspoken, garrulous advocate of support for Huguenot exiles in Britain, contributing generously to their needs himself. What Burnet could not abide was the rigid imposition of religious orthodoxy. Persona non grata during James' reign, Burnet had arrived at the Hague in 1686 and advised William of Orange to embrace pragmatic religious inclusion and to avoid the pitfalls of persecution once securely on the throne of England.

With a broad-minded Protestant model like Gilbert Burnet, James Welwood harbored none of the objections to the religious *via media* or to episcopacy that had enraged his brother John, a Presbyterian saint. Instead, Welwood leapt to the defense of his friend and fellow Scotsman. "Seventeen times in less than three quarters of an hour" had the vicar lambasted Burnet, a learned man whom Welwood said could not be touched by such expressions from so unworthy a minister. Implying that March was disingenuous, Welwood noted that even "the Black Robes" respected Burnet for his intellect and scholarship, referring to the cordial welcome Burnet had received from Pope Innocent XI.

Welwood denied that passive obedience and non-resistance were part of the Protestant tradition, insisting that the nations of Europe "forced their way to Reformation through rivers of blood." Queen Elizabeth, Welwood warranted, triumphed over tyranny by expending lives and treasure so that her subjects might be free. Welwood hinted at things to come when he wished for God to raise up "in our age another princess to act over again the part of her triumphant predecessor and make a glorious instrument to perfect that reformation which the other did so happily begin." Finally, Welwood reproved March for damning those who overturned King James II. He reminded the vicar that William rescued them all from slavery and the Pope, and that Parliament had approved his accession. What a shame that the noble corporation of Newcastle had been burdened with such an outburst, wrote Welwood, closing his epistle with the rather fawning, "your humble servant."

As soon as Reverend March received the missive, he could hardly wait to reply. He was in such a hurry that he omitted the customary polite salutation, denying he had defamed Dr. Burnet and insisting that passive obedience is founded in the Word of God and in the doctrines of the Church. Passive obedience did not preclude opposition, but it did require respect toward sovereign authority. Divinely sanctioned command provided the only safeguard against moral disintegration of society, therefore England was imperilled by William's illegitimate arrogation of the throne. March, like other churchmen and some laymen who adhered to the doctrines of divine right and non-resistance, refused to swear allegiance to William and Mary. Some openly identified themselves as Nonjurors, and many clergy among them lost their livings.

The lively and informed debate between Welwood and the minister was not confined to ideology; March had personal insults of his own to hurl and demonstrated knowledge of the Welwood family past. While violence is ordinarily to be avoided, March insisted, if someone were attacked by barbarous assassins, for instance Archbishop Sharp, he could in conscience defend himself. Skewering Welwood's Scottishness, March reminded Welwood that things were different in England than in the northern kingdom and surmised that Welwood was "of another profession" since he had so little skill in divinity. The vicar suggested that if Welwood wanted to quarrel on further, his scribblings should be about physick. The modern reader of these letters must be equally impressed by the level of classical erudition detectable in both and by the rapid descent into name-calling on the part of the correspondents. These letters demonstrate how, given the passionate nature of politics in the Augustan Age, two strangers could become instant antagonists.

Dr. Welwood took umbrage at the rude beginning of March's February 11th missive and construed the lack of greeting as an attack on his credentials. His lengthy riposte discussed limitations on monarchs and showed an understanding of the social contract theory of government, an understanding Welwood may have gleaned from discussions of John Locke's theories while in Holland.[22] Dr. Welwood reasoned that just as the Golden Bull protected the "German aggregate body against the incroachments of the Emperor, the same is the Coronation Oath in England against the encroachments of the King." He boasted of having read the works of some, including Quaker apologist Robert Barclay, who like March supported regal prerogative, but averred that even Quakers cite cases when protest is required. Welwood strongly resisted March's position ("from a minister in a corner of the nation") that passive obedience is a hallmark of the Church of England, given the patriotic obstinacy of good Anglicans in Parliament to James' maladversations. He justified his own interest in theology, refusing the notion that only the clergy can study "that sacred science," and defending his own education "at home and abroad…[as]…at least nothing inferior to yours."

Vicar March declined to recognize the slight inflicted by his previous letter, and in his reply of February 19 rubbed salt in Welwood's wounds. "Though perhaps you may have commenced Doctor in some foreign academy, yet you have no claim to the privileges of the same degree in England." March insisted that the doctrine of obedience to sovereign princes in the Church of England can best be gleaned "out of her own authentic monuments, than out of your [Scottish] country-men." But he also maintained that other Protestant examples abound supporting obedience to one's sovereign. Martin Luther openly opposed defiance of secular authority and even John Calvin in some cases impugned political revolt, argued March.

The vicar, who had a twenty-year tradition of observing the death of Charles I and damning resistance to divinely-chosen kings, clearly associated political revolt with regicide. Those who wished to usurp God-given rights to rule were not to be trusted including Welwood. March claimed that Welwood was lying in his defense of King William. "At the very time when the Prince of Orange was coming over to rescue the nation from popery and slavery...you merrily did in a certain house at the lower end of Westgate...drink a health to the success of King James' forces against all invaders whatsoever." March concluded that "it would be as easy to shape a coat for the moon as for your latitudinarian conscience." He reminded his readers that King James "has voluntarily divested himself into a private capacity," so resisting him now is not resisting a higher power but merely rejecting the man. By the end of the epistle, March had categorized Welwood's paragraphs as an Augean stable of such unkind falsities that his only response could be: "Get thee behind me, Satan!" He vowed in the future to ignore Welwood's impertinent calumnies and to burn his letters upon receipt.

March affixed this screed addressed to Welwood to the door of a Newcastle stationer's shop and neglected to send a copy to the good doctor. Welwood felt compelled to write at length again to March, given the unexpected attention in town afforded the public posting of their communication. In a letter dated March 3, Welwood labeled Vicar March's verbiage as "Billingsgate oratory," a reference to the coarse language usually associated with London's fish market. Though Welwood modestly agreed that the Herald's Office was unlikely to be familiar with either of their families' escutcheons, he boasted of his own university education and professional reputation. Paragraph by paragraph, Welwood debated the historical and contemporary examples provided previously by March, particularly denying the support of continental Protestants like Calvin and Melanchton for passive obedience to unjust authority.

Welwood's defense of the charge that he drank to King James' health was surprisingly tame; he stated that neither his friends nor his enemies would accept such a lie. Furthermore, he conceded that the transcriber of his last epistle to March made an error or two, but that there was no mistaking the desertion of King James from his throne. Despite the lack of a formal abdication, Welwood insisted that James' subjects had little choice but to follow a new leader. Besides, Welwood argued, when princes act in opposition to Christian principles God demands opposition from their subjects.

Among the final charges Welwood flung at March was the vicar's failure to preach a sermon of thanksgiving for deliverance on the day ordered, substituting for the congregation the homily against rebellion. Welwood said that he and the other parishioners were astonished by such rash behavior on March's part. Regretting his role in giving Vicar March a wider audience for his "fanatical" views, Welwood signed off with finality, vowing not to communicate with the vicar again. Within a few weeks, James Welwood had left Tyneside and relocated in London, not far from William and Mary's residence at Whitehall. He had the Newcastle letters bound together, licensed, and printed in London in April 1689 as *Vindication of the Present Revolution in England*. March parried quickly with his own published tract, *A Loyall Vindication of the Incomparable Prince, King Charles I*. It contained an "answer to some livres printed lately by Dr. James Welwood against a sermon." The Newcastle letters helped identify Welwood, heretofore an obscure Scottish physician, as an effective polemicist for the Glorious Revolution and the Whigs. Welwood's vigorous defense of William and Mary enabled the doctor to procure appointments during the reign of the joint monarchs. Previous acquaintance with some of the king's Dutch contingent and with the king himself doubtlessly influenced Welwood's rise to royal favor. The encouragement of the influential Gilbert Burnet, a close confidant of the queen and brother of Welwood's Edinburgh friend, demonstrably contributed to the doctor's success at court. Yet Welwood always insisted that he wrote "neither for bread or pension" and that no one should expect him "to be tied to the rules and interests of any one party."[23]

Gilbert Burnet, later Bishop of Salisbury, Welwood's most important and persistent champion after the Glorious Revolution, sponsored some of the doctor's political appointments. Burnet had himself spent considerable time with the royal couple in The Hague, having fled England after the accession of James II. By then, of course, Dr. Welwood was already back in Scotland, and it may have been Burnet with whom he was accused of corresponding. Welwood would have heard with alarm that James had initiated prosecution of his fellow Scotsman in the northern kingdom in 1687 for high treason, a charge based on Burnet's illicit letters to the rebellious Earl of Argyll. But Burnet secured naturalization as a Dutch citizen and even married a Dutch woman of Scottish extraction, thereby protecting himself from subsequent harassment. William and Mary became godparents to Burnet's firstborn child in April 1688, and Burnet knew full well about William's preparations. Burnet helped to write the prince's declaration and persuaded him to alter a passage about Scotland, pressed on William by the exiles around him, which seemed to support Presbyterianism. Burnet landed with William at Torbay, a site he suggested to the prince. Throughout the first days of the imbroglio, Burnet's advice proved invaluable to William. Burnet wisely counseled the humane treatment of King James and royal soldiers alike, and insisted as well that Catholics suffer no political discrimination. In sum, Burnet emerged as the new king's most trusted adviser, earning a bishopric for his service.

For his part, Bishop Burnet was grateful for Welwood's energetic endorsement of his own Williamite writing against the slurs of John March and was in a singular position to advance Dr. Welwood's name before the joint monarchs. Luckily for the good doctor, Welwood's need for monetary advancement happened to coincide with the king's need for effective propaganda. Tracts, prints, and commemorative medals appeared at every important step during and after the Revolution of 1688. In order to buttress his de facto kingship, William III had to successfully rebut damaging charges, such as those made by Rev. March, that he had usurped the throne from the legitimate monarch. Moreover, he required forceful justification for involving his new country and its Allies in the expensive War of the Grand Alliance against France so soon after gaining the English throne, a war William called the true beginning of his reign. In addition, William faced the challenge of managing a Parliament riven by faction and mistrust.[24] Knowing the power of the press, William's government practiced press control, ordering the Stationers Company to seize unlicensed works and prohibiting the printing of Parliamentary proceedings. Manipulating the news was an onerous task as hundreds of printed pieces were in circulation in the aftermath of 1688 and, since many of them sold for only a penny, they were within the reach of a wide audience. Moreover, the new king desired coordinated public affirmation for his actions. This was hardly a novel idea; Charles II had his own publicist in Dr. Robert Brady.[25] Bishop Gilbert Burnet, himself a publicist for the Prince of Orange, could orchestrate a campaign of written persuasion by Williamite publicists. Dr. James Welwood was a key element in that campaign, and for his contributions he was ultimately compensated with appointments to medical posts. However, Welwood was no hack writer; he was sincere in his devotion to the king and skilled in his expression of that devotion. He did not, like Daniel Defoe, sell his pen to the highest bidder. Nevertheless, Welwood knew that royal patronage came to him because of his politics and not because of his medical prowess. He expressed his gratitude later "since my good fortune rather than my merit procured me an honorable call from a crowned head to one of the best posts that a person in my profession could wish."[26]

Of course, Welwood's political beliefs and fondness for the new monarchs were hardly shared by everyone in Britain. Despite his own happiness in England, Welwood must have been at least troubled by the tragedy which brewed in the northern kingdom after the Revolution. The dethroned James II declared in April 1689 to the Convention of Estates in Edinburgh that while he would not have forced Protestants to convert to Catholicism, he had hoped to lead them to the true religion by example. Anticipating a return from exile, the king implied that a majority of the Scots' estates and most of the Protestants in Britain would be treated as rebels unless they joined with him in the fight to retake the kingdoms. This blustering warning effectively increased the natural majority in the Convention for William and Mary; James' supporters were consequently forced to seek a military solution to the affairs of state and Scotland plunged into a ruinous civil war.

Demonstrating keen interest in these political developments within his homeland, Welwood produced *Reasons Why the Parliament of Scotland Cannot Comply with the Late King James' Proclamation.*[27] In May 1689 James Stuart released a statement, countersigned by James' principal adviser, the ultra Catholic Earl of Melfort, striking back at the Scots who had defied "their lawful and undoubted sovereign," and promising to punish those who had allied with the Prince of Orange. Welwood dedicated his rebuttal to the Duke of Hamilton, a man who for a great many years "struggled against the encroachments made on a kingdom," with the hope that the 1688 revolution "may at last make us happy." The subtitle boasted that the author provided "an answer to every paragraph of the said proclamation" and vindicated "the said Parliament in their present proceedings against him." Again, as in his letters to Reverend March, Welwood demonstrated familiarity with a contractual theory of government although with his own particular emphasis. He repeatedly emphasized the mixed, balanced nature of the Scottish government, devised deliberately by "contract betwixt the King and People, equivalent to a Coronation Oath, at the very founding of our monarchy." Despite that contract, Welwood opined that the Stuarts' treatment of Scotland during the preceding twenty years was particularly egregious, the very definition of oppression, injustice and tyranny. Scots were not complaining of mere mismanagement, but flagrant violations of the law. Though Welwood counted himself "a great friend to monarchy, as being the best of governments," King James had subverted the cooperative law-making requirement of the constitution by unilaterally overturning the statutes of Parliament. Therefore, Welwood concluded, James II "ceased to be our King, and We to be his Subjects."

Reasons Why the Parliament of Scotland signals an important distinction that Welwood made in analyzing the Scottish Kirk vis-à-vis the Anglican Church. He explained English episcopacy by reminding his readers of the prominence of bishops in the English reformation, submitting that some even shed their blood for it; in Scotland because Presbyterians effected church reform, they overthrew episcopacy as well as the papacy. Welwood's appreciation of the historical relevance of bishops to the Anglican church may explain his sincere friendships with episcopates and his eventual membership in an English parish. Regardless, he insisted that the northern kingdom should be treated equitably by the Stuarts. Welwood seethed with anger over what he interpreted as "imperial language of annulling and disabling" the law used by James in his remarks to the Scots, and "softer words of dispensing with laws" addressed to the English.

Once William of Orange had arrived to take the throne of England, as Welwood saw it, the threats of Stuart Catholicism to Scotland dissipated but did not vanish. Despite the rhetoric of Williamites like Welwood, Highland Scots, some of them Catholic, remained loyal to James Stuart, preferring him to what they saw as a foreign usurper. Dr. Welwood called those Scots "a rabble" and insisted that most Scotsmen loved William. Clans under Viscount Dundee rose in support of James and in July 1689 demolished an army in Perthshire sent by William III to put down Scottish Jacobites, supporters of the deposed James II and his heirs.[28] Welwood confessed having himself been duped initially by the deceptive stratagems of Dundee, who claimed to be representing the interests of episcopates there. According to Welwood, he learned through correspondence with knowledgeable Scots that Dundee had really raised the rebellion in James' name to protect his own lands and fortunes, though he had nothing to fear from the House of Orange. Once again, William III personified for Welwood the righteous triumph over crypto-papists with all their plots, conspiracies, and selfish motives. Even the auspicious day of William's landing at Torbay, November 5, made clear to Welwood how saving was God's grace for Englishmen and Scotsmen alike; it was the anniversary of James I's salvation from the gunpowder plotting of Guy Fawkes, another Roman Catholic.

Later, in his newspaper, *Mercurius Reformatus*, Welwood commented that King William had possessed good fortune in the northern kingdom from the time of his arrival in the south of England. As Welwood saw it, the Scottish crown had been unanimously proffered to the dual monarchs in a timely fashion, various plots had been discovered and rendered harmless, and no single leader had emerged to forge a serious challenge to William after Viscount Dundee's Highland rising in July 1689. In reality, the period between 1688 and 1702 were years of affliction due to neglect on the part of the king and the incessant maneuvers of Scottish politicians. Scotland was of marginal interest to William of Orange, busy for most of his reign fighting wars with France. Yet he needed security in the northern kingdom, in addition to its monies and manpower, and wished to solidify his own executive prerogatives there. Unfortunately for the king, the complicated nature of Scottish affairs instead produced a divisive religious establishment and a weakened government in the north. His advisers, mostly self-serving émigrés, aggravated rather than alleviated Scottish crises.[29]

James Welwood was among those Williamites who optimistically believed that formal union of the two realms might provide a solution to the Scottish question. As early as 1690, he explicitly sanctioned consolidation. Welwood wrote that "ever since the Scotch race came to the crown [of England], it was always promoted by the wisest and honestest part of both kingdoms."[30] He deemed it unfortunate that union had not yet been accomplished by the time of the Glorious Revolution; in fact, Welwood thought the Scots might have something to offer their English counterparts. In 1689 when the Parliament of Scotland had discussed the wording of the oath to be taken supporting William and Mary, it insisted on including a provision on the legitimacy of the king and queen. Since so many Jacobites evaded swearing to the *de jure* right of the dual monarchs to rule by admitting their right *de facto*, Welwood hoped the English Parliament might follow suit and demand unequivocal allegiance. He suggested as well that King William might be able to effect union in the near future. Like Oliver Cromwell before him, William III had completed his capture of power in England by subduing rebels in Ireland and Scotland, and the king began to unite the Scots to the English Parliament.

Meanwhile, a new constitution for the Church of Scotland (its last until 1921) was crafted by a national conclave and ratified by William in 1690. This settlement was a fragile compromise which Welwood endorsed; Presbyterians were pleased by the abolition of bishops and the return to theology with a distinctly Calvinist character, while the church remained subject to Parliamentary control. Though the vast majority of Scotsmen embraced the Church as defined, several hundred clergy resigned rather than submit to it, seeding an Episcopal Church in the conservative north-east; a few Covenanting dissenters remained outside the establishment in the south-west. James Welwood thought too much had been made of divisions within his home country by those who knew nothing of it, and he called on other Scots to verify his claim that none of those parochial jealousies diminished national support for the dual monarchs there. As Welwood noted with pride,

20,000 Scotsmen would join William in Ireland to parry the thrust of the Jacobite uprising there.

Yet some Highlanders still resisted swearing allegiance to William, even refusing bribes offered to persuade them. After other savage encounters with William's troops and the failure of James' Irish campaign, the Highlanders were ordered by the government to swear allegiance to William and Mary or face the sword. Most clans did so, but the king decided to make an example of the Jacobite MacDonalds of Glencoe. In February 1692, government troops slaughtered the clan. Though William denied previous knowledge of the massacre, his reputation was ruined in the Highlands. Welwood, however, would never budge from his support of the king despite the resistance and death of his countrymen. In fact, even before Glencoe, Welwood isolated the Highlanders from other Scots, calling them "miserable men [who] skulk up and down their inaccessible mountains,...a wretched sort of people [who] take occasion of any revolution or disturbance to better their condition by robbing the lower countries."[31] Welwood evidently sloughed off what he regarded as exaggerated consideration paid to narrow Highland interests, judging Jacobite loyalty as misguided and dangerous to the rest of Britain. There is a curious emotional distancing of Welwood from his compatriots in Scotland, noticeable in his references to "that kingdom,...these people...that country." He wrote that even though they lived under the same king, the Scots were as independent from England in their actions as Holland was of Venice. He disavowed knowledge of persecutions against Episcopalians there, but explained that "experience has never made them wiser as to the inconveniences of persecution on either side."[32]

James Welwood had apparently moved on from his Scottish provenance, emotionally and physically, settling in London in early 1689, while continuing to publicize the virtues of William and Mary. By the time of Welwood's arrival, calm had been restored to a capital troubled by James' abrupt departure. In the vacuum between the flight of James and William's appearance in the city, indiscriminate looting and destruction had followed the ravaging of Catholic chapels, homes and businesses. Indeed, urban rioting may have been the decisive factor in persuading the peers and magistrates of London that it was in their best interests to support William, even before he was formally tendered the crown.[33] Welwood found in London a hospitable climate for his own political ideals, for there the meaning of the revolution was clarified in Whiggish terms. In the City elections that followed the revolution, London Whigs gained control of the Court of Aldermen and the Common Council where they tried to alter Corporation government through more direct election of magistrates, aldermen, and sheriffs.[34] In addition, the flow of Calvinist refugees from France accelerated after 1688 due to renewed persecutions in the southwestern provinces of that country. Huguenots constituted about five per cent of London's population just a decade following the Glorious Revolution. No wonder that Welwood felt among political and religious kindred spirits.

However, an old Newcastle nemesis soon resurfaced to disquiet Welwood's happiness. Unable to stomach the success of his Williamite antagonist, the Reverend John March sought revenge. In a letter dated February 10, 1690, from March to John Weld, a London bookseller, the vicar berated Welwood's character and professional credentials. Calling him both despicable and obscure, Vicar March asserted that Welwood only "pretended to be a doctor of physick" and that he "botched" a licensing examination by the Royal College of Physicians in Edinburgh. According to March, Thomas Burnet, "a fanatick himself," salvaged Welwood's first reply but could not cover-up another miscue and Welwood was denied the license. March said that Welwood lived in Newcastle "when we had no magistrates but papists and fanaticks," and insinuated himself with both, even arguing for repeal of the Test Act and the penal laws. Welwood, "drinking with great zeal," could not develop a decent medical practice and so he went to London (by sea because it was cheaper than overland) to escape debts in Newcastle. Welwood certainly owned no estate in Scotland and only maintained himself in London, said March, by political writing sponsored by the Bishop of Salisbury. Vicar March claimed that Bishop Burnet met Welwood in France when Welwood served as his travel guide and that Burnet had given Welwood some material "observables" to raise his ostensible reputation and sponsored him for club membership. Finally, March asked that his name be concealed because "there is no credit to be got by writing against such an adversary."[35] The *Dictionary of National Biography* understandably calls March's letter "an unreliable account" of Welwood's life; moreover, Welwood's name was hardly sullied by March's mudslinging. Nonetheless, the letter gives the modern reader an indication of the vehemence engendered by partisan difference. In July 1690 the Common Council of Newcastle cautioned Reverend John March that his pay would be halted unless he prayed for William and Mary. Like most High Churchmen, March took the required oaths and continued in place, mollifying his conscience by distinguishing between a *de facto* and a *de jure* sovereign.[36] He died in late 1692, having preached a final sermon in Newcastle the Sunday before his death. That sermon and others were published posthumously in London, favored enough by Jacobite readers to warrant a second edition in 1699.

CHAPTER FOUR

Welwood and Grub Street

*I*nspired by the reception afforded *Vindication of the Present Revolution*, in May 1689 Welwood inaugurated a popular newspaper of opinion, *Mercurius Reformatus or the New Observator*. For the next decade, Dr. Welwood demonstrated enormous personal energy by vigorously participating in several disparate activities. While practicing medicine in a new venue and entering into a vital collegiate relationship with other physicians in London, Welwood simultaneously attended to the occasional health-care needs of the dual monarchs, served on multiple governmental commissions, and wrote a significant body of political papers, tracts, and books. Although he earned his living primarily as a medical man in London, none of his work brought him greater pleasure than his writing, and it is that for which he is principally remembered.

Throughout the seventeenth century, England enjoyed an explosion of information as domestic and foreign news became accessible to the general public.[1] Literacy in the Augustan Age escalated as well. Estimates about the numbers of English literates, based on the ability to sign one's name, vary from twenty-five per cent to forty per cent of the population, but based on reading alone the percentage might be closer to sixty-five. Urbanites had higher literacy rates; perhaps eighty per cent of adult males in London could read. Even illiterates had access to information by gathering around those who could and did read aloud to them.[2]

Readers bought newsbooks or pamphlets of about thirty pages which were turned out quickly in response to newsworthy events and which usually covered a single topic; they purchased shorter broadsides and ballads about current happenings sold in public places to inform and entertain the educated man in the street. The London populace was especially engaged in the aftermath of the revolution by the debate over the allegiance controversy, and the presses spawned thousands of propagandist publications. In 1689 alone, some 2,000 individual titles were published. Undoubtedly, though the controversy may appear esoteric to modern sensibilities, the demand for allegiance pamphlets was voracious. William Sherlock's 1690 tract defending his own oath-taking scored a phenomenal publishing success, selling at least 30,000 copies, and generating forty-six responses. A reasonable estimate is that over 300,000 copies of allegiance pamphlets circulated in the six years following the Glorious Revolution. Of course we cannot know how many readers perused each copy nor how extensive the habitual reading of these works was, but the material is complicated and presumes a certain theoretical sophistication. Most of the publications were Whiggish, but nearly half of the pamphlets devised in the years following the Glorious Revolution were either Tory, Jacobite, or Nonjuror.[3]

Despite the popularity of pamphlets, there had been continuing efforts made to distribute the news in a more regular, composite format especially after mid-century. Attempts were made after the Restoration to impose rigorous controls on the printing of news; the Licensing Act of 1662 restricted printing to London, York, Oxford, and Cambridge. Although originally enacted for just two years, the statute was renewed until May 1679. It was brought into operation again in June 1684 and enforced by the Stationers Company, which enjoyed a printing monopoly in exchange for administering the government's orders respecting press control. As the principal agent for implementing the Crown's control of the press, the Stationers were empowered to search for and seize prohibited materials and arrest the suspected printer. However, a society which practices censorship induces writers to apply strategies in order to elude control.[4] Partisan clamber led to a relaxing of constraints, and the Licensing Act was finally allowed to lapse in June 1695. Independent newspapers flourished after that date, but even before then, the demand for news reflected the need of the London commercial community for trustworthy information about current affairs. Manuscript newsletters and coffee house news-sheets satisfied much of this demand. *The Cambridge Bibliography of English Literature* enumerates forty-five newspapers published at least once a week that started up in London between 1688 and 1695; one historian counts sixty printing houses there, averaging over two and a half presses per shop.[5] In many ways, Grub Street was the internet of its day.

Of course, Welwood did not actually inhabit Grub Street, now known as Milton Street near Barbican, then a poor neighborhood north of London notorious for its impoverished hack writers. Regardless, many seventeenth-century medical men did travel on the fringes of its trade. Welwood may have had some financial worries upon arriving in London, but good fortune and better connections kept him out of the poverty which prompted many educated persons to make a living out of scribbling for London's printers. Like many gentlemen of the time, Welwood denigrated the status of journalist, and so kept his authorship of *Mercurius Reformatus* unknown for as long as he could, "the province of a newsmonger [being] somewhat below me."[6] He viewed his journal of opinion as embracing historical as well as contemporary events, and therefore superior to a newspaper proper. Welwood's periodical was among the dozens of corantos, diurnals, and mercuries Londoners supported after the 1688 revolution. Through *Mercurius Reformatus*, Welwood became not only an outspoken propagandist for the Williamite Whigs but also a well-known and cogent critic of the Jacobites. But Welwood was no "hireling scribbler," as he put it. A few scholars of the period have assumed that *Mercurius Reformatus* was sponsored by the government, even though Bishop Burnet had to identify Welwood as a starving writer for William's secretary of state.[7] Besides, Welwood explicitly denied being the king's "mercenary pen." On April 9, 1690 he wrote:

> I never had from him or from any of his ministers, nor from anybody else except the book-seller to the value of one six-pence, for writing either this weekly paper or any other paper whatsoever. Yea, I declare likewise, that I never so much as acquainted any of his majesty's ministers with my being the author of this weekly paper but one single person; and that noble person will bear me witness, I did it under the seal of secrecy, and never asked nor received any money

or promise of money upon that account or upon any account whatever....

Welwood's disavowal of the mercenary label has the ring of truth. After all, he had begun to champion the validity of William's takeover against the slurs of anti-revolutionaries while still in Newcastle. The sole person who indisputably influenced his work after his arrival in London was the Bishop of Salisbury; Dr. Welwood attested to that influence on one occasion and published at least one document germane to the debate on Nonjuring views at Burnet's behest. Nevertheless, Welwood's paper started publication a full ten months before Burnet was able to garner an appointive assignment for the doctor.

Devoted to foreign affairs, current events, and partisan editorial comment, *Mercurius Reformatus or the New Observator* gave Welwood the opportunity to praise the government of the joint monarchs and to denounce the forces of despotism as he saw them, both foreign and domestic. After more than a year of dissemination, *Mercurius* additionally brought him some fame and a long-awaited governmental appointment. Bishop Burnet obtained placement for Welwood on a medical commission after repeated efforts. From Windsor Castle in May 1690, Burnet wrote to the Earl of Nottingham, Tory secretary of state for the dual monarchs and close confederate of Queen Mary, interceding for Welwood:

> He is a worthy and a learned man, a fine writter, a man zealous for the present government and is indeed one of vertuouest and politest men that our nation has produced this age....He is like to starve...and yet is more capable to doe considerable services than most men I know. I due therefore in a most humble manner beg of your lordship to move the King earnestly for him to see if that which i have so often proposed for him may be done....[8]

Queen Mary may have spoken up for Welwood, too. Historian Mark Goldie asserts that Welwood was in some trouble in 1690 for opinions expressed in *A Modest Enquiry into the Causes of the Present Disasters*, leading to tension within the ministry. The pamphlet in question, printed by Whig writer and bookseller Richard Baldwin, railed against a conspiracy of disaffected clergy and well-placed agents of Louis XIV who combined to make it possible for the French fleet to sail into the English channel. The diatribe placed particular blame on the Archbishop of Canterbury and specific Anglican bishops, who were understandably infuriated by the charges that they were Popish pawns. According to Sir George Mackenzie in a July 1690 letter to Nottingham, the Episcopal clergy erupted with righteous anger at "fixing a third plot upon them, and at the imprisoning of many honest men in our neighboring counties, though they were more affectionate to the present government than those who imprisoned them." Mackenzie, Scottish physician and Tory, applauded Nottingham for punishing "Baldwin and Walwood" because that would please Church of England adherents in Scotland, where *A Modest Enquiry* was being read and admired in conventicles. Some rumors fixed authorial connivance with the secretary of state, but by jailing the writers, Mackenzie thought that Nottingham had freed himself from that imputation. Mackenzie wanted them punished as well.[9]

However, James Welwood did not write *A Modest Enquiry*. Its style is banal and its contents inflammatory, without any of the graceful classical and historical references that identify Welwood's distinctive style. Welwood himself critiqued the thesis of the pamphlet and its use of evidence in *Mercurius Reformatus*. *A Modest Enquiry* must have been written by an English Dissenter, as it evinces great empathy for Protestants persecuted by the Church of England. Furthermore, the booklet refers to "the accession of the crown of Scotland to *ours*," italicized in the original text. Welwood's friendship with Bishop Burnet and his moderate Whiggery precluded the wholesale slandering of Anglican leaders. Throughout the run of *Mercurius Reformatus* he repeatedly advocated "a happy union among all Protestants," and admonished sectarians that their enemies would exploit any division to defeat them, "a breach that shall never be widened by my pen." Nevertheless, in the July 18, 1690 issue, Welwood did hold that there was validity in questioning the loyalty to William of some leaders in the Church of England, the charge which was raised in *A Modest Enquiry*.

Richard Baldwin, a radical Whig and an avowed Presbyterian, is credited with writing *A Modest Enquiry* by the editor of the Finch papers and by Baldwin's biographers. Baldwin alone was sent to Newgate prison two days before Welwood's column appeared, and he was released shortly from sentence by posting bail.[10] Probably because of Welwood's endorsement of the theory that some Anglican clergy were involved in a plot against the king, Nottingham urged that charges be brought against Welwood and parliamentary condemnation of his writing. However, Queen Mary prevailed with the secretary of state to leave Welwood unmolested.[11] Someone in a position of importance was undeniably in Dr. Welwood's corner, because in January 1691 he obtained his first appointment to become superintendent of the surgeons of the fleet. He would receive others. A 1691 newsletter which identified Welwood as the new superintendent described him as the writer of the *Observator*, the alternate title for *Mercurius Reformatus*.

Concurrent to his newspaper writing, Welwood authored other tracts. In 1689 he composed in London and in Edinburgh *An Answer to the Late King James' Declaration to All His Pretended Subjects in the Kingdom of England*, a brochure published "to silence the impertinent clamors of repeated provocations of the Jacobites." Welwood energetically urged that the king's propaganda should be "buried in eternal oblivion," and the House of Commons followed suit by ordering that James' declaration be burnt by the common hangman.[12] In this work Welwood identified the ways in which James II had lost the right to rule his subjects. First, despite James' claim that he pledged to protect all Protestants and the Church of England Welwood accused the quondam king of imposing Catholicism upon Protestants because Catholics are required by their pope to extirpate heretics. To do this, James was clearly following the heinous example of Louis XIV whose "fatal days of the dragoon conversions" Welwood recalled from his sojourn in France. In fact, James had become little more than a puppet of the Gallic sovereign at the same time that the pope called Louis "the common enemy of the Christian part of Europe." Second, having been ousted from Britain, James sought to use Catholic Ireland as a base for his anticipated recapturing of the throne. Welwood rebuked James for abandoning Irish Protestants "to the merciless rage of an enemy irreconcilable" and thereby jeopardizing English control over the island. Welwood fumed that all of the field offices in the Irish army had been turned over to the French or James' "darling wild Irish...that they might in time shake off the English government." Third, Welwood chastised James for hypocrisy in extending simulated toleration to Protestant dissenters. Either the perfidious Stuart wanted to divide Protestants among themselves or lull them into a false sense of security, but he certainly did not intend to exalt freedom of conscience in Britain. Welwood warned his fellow citizens to wake up to the historical record of Catholicism and to recollect the martyrdoms inflicted by the masterminds of the Roman Inquisition on men of faith in Europe. Welwood blamed the Jesuits for killing "millions of souls in Japan and other parts of Asia," and claimed that passive resistance to the government was not enough; James had brought his three kingdoms "to the brink of ruin and his fate upon himself" through the unlawful exercise of arbitrary power.

Some scholars have attributed *An Answer to the Late King James' Declaration* and a parallel broadside in 1693 to fellow Williamite Daniel Defoe, their confusion due to the avalanche of anonymous leaflets emanating from all spots on the political spectrum. But the good doctor never denied his authorship of this work; his contemporaries surmised that he wrote it and the later companion piece, so consequently Welwood's honor and celebrity soared among those who agreed with him. For those who opposed his message, Welwood became merely notorious.

However, it was *Mercurius Reformatus* that made him famous throughout London. More than any other of his writings, Welwood's newspaper gave voice to his particular combination of political beliefs. Above all, Welwood was loyal to the Glorious Revolution. He wanted to be confident that the historical record of the watershed event of his life was accurately written for posterity, and he feared that somehow minions of the French king, "counterfeiters of history," might distort the truth. He insisted to his readers that "I disdain to write anything but what I back with authentic proofs." *Mercurius Reformatus* complimented the martial genius of the House of Orange and likened William in greatness to heroic emperors such as Constantine and Justinian. On the other hand, Welwood speculated that ex-King James lacked the courage to hazard a campaign in person against William's Irish forces. Reflecting in late July 1690 on the successes of King William's military engagements in Ireland that summer, Welwood wrote that "when I fancy to myself, I see him in the action at the Boyne." Welwood lauded the English people for undertaking an expensive war and financially supporting the king's mighty effort against the forces of tyranny and injustice. During those bleak periods in the War of the Grand Alliance when English fortunes did not advance, and when even the weather seemed to conspire against England's fleet, *Mercurius Reformatus* urged steadfastness. Assured of ultimate victory over their enemies, Welwood admonished his readers that there was plenty of oak and money left in England to build new ships.[13]

While asserting his devotion to the king on nearly every question, Welwood often conceded the necessity of finding the golden mean in the midst of rancorous partisan bickering. "Moderation is able to curb the fiery and inconsiderate zeal of the uncharitable bigots of either party," he wrote in the February 19, 1690 issue of *Mercurius Reformatus*. He perceived party politics as detracting from substantive discussion of the nation's concerns: "We play the fool with the nicknames of Whig and Tory." Welwood wrote, he pledged to his readers, "not to please any particular party [and] never to widen our differences by a bitterness of style, but to use the calmest measures in my reflexions upon the most disallowable practices and papers." Welwood warned that party factions threatened to diminish England to the level of another Venice, "that epitome of politicks," brought down by partisan divisions.

Welwood's advocacy of the middle ground is apparent in his various remarks in *Mercurius Reformatus* about organized religion. He tried, he wrote, not to categorize men by their denomination, because "a good God approves us both." Dr. Welwood specifically avoided classifications like Calvinist, Lutheran, Church of England-man, and Presbyterian. They were all just Protestants as far as he was concerned, but their adherence to reform did not protect them from error. Welwood labelled "ignorant religious zealotry" as dangerous to the whole world. Noting that there was "villainy in all parts of Christendom," Welwood asserted that some Roman Catholics had greater respect for John Calvin's theology than did "English bigots." Indicating that he had Catholic friends at home and abroad, Welwood pronounced himself "very unwilling to lay the blame of the miscarriages of a few, or of a particular order among them, at the door of their whole church." Among the Catholics he praised was the Prince Palatine, who "gave proof of the possibility of a Popish prince being really kind to his Protestant subjects." Welwood cited the Prince for fostering charity between Papists and Protestants and for punishing one of his own officers for attacking a German meeting house. *Mercurius Reformatus* contained words of admiration for the recently deceased Queen Christina of Sweden, a convert to Catholicism, who nonetheless condemned religious persecution in France. Even the Papacy itself might be absolved of the charge of perpetual tyranny; Welwood complimented Pope Innocent XI for opposing the revocation of the Edict of Nantes, for blocking the friendship between James II and Louis XIV by supporting the Grand Alliance against France, and for asserting that James had been the author of his own misfortunes. Although he worried initially about the influence of the French faction on the Papal election to succeed Innocent XI, Welwood later congratulated the Spanish contingent in the College of Cardinals for engineering the vote for an anti-French pontiff.

Mercurius Reformatus conducted a campaign to demonize Louis XIV, reporting stories that the French ruler was born with a full set of teeth. Welwood surmised that bloodshed was second nature to a monarch who had as a baby drawn blood rather than milk from the breast of his wetnurses. Welwood made clear that he felt the French king was as much an enemy to freedom-loving Catholics as to Protestants, and that all persuasions in England were better off with the benign influences of William and Mary's government. Louis could not be trusted by other Christian sovereigns even as they waged war against Islam; he had invaded the Palatinate while the Holy Roman Emperor was off campaigning against the infidel Turks. Direct French aid to the Turks two years later meant that "Christian churches in eastern Europe [would be] turned into mosques," wrote Welwood, claiming to have seen correspondence between Louis and the Grand Vizier. The Sun King especially victimized his own people by constant warfare and had lied to them in broadsides which purported that the English themselves desperately invited his intervention after a few Gallic victories. Welwood reserved particular opprobrium for the Jesuit order and its fanatical influence on the policies of some states. He wondered how people who acknowledged Jesus could do the things that the Jesuits did to other Christians. Welwood mused that English Catholics need reminding that they should be grateful for their own "mild government." As for the exiled James II, Welwood viewed him as having been destroyed by the Jesuits, just another "victim of Loyola's principles."[14]

In a series of *Mercurius Reformatus* issues, Welwood rebutted the revisionist Catholic argument that religious reform in England had been precipitated by frivolous and immoral royal behavior. The English Reformation had come about in the sixteenth century because the people sought metamorphosis of their spiritual lives and not, Welwood urged, because of Henry VIII's lust for Anne Boleyn. The people demanded something better than an ignorant, corrupt clergy, a litany of mutually-excommunicating popes, and fractious doctrinal pronouncements. As he examined each reform, Welwood urged his readers to follow the sequence of his report in the next edition of the publication. Typical of the chauvinism of its era, Welwood's newspaper catalogued non-Britons as inferior. Speaking of James' Italian queen, Mary of Modena, Welwood said that her participation in plots against King William were crimes "so suitable to her genius and country." To Welwood the Venetians were unprincipled and overly pragmatic "Trimmers (to adapt an English phrase to an Italian politick)." The Irish were routinely earmarked for ridicule by Grub Street writers; Welwood called them "naked, stupid, and cowardly," as much for their support of James II as for their intransigent Catholicism. On the other hand, Irish soldiers might be excused, stated Welwood, since they had been prevailed upon by their priests to enlist.

Of course, most Englishmen would have naturally lumped Scotsmen into the same category as the Irish, part of the invading Celtic fringe. Popular prints in London portrayed the Scots as backward and provincial, haughty and overbearing, scarcely better than dirty and penniless savages. Writers parodied the Scots as suspicious buffoons; Samuel Johnson was a notorious Scot-baiter. Bishop Burnet was the target of mockery because of his ethnic origins. One wag wrote of him as:

...a big-boned northern priest,
With pliant body and with a brawny fist;
Whose weighty blows the dusty cushions thrash,
And make the trembling pulpit's wainscot crash.[15]

Scottish physicians like Welwood, who made their entry into English society after the Glorious Revolution, aroused acute jealousy. Satirists depicted Williamite Scotsmen as "a swarm of locusts from the north in search of profit and preferment."[16]

Although he occasionally flaunted cultural bias against any non-Briton that is shocking to today's reader, Welwood was typical in his day. He did have some encouraging if qualified words for other ethnic groups. He often enthused about the Dutch auxiliaries stationed in England, and mocked the outrageous rumors that any of them had been involved in nefarious activity near Hampton Court in early 1690; he also lauded William's Danish forces in Scotland en route to Ireland. He called the "barbarians of Monotopa kind and compassionate Africans," and sketched a sympathetic history of the Jews in Britain, decrying their persecution in England and elsewhere until Oliver Cromwell gave them liberty of residence. Yet Welwood approved of a £100,000 House of Commons levy on the Jews in late 1689 as part of a larger subsidy for the war against France because, he wrote, they enjoyed greater freedom in Williamite England than anywhere else. Welwood exposed his own anti-semitism when he called the Jews a "poor deluded people [who] rather should be the objects of our compassion than our hatred as being once the peculiar people of God for above two thousand years."[17]

Welwood continued every Wednesday to publish *Mercurius Reformatus* which flourished amidst controversy. Many newspapers imitated the format of *The London Gazette*, a single unfolded half-sheet folio printed on both sides, with advertisements grouped at the end; Welwood's publication roughly followed this model. *Mercurius Reformatus* was printed in double columns on both sides of a standard sheet of paper (roughly 11 inches by 7 inches) with a fairly elaborate heading and abstract. As much as a half of the final column was occupied by miscellaneous advertising, and the printer's identity and location took up the bottom lines across both columns. The advertisements are often as political as the panegyric reflections they supported. For example, in the July 17, 1689 edition readers are exhorted to buy "Orange Cards," a series of collectibles that includes pictures of a "Jesuit preaching against our Bible," trials of Protestants, the birth of the Prince of Wales replete with a suspicious midwife, and effigies of

William and Mary, "curiously illustrated and engraven in lively figures; done by the performers of the first Popish Plot Cards." Precursors of the comic strip, these playing cards provided a pictorial text to a broad spectrum of people.

How many readers did Welwood attract? Unfortunately, many aspects of distribution remain obscure. People could purchase copies of *Mercurius Reformatus* from various distribution points for the standard price of a penny a piece or from one of the many newsboys who sold a variety of papers in the streets. Welwood's paper likely attracted a better if eclectic clientele, given the erudition of its author and the sometimes recherché historical and literary allusions on which he relied. Its advertisements provide us with additional clues about readership. They touted expensive, esoteric religious and political books, as well as quack medicines and frivolous kickshaws.[18]

Among the disparate and intriguing commercials is one for language instruction in Latin, High Dutch, French or Italian; another celebrates "German Balls, so much used for the beautifying of boots and shoes, and keeping the feet from wet and taking cold;" yet another peddles fortune-telling cards which answer "twenty of the most significant astrological questions." Two adjacent if antipodal advertisements for reading material in July 17, 1691 deserve consideration. The first promotes *Academia*, a book full of "pleasant humours of the universities with pranks of younger students" for 13*s*; the second work, only sixpence, is a sermon exhorting youth to prepare for Judgment Day. There were occasional personal ads, such as one in June 1691 which requested that the person sending a letter "by the penny post without date or subscription to a citizen living not far from the Exchange" come forward to speak with the recipient. Another proffered a ten shilling reward for a cane with an agate and silver head lost at Jonathan's Coffee House. One can find advertised forerunners of self-help and demotic psychology manuals, for example *Nosce Teipsum, a Leading-Step to the Knowledge of our Selves*.

Welwood's readership unquestionably extended beyond the city's bookshops. The penny post delivered in London and the suburbs, but the cost of paper and delivery twice-weekly was too much for an artisan or shopkeeper. Besides, since houses and apartment buildings in Augustan London had no numbers, a man had his mail or any other correspondence delivered to his coffee house. More than 500 licensed coffee houses in London provided newspapers, usually buying four copies of each leading paper for the use of their customers. By 1700, there may have been 1000 establishments, meaning half the men in London visited a coffee house every day.[19] Runners were dispatched to the coffee houses to relate major events of the day, such as victory in battle or political upheaval. Open from 6 a.m. to 10 p.m., coffee houses provided space for reading and writing. Customers paid a penny for admission, and might be charged more for the use of pen, ink, and paper for the season. The coffee houses themselves, "nurseries of sedition," became a problem for authorities intent on managing the press. Booksellers had their favorite establishments, as did political factions, and various other business activities took place there, such as auctions, the buying and selling of copyrights, and the insuring of shipping and foreign trade. Apothecaries often found physicians "keeping office hours" in a coffee house, and leisured rakes passed the hours at cards in its gaming rooms. Most importantly, during the various crises of government in the Augustan Age, coffee houses were the preeminent meeting places for men of letters to engage in partisan discussions. Political and religious moderates, as well as the more fervent Whigs who would not endorse popular sovereignty, staunchly defended coffee houses, the notion of the public sphere, and meaningful citizen discourse. James Welwood knew that *Mercurius Reformatus* would be read aloud and tacked up on the walls of the informal Whig clubs in coffee houses like Graecian's in the Strand near his home and the St. James in Westminster, both of which he himself frequented.

After each thirty issues of *Mercurius*, Welwood had them done up in marbled paper, bound, and sold as a discrete volume at his printer's shop. He provided a table of contents and a foreword summarizing events of the previous seven months. Welwood's gazette sought to inform educated readers, those with some training in language, history, and religion. Issues are sprinkled with untranslated Greek, Latin, and French maxims attesting to the author's erudition and respect for his audience; Welwood used sources which he translated from the original Italian, German, and Dutch. He freely paraphrased such diverse authors as Demosthenes, Plutarch, Cicero, Tacitus, Procopius, and even Herodotus, "a heathen historian."[20] Welwood in his columns referred to opera, to *belles lettres*, and to his readers as "persons of quality." Of course, the dynamics of periodicity require the flattering of readers, especially readers who show up at the printer's establishment to buy their papers.[21]

There are production factors, however, which support the conclusion that Welwood's regular readers were advanced readers. Paper size signalled the importance of a work. Folio sheets, such as those used for *Mercurius Reformatus*, targeted politicians and the professional class. Smaller publications, printed in octavos or twelves and usually un-stitched, cost less and appealed to a lower economic stratum. The kind of typeface used in seventeenth-century printing also indicated what the potential audience was for a specific publication. Roman type was associated with better-educated Englishmen, while black-letter font remained the type of the lower class and the marginally literate. Black-letter persisted as the typeface for ballads, broadsides, and jest books. Paradoxically, it endured as the print of the Crown; statutes, proclamations, and plague bills utilized black-letter. Layouts often employed italics for decoration and emphasis. The most elaborate format, meant for sophisticated readers, manifested all these typefaces. *Mercurius Reformatus* used that format.[22]

Besides the complex content and varied fonts displayed in his mercury, Welwood probably attracted cultured readers because of his style. He introduced a new journalistic diction, smoother and more literary than any seen before. His language would influence later essayists, although the substance of *Mercurius Reformatus* was devoted to harangues about French hegemony and threats to freedom. In addition to drawing on documents and printed works, Welwood based his commentary on personal letters from correspondents abroad and conversations with governmental officials and London insiders. For instance, in the October 1, 1690 issue he referred to a communication from a professor at Leipzig concerning the poisoning of the Duke of Lorraine. On another occasion, he explained his conclusion, based on personal observation and discourses with courtiers, that King William's fondness for hunting at Windsor or Richmond was an excellent diversion from his pressing duties.

Welwood presented his arguments for a specific position after careful explanation of the problem's history. Advertisements at the end of each paper often refer to supplementary reading in texts mentioned in that edition or books penned by Welwood himself. For example, the July 2, 1690 *Mercurius* suggests reading in Irish history to fully appreciate the military challenge posed to the king by Jacobites in Ireland. Evidently, there was sufficient demand to warrant twice-weekly publication of the mercury after just two months of publication. A regular Saturday edition was added to the Wednesday schedule at the insistence of Welwood's booksellers.

For two years, the regular appearance of *Mercurius Reformatus* was a given. Then, for a short time, on Wednesdays from March 25, 1691 to May 13, 1691, Welwood concomitantly produced another journal of opinion, *The Weekly Remarks*. During the run of the second paper and until the cessation of *Mercurius Reformatus* later in that year, Welwood generated *Mercurius Reformatus* only once a week, mostly on Fridays. Clearly, the crush of deadlines for all of his varied writing projects overwhelmed Dr. Welwood. In the second of the six printings of *The Weekly Remarks*, he apologized for missing the previous week's edition, explaining to his readers that despite his hectic schedule producing *Mercurius Reformatus*, he felt an obligation to counter all the hands employed to disturb William's government. He wrote he would "throw all his mite, desiring no greater happiness or reward than to do his country what service he can."[23]

The premise of *The Weekly Remarks* is very similar to that of *Mercurius Reformatus*: Welwood continued to assail Louis XIV and exalt King William. The style of *The Weekly Reader* likewise paralleled *Mercurius Reformatus*, as Welwood relied increasingly on his classical repertory for examples and quotations. Sprinkled in the columns are well-known passages from illustrious ancient commentators like Julius Caesar, Plutarch, and Suetonius as well as more arcane references to the Roman historians Appian, Curtius, Justin, and Cornelius Nepos. Welwood pondered as had Cato whether France like Carthage would have to be destroyed before its threats to the peace were eliminated. He made allusions to the Augustan Age of Rome with its lessons for Augustan Britain and attacked his pet *béte noir*, the theory of passive obedience, with the suggestion that it was "as pernicious to a civil society as the heresy of Arius was to the Christian church."[24] Welwood cited far fewer modern scholars, just quoting Hugo Grotius, a seventeenth-century Dutch jurist and near contemporary of Welwood, in passing.

Of particular concern to Dr. Welwood during the brief life of *The Weekly Remarks* was the course of the continental war, especially the failure of the Allies in the siege of Mons, a Meuse river garrison which fell to the French general Vauban in April 1691. He contended that the loss of Mons provoked two equally inappropriate but opposite reactions in England: enemies of William's government grinned with glee, while weak-willed supporters of the king panicked at the possibility of total defeat. Welwood exhorted the latter to rally behind the war effort, assuring his audience that the virtuous side would be victorious in the long run. He reminded readers that persevering Britons had often overcome initial losses to enemies in the past, citing as one example the ninth-century infestation by Danish pirates and the heroic response of the indomitable admiral, Earl Ethelworth. Moreover, Welwood argued that the success of France at Mons might prove to be Pyrrhic, since so many of Louis' troops had been dispatched from the Rhine to Dunkirk to join the besiegement of Flanders. "Gold itself may be bought too dear," he wrote, gauging that the French had lost thousands of soldiers, "the very flower of their army."

In another issue, Welwood addressed the possible restoration of James II, an exceptionally frightening prospect if it came about through the mediation of Louis XIV. To many Englishmen this horror seemed a distinct possibility after the fall of Mons, because that defeat on land came after an embarrassing naval setback the previous summer. However, many Members of Parliament, whose outlook was decidedly provincial, balked at the government's demands for extra money to fight "King William's War" with so little evidence of success. Welwood tried to reassure both the skeptics and the anxious that the Grand Alliance would emerge triumphant with the solid backing of England. At the same time he blamed the council of allied ministers, which sat at The Hague throughout the war, for failing to act in a unified manner. He accused some of the allies of lacking fortitude, especially the Imperial and Spanish states, which were uncomfortable collaborating with a Protestant against the interests of the Catholic claimant to the throne of England. Welwood was right in his assessment of the internal diplomatic problems facing the Grand Alliance, but his accusatory words may have ruffled rather than smoothed feathers. Without explanation, perhaps presaging trouble for his other newspaper, Welwood suddenly discontinued *The Weekly Remarks* after the sixth imprint.

Dr. James Welwood valued liberty above all else, and he reveled in the ability to express his views freely. He associated the Glorious Revolution with openness and happily contrasted the era of William and Mary with the closed, repressive years of James II. Though he rejected the principles of the Tories and belittled the distrustful Country faction, Welwood directed most of his invective at Jacobites, supporters of the exiled Stuarts who were ideologically inclined toward Toryism, and he wrote most of his political works during a great wave of Jacobite activity.[25] As a Protestant himself, Welwood insisted that Protestantism, personified by the Dutch Calvinist William, guaranteed Englishmen liberty of conscience, while Catholicism generally suffocated freedom by imposing religious and political orthodoxy. Of course, from the Catholic point of view the "Glorious Revolution" had nothing to do with timeless conceptions of liberty but rather with virulent anti-popery. To them (and to many historians today) William III was just as autocratic as James had been. The new king saw little advantage to open debate, particularly in coffee houses or in the press.

The Bill of Rights about which Welwood rhapsodized insured Members of Parliament their free speech, but said nothing about freedom of the press. William's government did not sanction partisanship in the press because it did not want to lose the support of influential politicians on account of a few fanatical writers. Furthermore, all honeymoons must end, and the legitimacy of William and Mary's coronation proved a sticking point for many. Some Anglican clergy balked at swearing allegiance to a foreign interloper; these Nonjurors were deprived of their benefices and joined the Jacobite cause. Because of the controversy engendered by the War of the Grand Alliance against France, radical Whiggish sentiment in Parliament for William began to cool rather quickly, even causing some former revolutionaries to find common ground with Jacobites. Complicating the political scene even more, there existed another division of opinion between the resurgent Country-opposition ideology and that of the Court which cut across the Whig-Tory political alignment for over a decade. Though the Country faction, led during William's reign by Robert Harley, did not have the cohesion of a party, it tried through Parliament to limit the crown's ability to determine the outcome of treason trials and to remove judges at will. Despite his stature as a "toppler of tyrants," William III did not want statutory restrictions on the royal prerogative, but in order to procure appropriations for the war he had to relinquish some of his independence. While the old parties disintegrated, the king used his veto power as Country Whigs conjoined with the Tories to exclude placemen from the House of Commons. When Welwood had the temerity to criticize fair-weather supporters of the king in print, the House of Commons found portions of his publication objectionable.

Like many other revolutionary enthusiasts, Welwood was caught off-guard by the rapid changes in the political landscape. Fear of excessive radicalism in London and elsewhere caused a reaction among established Whigs in Parliament against wholesale changes in the constitution. Disdaining any sort of commonwealth designed even by Whigs, James Welwood confirmed for the readers of *Mercurius Reformatus* that "monarchy is rooted and interwoven with our laws and institutions." King William himself became apprehensive about urban republicanism and as a result effected a surprising rapprochement with the Tories by 1690. The needle on England's political compass moved so erratically that Welwood and others lost their way in dangerous, uncharted territory.[26]

The good doctor tried to fathom the shifts in public and Parliamentary opinion of the king. He was surely aware of the customary xenophobia of the English toward emigrant noblemen and commoners alike, and attributed William's loss of support to his foreignness. William found spoken English hard to follow and admitted few Englishmen into his confidence. Ironically, though he despised politicians, as a foreigner he had to depend on them, thereby devaluing the monarchy. Even Bishop Burnet later criticized the king for taking "little pains to gain the affections of the nation." Throughout his life, William's heart lay in the Netherlands. He would not abjure his position there as stadtholder, and he designated two Dutch favorites his primary advisers in England. One of them, Hans Willem Bentinck, the king's closest confidant, was created Earl of Portland even before

William's coronation. For some years foreigners persisted as commanders of English troops in the field, and William kept Dutch guards around him in England. Many Englishmen were envious of the Dutch and French Protestant émigrés who had come with the Prince of Orange to England, later obtaining lands and high offices from him. Holland-style geometric gardens, evergreen shrubbery, and neat red-brick houses, so popular after 1688 with Englishmen, quickly assumed political meanings and attracted criticism; Tories even denounced topiary because it was associated with Dutchmen. Of course, some English indignation stemmed from nativist cultural arrogance, but much of it signaled partisan animosity. Everyone knew that complaints about aliens were really thinly disguised assaults on the government and the king himself. Daniel Defoe later noted that "the word Foreigner was the shibboleth of a party, who made it popular, that they might better affront that great foreigner, that had made them all denizens. I mean King William."[27]

William may have further exacerbated the growing common disaffection with his regime by refusing to perform some of the traditional rituals of English monarchs, such as washing the feet of the poor on Maundy Thursday or laying hands on scrofulous victims of "the king's evil," a tubercular affliction. In 1682 Charles II performed the touching rite 8,500 times, and James touched 800 in Chester Cathedral during one of his progresses. Gold talismans were distributed by the monarch, and so the expense of the ceremony was significant, but the crowds were immense.[28] Failure to recognize the potency of the people's belief in sacred royal powers, ludicrous though they may have seemed to the practical Dutchman, undercut popular admiration and awe for his kingship. By the end of his reign Parliament was so disenchanted with William that it passed an Act of Settlement forbidding an English monarch of foreign birth from taking the country into "any warr for the defence of any dominions and territories which do not belong to the crown of England," and from leaving the kingdom; the same legislation disqualified any alien from a governmental or Parliamentary position.

Given the instability of the political landscape after the Glorious Revolution, Welwood understandably chose printers and booksellers with whom to work whose partisan view mirrored his own. Readers associated specific printers with authors and remembered their politics. James II's hapless publisher, Henry Hill, became a marked man during the London disturbances which accompanied the revolution. Welwood often relied on the presses of Dorman Newman, who published *Reasons Why the Parliament of Scotland...* in 1689 and printed the first months of the mercury, selling it at several locations in London. Dorman Newman's first imprint appeared in 1665 and by Welwood's time he was one of the city's largest publishers with locations at the King's Arms in Poultry Lane, in Little Britain, and on both sides of London Bridge. Dorman Newman ceased publishing *Mercurius Reformatus* in March of 1691, and Dr. Welwood claimed that Newman had printed a spurious paper under Welwood's name. Curiously, however, Dorman Newman published the entire if short-lived run of *The Weekly Remarks*, its inaugural number begun by Welwood just two days before he shifted the job of printing *Mercurius Reformatus* to Richard Baldwin. Their rift could not have been too serious if Dr. Welwood continued doing some business with Newman. Due to unwise speculation, Dorman Newman went bankrupt in 1694.

Richard Baldwin, printer, bookbinder, and bookseller, handled the last eight months of Welwood's tenure as author of *Mercurius Reformatus*. He also assembled one edition of Welwood's 1689 *Answer to the Late King James' Declaration* and a later medical report of the doctor's. Among the best-known controversialist publishers of his day and a staunch Whig, Baldwin specialized in divisive political pamphlets and broadsides, as well as satires on social life and contemporary culture. His principal editors were Huguenot exiles; his target audience included Irish Protestants and Scotsmen in London. Baldwin advertised his house's lists extensively in newspapers and for a time published a periodical of his own, *Mercurius Anglicus*. Books and papers with his imprint were distributed at Will's Coffee House in Russell Street, at the Hermitage in Wapping, and for over seventeen years from the Oxford Arms in Warwick Lane near the Old Bailey. Baldwin's employees routinely posted the titles of forthcoming works on the Saturday night before publication, causing some excitement if the pieces were controversial. His apprentices were beaten up on a couple of occasions by men unhappy with Baldwin and his books. The critical tone of many of Baldwin's titles in the 1680s led to trouble with political opponents and with the government. The secretary of state in 1682 demanded security and a copy of one offensive tome, *Rights of the Kingdom*. Complaints another time were lodged against him with the judges of the King's Bench for a newspaper, *The Protestant Courant*, but evidently no action followed. From 1689 through 1698 Baldwin published approximately 240 books including 150 political titles, seventy-five of which were Gallophobic. Stimulated by the protracted Anglo-French conflict, Baldwin poured out works lampooning Louis XIV, James Stuart, and the Papacy. Furthermore, he wrote whole works and prefaces to others which enthused about the rights and liberties of the people. The greatest tribulation for his business came in 1691 as a result of his association with James Welwood, a client with whom he shared an abiding love of King William.[29]

Although Parliament had generously appropriated sufficient grants (some £4,600,000) for the conduct of the war with France in its 1690 sessions, a commission of public accounts with members chosen by Parliament had been set up to supervise expenditures. The commission's report, made public in November 1691, chided the government for waste and recommended specific appropriations inaccessible to corrupt ministers. Furious with this turn of events, Welwood excoriated unnamed Members of Parliament in the November 5, 1691 issue of *Mercurius Reformatus* for betraying the nation. "The King has done his part, and has done all that man can do: if any of our selves do not ours, it's our own fault, and there ought an atonement to be made to our country for the crime." He called it "sacrilege to purloin money given for carrying on this war," and compared reducing supply money to stealing the utensils of a Christian temple. Those appropriations made by Parliament should "deliver us from religious and civil slavery [and] redeem three nations from captivity and thraldom," so Welwood demanded that any misapplication of "sacred treasure" should be punished as a heinous offense. Members of the House of Commons were sensitive about any public discussion of their proceedings, and had even refused since 1689 to authorize newspapers to publish their votes, fearing that individuals' decisions would become fodder for coffee house gossip. As a result, the early Williamite press was usually silent about Parliament, barely publishing the names of those elected;

printed criticism of its members and their motives would not be tolerated.

Accordingly, under its licensing prerogative, Parliament summoned *Mercurius'* printer Baldwin on November 7 to appear before a session of the Commons. He was compelled to do penance on his knees and received a reprimand from the Speaker for the paper's intemperate language. However, Baldwin made his peace with the legislature by declaring that Dr. Welwood was the sole author of the paper. After paying a fee, he was released from custody, but now Welwood was charged with breach of privilege. Placed under custody of the Sergeant at Arms, Welwood found it prudent to acknowledge his offense to the House, while "humbly praying to be discharged of his imprisonment." Brought to the bar of the House two days later, Doctor Welwood fell to his knees and absorbed a reproof comparable to Baldwin's. Having groveled to the Houses' satisfaction and demonstrated obeisance, he, too, paid the obligatory fees to be free again.[30] Welwood, much to his chagrin, had discovered belatedly that erstwhile friends now took umbrage at his libertarianism, and that his standing in the medical profession or as a commissioner for the government meant little. Clearly shaken by what had happened, the doctor later expressed both shock at the drift of Parliament away from the king and sadness at the censorship imposed on him. He had castigated the Stuarts for their inflexible authority, but now was subject to the power of an equally brittle Parliamentary majority. He immediately ceased publication of *Mercurius Reformatus*, closing with a lengthy appendix reaffirming his belief in William and Mary.

In the *Appendix to Mercurius Reformatus*, Welwood described the "accident" that obliged him to concede authorship of the paper. Although he insisted that Parliament did not make him stop publication, Welwood voiced fear that "lest some time or another, in tracing truth too near, I may come to have my teeth struck out." Besides, he argued, William and Mary hardly need his pen, or anyone else's, to assert their rights to rule. Welwood unapologetically insisted on the point he had made in the offending issue of *Mercurius*, that England must do all in its power to debilitate France or risk losing everything at home and abroad. Somewhat disingenuously, Welwood vowed "to trouble the world with no more Observators," yet offered from time to time to serve king and country with his pen when called upon.

Some of the pragmatic members of William's government may have welcomed Welwood's retirement from journalism, certainly those who felt his sentiments endangered the political co-operation which the war with France necessitated. Even the king may have entertained the idea of grounding his rule on the Church bloc, which he regarded as situated safely between the Jacobites and the radical Whigs. Secretary of State Nottingham tried to propel William on this course, encouraging the princely suspicion that Whigs like Welwood might be closet republicans. However, Bishop Burnet still approved of Welwood's work and even collaborated with him, editing and vetting at least one of the doctor's polemics. As Welwood cheerfully continued to blast colluding foreign and domestic enemies of the king, Secretary of State Nottingham cracked down, exhibiting signs of stress in the administration during at least one anxious episode.

Jacobite plans for a domestic counter-revolution had fizzled, and all their hopes depended on Louis XIV. In 1692 during one of the many extended periods William spent away from England commanding the Allied forces during the war with France, an assassination scheme against him was hatched in the French court, refuge of James II. The plot had originally been the brainstorm of Louis' Minister of War, the Marquis de Louvois. When Louvois died in 1691, his twenty-four year-old son, Louis Barbézieux, took over his post, determined to carry out his father's Machiavellian design. The conspiracy centered on a young French officer, Barthelemy de Linière, chevalier de Grandval, who was to make his way to William's headquarters in Flanders and to shoot the king while he was making the rounds of his troops. Before leaving Paris, Grandval was presented to James. However, Grandval's two accomplices betrayed him to the Allies and he was arrested as soon as he reached Brabant. Monsieur Grandvall (as he was known in England), who made a full confession at his court-martial revealing that James had given his approval to the strategy, was executed soon afterwards.

Cabinet Whigs urged the queen to publish the details of Grandval's sensational trial in order to discredit the Jacobite cause, but Mary herself was reluctant because of her father's ignoble involvement in the murder attempt.[31] While visiting Salisbury, Bishop Burnet wrote to Nottingham that Dr. Welwood had fashioned "a very pretty paper upon this matter of Grandvall which I have revised with great care and dare answer for it...." Burnet assured Nottingham that no one could object to the piece and that the complaints it lodged against the French king should be published right away. Nevertheless, Nottingham voided Burnet's approval of the leaflet, refusing to license or make public in any way Welwood's reflections on an anti-Williamite conspiracy. Welwood promised the secretary that he would not publish the provocative piece, but did request that his reflections be sent to the king; Nottingham felt confident the king would agree with his judgment that some "passages were so indecent that they are not fit to be printed."[32] But Nottingham's conservatism made him suspect with Whigs, and he himself faced a vote of censure in the House of Commons in the autumn of that year. Perhaps his influence had waned to the point that he could not suppress Welwood's polemic; surely the public sympathized with a monarch at risk from foreign agents. Two anonymous brochures about Grandvall appeared in 1692: one, an eight page tract called *A True Account of the Horrid Conspiracy against the Life of His Sacred Majesty William III*, was published by Edward Jones. The other, *Reflections upon the Late Horrid Conspiracy Contrived by Some of the French Court to Murther His Majesty in Flanders*, thirty-five pages in length, bore the imprint of Richard Baldwin; it is patently the work of James Welwood.

Reflections upon the Late Horrid Conspiracy bears all the hallmarks of Welwood's content and writing flair. It is polished prose, brimming with references to Roman history and with familiar phrases from the Welwood lexicon. The author had access to correspondents in France and Holland, as well as to the letters and papers of the Bishop of Salisbury. He was familiar with various continental cities, Paris in particular, which he suggested he had visited around 1682. He specifically mentioned undisclosed information known by several influential people in France including the Archbishop of Reims, whom he impugned as complicitous in the assassination intrigue. While shocked at the assassination conspiracy and the role played by the French king, the essayist made clear that he is respectful of all monarchs and sympathetic to James Stuart, a mere pawn to Louis XIV. As in

Mercurius Reformatus, Reflections upon the Late Horrid Conspiracy referred to Louvois with surprising esteem, lauded the House of Nassau, and elevated Queen Mary to sainthood. No charges are made in the pamphlet against anyone in England, and no Williamite could find the description of the French conspiracy against the king remotely controversial or offensive. This booklet is indubitably the "very pretty paper" by Welwood about Grandval to which Gilbert Burnet alluded in his letter to Nottingham, but if the bishop did edit it, he did little to obscure the Welwood style.[33]

Regardless of Nottingham's views, Welwood's quill apparently remained useful as an antidote to Jacobite sentiments and criticism of Williamite policies. Most of his replies and answers to the Stuart faction arose spontaneously from his belief system, but on at least one occasion Welwood's comments were purposefully solicited by the government. Although many unlicensed printers had been tried for violating the Licensing Act in the early 1690s, censorship was hard to impose and Jacobite libels against the government continued. The Licensing Act was allowed to lapse because the Crown found a new weapon for controlling the press, the treason law. William Anderton, a Nonjuring Jacobite who ran the most important of all the unlicensed presses in London, became the first person to be charged with treason for a seditious publication since 1663.

Anderton had written, printed, and published two jeremiads that led to his indictment. In *Remarks upon the Present Confederacy and Late Revolution in England*, Anderton repudiated the removal of James II and the destruction of the doctrine of non-resistance, predicting divinely-ordered catastrophe for England as a consequence. Providence had not brought William of Orange to the throne, he wrote, men had, and in the process had offended God. Anderton maintained that "...Instead of blessings we have plagues and judgments," an intimation of the economic hardships caused by King William's incessant war against France. Anderton argued as well that in his Declaration and the terms of the offer of the crown, William was contractually bound. William, not James, had violated the compact by his tyranny, bloodshed, and taxation.

The king's counsel had to prove that these infamous papers incited rebellion and war. In court the printer insisted that mere printing could not lead to the monarchs' deaths, but Chief Justice George Treby of the Court of Common Pleas found that writing was an overt act and could be treasonous. Anderton was found guilty on June 8, 1693, and sent to be executed on June 16. Queen Mary, acting as regent during one of the king's many military absences, refused to pardon him.[34] On the scaffold, Anderton asked to read his last words in defense of his actions, but according to witnesses he was not allowed to do so. The document was distributed at Anderton's request, making an effective and disturbing case for judicial murder. Defiant to the end, Anderton begged for England's deliverance from "our present deliverers [who under pretext] of war, deliver us from our money,...kidnap our young men,...and murther those who disapprove of these proceedings." He maintained that his "crime" was not treason but only reproducing material with which the government disagreed, hardly a capital offense. With his last breath, Anderton had insisted that the government had suborned witnesses and refused him counsel, all for calling the Prince of Orange "hook-nose."[35] He branded Robin Stephens, barrister, antiquarian, and the ministerial factotum who seized the publication and testified against him, a perjurious witness. Stephens was the government's veteran "messenger to the Press," armed with warrants to arrest those who dispensed "idle and mistaken relations of what passes."[36]

Moreover, Anderton charged that when the jury refused to convict him, Lord Chief Justice Treby had instructed the panel to find him guilty, threatening them with dire consequences if they did not. A guilty verdict was procured, and for a first offense Anderton faced the severest punishment; he maintained that his sentence amounted to cruel and unusual punishment in violation of the law. In a prayerful coda, Anderton asked God to restore King James to the throne and forgave even "my most false and perjured witnesses...and my most unjust and unrighteous judges." Copies of Anderton's scaffold statement along with a description of his execution were disseminated throughout England. In addition, Samuel Grascome openly accused "certain unjust judges lately sitting at the Old Baily" of killing Anderton for "pretended treason."[37]

The furor spawned by Anderton's treason conviction could not be ignored by the Crown. Bishop Burnet noted with some alarm that the traditional parties had changed places: the Whigs had to argue for prerogatives and the Tories became zealots for political liberties. Government Prosecutor Edward Cooke (sometimes called Cooke of the Middle Temple) was particularly disturbed about repercussions from the trial. An ardent Williamite, Cooke in 1689 had provided a historical justification for a claim by the Prince of Orange that his conquest was based on popular consent. Cooke found a precedent for one William's title in the actions of another conquering William; he argued that William I similarly arrived with force, but obtained the throne by winning the support of the people. In August 1693, Cooke wrote to Justice Treby that he had asked an agreeable Welwood to compose an appropriate response to Anderton's charges. Cooke reported that John Trenchard, secretary of state, concurred with him that a riposte was needed against all charges, "provided it were done by a good hand (and that) there could be no better person to do it with smartness...(to) prove a good service to the government." Treby was to inform Welwood about the circumstances of Anderton's trial and jury deliberations.[38] Dr. James Welwood, himself reproached by Parliament for overstepping the boundaries of printed criticism, was expected to dispute a dead man who sought to publish his version of the truth. No record, however, of any such retort remains, and it is probable that Welwood ultimately declined Cooke's suggestion. Edward Cooke was rewarded for his strategic contributions with appointment to the bench in 1694, and Robin Stephens was renamed messenger-in-ordinary that same year for his effort testifying against the printer.[39] But the implications of Anderton's execution at Tyburn could not have been lost on Welwood, nor presumably the collusion of the prosecutor and judge in the case, but he later sneered at those critics, "gentlemen, who in former reigns hurried on our ruin by stretching the prerogative, so now stand up champions for liberty."[40] However, Welwood knew that relying on treasonous prosecutions as a regular means of controlling the press was hardly a characteristic of a liberating government and was even harsher policy than employed by William's predecessors.

James Welwood continued to refute Jacobite propaganda emanating from the continent. Between 1689 and 1715 the exiled court dispersed at least fifteen declarations, creating a veritable cottage industry for Welwood the wordsmith. One of his most widely read and circulated rejoinders analyzed a paper released by James II from France in April 1693 and published in the Paris *Gazette* two months later. An atypically irenic text, James' declaration swore that if he were allowed to reclaim his throne there would be no retribution exacted for crimes against him and that Parliament's decisions on all matters would be binding. He similarly vouched for Protestant hegemony in England, pledging to maintain the Church of England, a vow which upon reflection caused a distinct twinge of conscience in the monarch. Two London printers, Newbolt and Butler, published *King James' Declaration*, and in 1695 were found guilty of treason, another attempt by the government to deter anti-Williamite literature.[41]

Welwood's *Answer to the Late King James' Last Declaration to All His Pretended Subjects* was printed by the indefatigable Richard Baldwin in 1693; forty pages long, it sold for sixpence. Despite the harsh judgment of Newbolt and Butler, Welwood's *Answer* included the king's manifesto in its entirety, interspersed with criticism and rebuttal. His tone acidic and sarcastic, his style more colloquial and conversational than usual, Welwood's persiflage ridiculed both the frequency of James' pronouncements and the about-face signalled by this new document. Just as many had believed the 1688 birth of a Stuart son to be suppositious, Welwood viewed this Jacobite document as fraudulent. Far from the thunderous expressions of previous statements, wrote Welwood, the 1693 declaration was serene in temper albeit based in treachery. Welwood calculated that it had not been long since the French army was ready to invade Britain's coasts with King James in tow. Buoyed by the prospects of retaking the throne, James had spoken plainly about his intention to punish all rebels, but as no invasion had taken place, Welwood accused the former king of feigning benevolence and forgiveness. He warned his readers to eschew any reconciliation grounded in "the old passive-obedience principle trumped up upon us, which was once within an ace of ruining us all." Most Britons, however, could not forget the hazards posed by James' tyrannical rule and like "the shipwracked mariner retains the impression of the shelve on which he once was in danger to split." One had only to recall the former king's broken pledges to Parliament, to prelates of the Church, and to Protestants who served him during Monmouth's revolt; Welwood bitterly referred to abolition of the Irish Act of Settlement as the king's masterpiece of betrayal.

Welwood's *Answer* rehashes most of his standard grievances against James II including the grave charge that James' perfidy encouraged French aggression against Britain. Of course, Welwood noted, whatever laughable promises of reward Louis XIV made to James were hollow, given the French monarch's penchant for deceiving even members of his own royal family. No wonder, posited Welwood, that other European states including Catholic ones abhorred the nation of France. Apart from the French threat, however, James Stuart himself accumulated quite a list of offenses including improper appropriation of Charles II's revenues, Catholicizing the army, packing Parliament with his supporters, and asserting a "paramount, all devouring power" which would destroy all laws. According to Welwood, the king's supposed concessions in the 1693 declaration, such as relinquishing chimney money, were bogus; so many of his subjects would flee England if he were restored to power that there would be no chimneys to tax! Ever the Williamite, Welwood maintained that whatever taxes Englishmen paid for national defense were small compared to the misery they would know if their enemies triumphed.

So that Welwood would not have the last word on the subject, an unsigned comeback to his broadside rolled from the Jacobite press. *A Reply to the Answer Doctor Welwood Has Made to King James' Declaration*, forty-seven pages in length, was printed in London in 1694.[42] In his preface, the essayist jeered at Welwood's contention that William of Orange had come to the rescue of millions of Protestants beset with "five or six thousand" papists. Instead, he asserted that the Dutch government did not care about religion or the English, but about using the power and resources of Britain for its own purposes. Panicked by false rumors, the English had deposed their "lawful home-born monarch" for a "little foreign prince" who never wished England well, and for their pains ended up giving the usurper prodigious sums of money and incurring excessive debts. The writer had harsh words for the States of Holland, "generally enemies to all mankind and particular to us," and accused the Dutch of prospering from the misfortunes of their neighbors by breaking treaties. *Reply to the Answer* posited the view that William's incessant wars diminished England at home and exposed its colonies to ruin abroad; likewise, the vibrant trade of London was being transfused into the "veins and sink of Amsterdam." Continental war, estimated by the author at "six or seven and twenty millions," sabotaged the maxim that an economy dependent on trade should pursue balance among its neighboring states. To restore peace, trade, and plenty, contended the anonymous polemicist, restore James to the throne.

Whoever penned *Reply to the Answer* knew Jacobites in high places on both sides of the English Channel. He denied Welwood's assertion that James' declaration had been a volte-face by divulging 1692 correspondence from the Earl of Melfort to himself which outlined the intent of James' conciliatory policy once the Stuart king was restored to the throne. Of course, he pointed out, pamphleteers like Welwood, "a mannerly pupil of Titus Oates," made that event less likely. Besides, if James' declaration had been a fraud, why had industrious hawkers carried Welwood's *Answer* all through London and the country? The author also knew how best to wound the doctor's pride. Welwood's writing is dismissed as "weak and quibbling sophistry...[filled with] Billingsgate flights," his "intimate friends [as] lewd whiggs," and his knowledge of English law as flawed because Welwood was a Scot. Denying Welwood's emphasis on a king's contractual obligation to rule justly, the Jacobite writer invoked Thomas Hobbes' version of the social contract: the king is not a party to any original contract, but simply a beneficiary.

The penman of *Reply to the Answer* saved his nastiest slur for Welwood's own authorial troubles at the hands of arbitrary power.

> Especially of all their Scriblers, it little becomes Doctor Welwood to exaggerate matters against King James, since his discourse about a dictatorial power brought him for his arbitrary doctrines under the censure of the House of Commons.

However, he noted, Welwood's penalty was nothing like that afforded poor William Anderton. *Reply to an Answer* had made its points well.

James Welwood never returned to Grub Street and his *Mercurius Reformatus*, even after the lifting of censorious restrictions and amidst the flowering of the political press. Perhaps some of the fire went out of his passion for politics when Queen Mary died suddenly of smallpox in December 1694. That same year brought him the disagreeable task of petitioning for monies he felt were due him from his service on medical commissions. Another unrepentant Williamite took over the title of the paper and published it as "The Weekly Observator," maintaining its format of current events and history. Welwood denied any involvement with that project. He tried to understand the motives of those onetime partisans who now opposed the king's policies and prerogatives. In a 1701 letter to a lifelong friend in Newcastle, Welwood wrote: "It may be they are earnest to lower the value of a crown merely because it fits upon one's head they do not love."[43]

CHAPTER FIVE

Welwood's Prolific Pen

Stung by Parliamentary critics of his journalism and surprised by ministerial censorship of his anti-Jacobite tracts, Dr. James Welwood turned to the writing of less political books. During William III's reign the book trade in England flourished. A dictionary of printers and booksellers in Augustan Britain lists over a thousand publishers and booksellers active in London alone; there were also bookshops in most provincial towns. Titles fairly flew off the presses, and during one three month period in 1690, the Stationers Company tallied 117 new works produced by fifty-three different publishers.[1] Welwood was among many erudite men who took advantage of the opportunities afforded by this vibrant market. His most successful project was a history suggested by Queen Mary. Though Welwood was by then winning plaudits for his industrious medical administration, she was clearly more interested in his writing talents than in his medicine or management skills.

According to Welwood, a few years after the coronation of the joint monarchs, Mary read a disturbing account of the reign of Charles I which painted a villainous portrait of her grandfather. Welwood identified the popular pamphlet as "A Letter from General Ludlow to Sir Edward Seymour," printed in 1691. Edmund Ludlow, republican and regicide, had penned his memoirs while in exile, though they were yet unpublished; in them, he expressed an abhorrence of monarchy and impugned Charles I as the Antichrist. He lived in London after the Glorious Revolution, where his presence infuriated the Tories and ostensibly upset the queen.[2]

Perhaps hoping to curry favor with Mary in the face of Ludlow's affront, defenses of the executed king by a variety of men came forth quickly from Parliament, press, and pulpit. By royal mandate after the Stuart restoration, an addition to the *Book of Common Prayer* recognized Charles I as a martyr, commemorating the anniversary of Charles' beheading with a special liturgical service and a day of national fasting and atonement. Beyond the required annual ecclesiastical remembrance, however, the politically-charged legend of Charles the Royal Martyr enjoyed periodic resurgence. Royalists in the last decades of the seventeenth century earnestly declared him a "blessed saint," although the Church of England has no mechanism for official canonization. A wave of veneration for the deceased king swelled during the months of the Popish Plot and surged again in the 1690s.[3] Richard Hollingworth preached a notable sermon in 1693 at St. Botolph, Aldgate, published soon afterwards, which termed Charles' death murder; Edward Pelling and Anthony Walker also drafted separate accounts sympathetic to the king.

Everyone, it seems, had an opinion about the events that led up to the Civil War. The trouble for Whiggish writers like Welwood was that Charles I's situation paralleled that of James II; Tories argued effectively from historical example that reckless political dissent could inexorably lead to republicanism. High Churchmen often used the cult of Charles I in their January 30 sermons to expose inconsistencies in the Whig arguments, as John March had done in Newcastle. James Welwood had recorded his own assessment of the character of Charles I in the September 11, 1689 issue of *Mercurius Reformatus*. Welwood's distinctive interpretation buttressed both Whig and Williamite agendas. He had called the king a martyr who had done all that he could to aid Protestants in France, and had printed portions of two 1628 letters from Charles as proof to his readers of that effort.[4] By emphasizing the late king's French design, Welwood justified the present king's military campaigns against Louis XIV. Clearly, Welwood early on had enjoyed access to unusual archival materials for use in his newspaper against critics of William's policies.

Furthermore, he had unusual access to the royals themselves, especially the queen, whom Welwood saw in his capacity as her doctor. King William suffered from asthma, and the damp, smoggy air of London made breathing difficult for him at Whitehall; moreover, he disliked the city crowds, however fashionable they might be. In late 1689 the monarchs moved to Hampton Court and Queen Mary threw herself into rebuilding the palace with famed architect Christopher Wren. Wren constructed new pavilions, symmetrical gardens, and a Water Gallery by the Thames that Mary especially loved. Hanging in the gallery were formal portraits of eight "Hampton Court beauties," painted by Court Painter Godfrey Kneller for her pleasure. Dr. Welwood often visited the queen at Hampton Court and at Kensington House, bought by William and Mary and renovated by Wren for them as a nearby retreat from urban congestion; fires at Whitehall in 1691 and 1698 reinforced the king's distaste for the city. Welwood took particular delight in Kensington's botanical garden and his conversations with the queen. After discussing various new publications with Welwood, Mary asked him to write a short history of Charles I's reign for her private edification. She wished, Welwood said, to know the truth, having read "either panegyrics or satire."

Welwood adored the queen, having on more than one occasion compared her style of rule favorably to Elizabeth I. According to Welwood, the Virgin Queen had a much easier assignment in reigning than did Mary II, especially with the king abroad during wartime. In the July 25, 1690 issue of *Mercurius Reformatus*, Welwood enumerated Elizabeth's advantages: first, she was thirty years on the throne before England was threatened with invasion; second, there were few Catholics in England at the time of the Armada and half of them hated the Spanish; and third, the fleet Philip II sent against her was no match for the English navy. With all things considered, Queen Mary's task was much tougher. Welwood could not deny so dear a monarch any request, and pledged to pen the history for her exclusively. The queen in turn promised to show the manuscript to no one without the author's consent. Obviously, Welwood was still smarting over his treatment by Parliament.

Assured of the queen's reticence, Welwood took up the pen to write a narrative that would be both ethical and instructive, convinced that the study of history held moral and didactic value, particularly to statesmen. Bishop Burnet opined that Plutarch's *Lives* ought to be required reading for English aristocrats, but history was not yet part of a university curriculum. Princes actually read history, and tutors of princes, like the Earl of Clarendon to Charles II and Bishop Burnet to the young Duke of Gloucester, actually wrote them. Courtiers dedicated historical works to royalty, too. Many Augustan Age writers who dabbled in the genre praised history as the highest form of literature, but learned Englishmen often complained about the quality of their historical writing. Good historians needed to be sophisticated gentlemen; good history needed to meet the coupled criteria of diversion and instruction if it were to find an audience, regal or otherwise. Books of history were also written by clerics, journalists, and political propagandists, but not often by professional historians. History was not yet a specialized academic discipline in Welwood's time, and little historical research could be done before repositories and libraries were established.[5]

Therefore, Dr. Welwood's scholarly task was a difficult one. His work needs to be properly situated in the transformation of partisan propaganda into history. For Welwood, the muse required not only a clarification of the interplay of faction and self-interest, but an exegesis of ideals and conscious purposes, too. Historical meditation could then become a resource for action. By turning to the past, Welwood thought, one could find both explanations for and solutions to present problems. As requested by Queen Mary, Welwood's first goal was to write the life of Charles I, and because of its difficulty, biography commanded respect in the literary hierarchy. "The hardest thing," Welwood wrote in an edition of *Mercurius Reformatus*, "is to write history, especially the secret transactions and personal faults of great men." Even more exalted than biography was the general history or a "complete" history, as Welwood's contemporaries designated it, of a panoramic past unwitnessed by the writer. Legitimacy in general history required that evidence be accurately weighed and analyzed by an impartial author who was detached and balanced in his approach.

"Particular" history, that is, a history of one's own time, had less cachet because the writer was a participant and thereby biased in his reportage. However, Dr. Welwood had unusual access, through his friendship with the king and queen, to the secret papers of the hastily-departed James II, which had fallen into the hands of William's military staff. The good doctor not only perused these secret documents but obtained permission to copy and publish their contents.[6] Moreover, he relied on his considerable personal acquaintance with individuals connected to the earlier Stuart reign, with the Interregnum, and with the sequence of chronology up to 1688. However, memoir was seen by critics as inferior to authentic history. As a memoirist Welwood drew upon interviews and past conversations at the Court of the Prince of Orange, including one with Charles II's illegitimate son, the Duke of Monmouth. In sum, Welwood's book was researched narrative history, biography, and memoir, an unusual combination of genres that set it apart from the field.[7]

Dr. Welwood scrutinized whatever registers and letters he could find in the State Paper Office, the Tower of London archives, and at the Cotton library. He possessed some copies of original documents, but admitted that he had lost at least one important piece of evidence, a letter to the Earl of Rothes which figured prominently in his book. Unwittingly, the usually meticulous Welwood demonstrated the need for professional archivists and permanent repositories. Welwood read extensively in the chronicles and anecdotal histories, probably digesting more than just descriptions and chronology. He referred specifically in *Memoirs* to several seventeenth-century historians whose work influenced his: Friedrich Spanheim, Samuel Pufendorf, and Bulstrode Whitelocke. There are only two citations in the text: a Latin citation from Pufendorf's biography of the Elector of Brandenburg and a three-page excerpt from a translated life of the French commander Turenne by "Monsieur de Buisson," pseudonym of Gatien Courtilz de Sandras. Welwood admonished his readers not to expect "that I should have observed the rules of a regular history, much less any niceness of method or exactness in the narration."

Welwood certainly discussed historical questions with his friend, Bishop Burnet, who had written a *History of the Reformation in England* sometime before accompanying the Prince of Orange to England in 1688; it is counted the first historical narrative published in England which was based on extensive documentation. He is deemed a pioneer in recognizing the complexity of causation, not seriously considered again until the nineteenth century.[8] Burnet began to write the more problematic *History of His Own Time* in 1683, recasting it several times before its posthumous publication in 1724. With good Whig technique, Burnet's history upheld the right of resistance, parliamentary monarchy, and religious freedom. He did not chose to write about battles or foreign affairs, but "let his exaggerated sense of personal importance lead him away from public events to personal details of his own life."[9] Although the historical literature of Augustan England usually reflects Whig or Tory biases, those books limning the most recent phenomena included oral testimony and personal experience to a greater extent than documentary evidence and are even more politically flavored than most tomes.

Understandably, however, James Welwood claimed to admire Burnet's scholarship and referred to the bishop as "an historian for whom I have the highest veneration." In fact, Welwood quoted extensively from Burnet's *Memoirs of the Dukes of Hamilton* in his narration, and, as if to confirm his own historical analysis, Welwood followed his recounting an incident with the same story verbatim from Burnet. Welwood's work shows the influence of Bishop Burnet's style, especially in their mutual fondness for comparing England's greatness with Rome and certain Englishmen with their Roman counterparts. For his *Memoirs*, Welwood borrowed a story Burnet had imparted of walking in the Farnese Gardens in Rome and being startled by a sculpted likeness of the Emperor Tiberius which bore a striking resemblance to Charles II. Welwood discerned similarities between Tiberius and Charles in their style of governance, too. Contrasting pairs of imperial lives was one of the standard pedagogical ploys used during the Augustan Age. Roman emperors like Marcus Aurelius and Commodus provided clear archetypes of virtue and vice, as well as the consequences of their example. All of Welwood's writing exemplifies the impact that classical literature had on the judgment of Augustan Age writers.

Though Welwood's history came to encompass a longer range of chronology than he originally intended, starting with the defeat of the Spanish Armada and ending with the Glorious Revolution, the author was pleased with the narrative. He aimed for an unjaundiced account: "I hope I may venture to say that I have tread as softly as was possible over the Graves of the Dead and have not aggravated the Errors of the

Living." One commentator on Welwood's *Memoirs* tried to explain how the good doctor was able to achieve a modicum of historical objectivity. Henry Imbert-Terry investigated James Welwood's family background and tumultuous youth; he decided that Welwood's actual experience "modified and mellowed" all the old opinions, even obliterating those formed in the social and religious environment of Caroline Scotland.[10] Although Welwood aspired to neutrality, he evinced at all times profound admiration and allegiance to William III. In fact, he declared that the best thing Charles II ever did was to marry his niece to the Dutch prince "by which he made sufficient atonement for all the errors of his reign." A dedicatory epistle lays the history at William's feet "with the most profound submission and duty."

Welwood did not publish his history for nearly a decade, and said he only did so then because he feared an altered, surreptitious copy might find its way to a printer. By then the queen had died, felled by smallpox in 1694; she was only thirty-two. A bereft King William dispatched Welwood the manuscript, found in Mary's cabinet, upon which she had written her promise of confidentiality. Welwood noted in a preface to the published edition that if the queen were still alive, he would have added new sections,

> wherein some dark transactions of those times might possibly have been put into a truer light than hitherto they have been. And indeed it's a pity that, of all the nations in Europe, the history of ours alone should seem most covered with the clouds of darkness and partial-ity.[11]

At least Welwood could feel justified in his long support for the Glorious Revolution, for by the time his history reached its readers, the protracted war between England and France had ended in 1697 with the Treaty of Ryswick. He also surmised that his reading public had changed its commitment to the principles of the revolution, as the end of hostilities released a latent and conservative partiality among Englishmen for pacifism and provincialism. The polemicist in Welwood may have needed the Sun King functioning as freedom's assailant to give meaning to his own message. Perhaps an exhausted Louis XIV's ultimate recognition of William as King of England in 1697 contributed to Welwood's shift from fractious contemporary milestones to more contemplative history.

Memoirs of the Most Material Transactions in England for the Last Hundred Years, Preceding the Revolution in 1688 is James Welwood's most important book for several reasons. First, though colored by personal predilections and prejudice, Welwood's history supplied original information on important episodes unavailable in the narratives of other writers. Next, compared to other historical accounts, *Memoirs* demonstrates considerable impartiality, even sympathy towards the Stuart monarchs. Finally, despite that relative moderation, Welwood's book presaged the development of the Whig interpretation of history. No less a figure than Thomas Babington Macaulay relied extensively on his scholarship. Because of its unique place in British historiography, careful summary and appraisal of Welwood's book is necessary.

The first edition of Welwood's *Memoirs* was printed in 1700 by the eminent bookseller Tim Goodwin and was dedicated to King William. It appeared two years before Lord Clarendon's influential *History of the Rebellion and Civil Wars in England* and more than two decades before Burnet's *History of My Own Time*. Second and third editions of Welwood's work quickly followed in a few months, although the author had not anticipated such success. "I can hardly expect that [the memoirs] should please in an age like this, that is fond only of what is writ for or against a Party." On the frontispiece Welwood is identified as "physician-in-ordinary to His Majesty." Welwood took the trouble in the preface to eschew authorship of an anonymous pamphlet, *Cursory Remarks about the Last Session of Parliament*, which had circulated in London the previous summer. He reminded his readers that he had avoided political rhetoric since the *Mercurius* shutdown, and that if he had written anything, he would certainly have put his name on it! Anyway, he asserted, he had "but little leisure, and yet less inclination, to appear again in print."

In *Memoirs*, Welwood included a detailed table of contents which shows the chronological boundaries of his narrative and the author's emphasis on the character of English leaders. Within reigns Welwood roamed topically, often pursuing lines of thought without regard to the sequence of events; he rarely affixed dates to the anecdotes he described. He began his review with a reflective query about the cyclical political convulsions suffered by England despite the excellence of its laws. "Brittle fate" had caused intermittent struggles "between king and people for prerogative and liberty or between competitors for the crown itself." The pattern of chance emerges repeatedly throughout Welwood's history: fortuitous timing, counterfeit messages, plots exposed, opportunities missed.

Welwood commenced his historical study by evaluating the days of Elizabethan constitutional bliss, which he called the "high pitch...[when] people lived at their ease and were happy." Queen Elizabeth's value rested not with her beauty but with her intellect. Welwood savored her intelligence and erudition, noting her youthful mastery of multiple languages and her translation from Greek into Latin of two of Isocrates' orations. Welwood claimed to have seen those translations in the queen's own handwriting, and commented that her tutor had made only three corrections on the manuscript. Welwood congratulated Elizabeth on the industriousness she showed as a teenage pupil: "She was indefatigable in the study of learning especially philosophy, history, divinity, and rhetoric, not forgetting both vocal and instrumental music, as far as it might become one of her quality."

After her near-miraculous accession, Elizabeth developed "to perfection the art of pleasing her Parliament, and she and they never parted in discontent, but with the highest proofs of mutual confidence." Welwood did not choose to focus on any discontent that might have surfaced against "Gloriana's" administration during the whole of her forty-five year reign. Instead, he concentrated his analysis on her successes. Welwood credited Elizabeth's achievements to the wise appointment of skillful ministers, glossing over much mention of any personal anguish she experienced due to the Earls of Leicester and Essex. Welwood spotlighted Francis Walsingham as Elizabeth's most valuable and ubiquitous statesman, a man who saved the "Virgin Queen" from diurnal murderous conspiracies and her subjects from epochal invasion. Over several pages, Walsingham's character and role as Elizabethan foreign policy mastermind is explored with nary a mention of Lord Burghley, Elizabeth's lifelong chief minister. Welwood's own predilection for foreign affairs, and his own alienage, shaped the heart of his historical examination.

Welwood derogated "Gloriana" for only one action, her part in the death of her cousin, Mary, Queen of Scots. Although he charges Burghley with deceiving Elizabeth, tricking her into signing Mary's death warrant, Welwood reminded his readers that Elizabeth was "not altogether excusable." The unfortunate Queen Mary had come into England upon a promise of protection made to her long before, wrote Welwood, a promise Elizabeth had sealed with a ring. Welwood obviously sympathized with the plight of the Scottish queen, driven from her kingdom and desperate for sanctuary. Welwood remarked that he had read several moving letters to Elizabeth in Mary's handwriting in the Cotton library, but these missives evidently did not allay Elizabeth's fears or oblige her to guarantee Mary's life forever. Concluding his segment on the last Tudor monarch, Welwood lauded Elizabeth for upholding her own prerogatives without curtailing the liberties of her subjects.

Welwood tracked through the early Stuarts the joint themes of Protestantism and liberty, an intersection accepted by most Englishmen. Welwood theorized that James I was too fond of royal prerogatives, because he had been denied them as James VI in his native Scotland. Paradoxically, "though his mother had been dethroned to make room for him, and consequently he could have no right but the consent of the people while he lived; yet upon all occasions he was fond of being thought to have a divine right to the crown." Despite his claim of divine right to rule, James was a painfully undivine king, and his gaffes cost both kingdoms peace and security. The powerful states of England and Scotland were united under one king after James' 1603 coronation in Westminster, a circumstance that Welwood presumed should have created an even more potent integrated state, but the reputation of the two kingdoms actually dwindled from that of former years. Welwood affixed blame for this predicament on the king, not on his ministers. In particular, Welwood emphasized the misfortunes visited on James' subjects at home and his allies abroad. He called into question the king's religious consistency as well, noting that although James had been raised Calvinist, he became an ardent advocate for episcopacy. In a curious aside, while registering the king's homeliness, Welwood remarked upon the physical beauty of James' parents. He may have been hinting about the canard that James was really the posthumous child of Mary's Italian private secretary, slain by her jealous husband.

Welwood seemed especially taken with the lives of James' four offspring, and went into detail about each. Capturing much of Welwood's attention is the Princess Elizabeth, a woman both admirable and ill-starred, who married Frederick V, the Elector Palatine, and was forsaken by England. Welwood gleaned material for his dissection of King James' conduct in the business of the Palatinate from a biography of Frederick's mother, the Electress Louise Juliane, written by Friedrich Spanheim in 1645, hardly the most current text he could have consulted. Welwood told a familiar story. After Frederick was chosen King of Bohemia in 1618, he was beaten in battle at Prague by the forces of the Hapsburg emperor and obliged to abandon both titles. Although the English Parliament wanted to reinstate the Palatine family by warfare if necessary, King James opted for negotiations that undermined his son-in-law. Even worse than selling out the Palatinate, according to Welwood, James' feebleness of purpose cost the Protestants all of Bohemia, a loss of liberty for his co-religionists that Welwood could not abide. In his assessment of James' reign, Welwood scornfully dismissed the first Stuart king as more interested in "his standish, his bottle, and his hunting" than in wise statecraft. Welwood, the Presbyterian minister's son, remained silent on rumors of corruption and sexual decadence thought by his contemporaries to be endemic to the Jacobean court.[12] Instead, *Memoirs* staunchly defended James' controversial favorite adviser, George Villiers, Duke of Buckingham. Welwood called it "a vulgar mistake" to credit Buckingham's rise to the position of first minister merely to the king's caprice. Welwood reminded his readers that the court unanimously promoted Buckingham's interests and recommended him for the highest favors. Moreover, Welwood hinted that his enemies were jealous of his visible successes:

> No servant did his master more honor in the magnificence of his train and the splendid manner of his living,...the gracefulness of his person, and in the nobleness of his behavior and equipage, he outdid anything that ever was seen of that kind before.

In 1625 Charles I inherited the problems bequeathed to him by his father; he also acquired the dangerously incompetent Buckingham. Dr.

Welwood did recognize that Buckingham was out of his element on the field of battle, admitting that he was "more formed for a court than a camp." In 1628 at La Rochelle in western France, Buckingham lost the only military expedition he headed. Even then, asserted Welwood, he tried to repair that disgrace and might have done so, had he not been murdered.

In Welwood's *Memoirs*, the young king was saddled from the start with fratricidal religious grievances and economic discontent which intensified after the assassination of Buckingham. Welwood completely exonerated Charles I of any wrongdoing as divisions deepened, even excusing the king's "unwarrantable methods of raising money" and his alliance with Roman Catholics as the fruit of urgency necessity. Reflecting the views of many Scotsmen, Welwood sketched Charles I as a wise, decent, and solidly Protestant ruler. Unfortunately for the king, in 1637 the spark of rebellion that led to his undoing originated in Scotland. The Scots vehemently rejected the newly-composed Anglican liturgy, embracing instead exclusive Presbyterianism, which resulted in declarations of rebellion and war. Welwood insisted that the Scots were inviolately faithful to the crown, wanting only to enjoy their religion and liberties without interference. Charles raised money through loans and benefices to fight the Scots, but through the intercession of moderates on both sides of the border, a solemn pacification was signed in June 1638.

Welwood lamented that the treaty was short-lived and that the resumption of belligerence forced the king to summon Parliament to procure military appropriations, opening a Pandora's box of legislative demands. More bad advice from the king's inept ministers, coupled with the abilities of the Parliamentarians, produced grievous domestic conflict. The complaints presented at Westminster soon overshadowed the troubles with the Scots and cost the king the lives of two of his chief ministers, Archbishop Laud and Thomas Wentworth, Earl of Strafford. Welwood regarded Strafford as a statesman of the first rank, but one who succumbed to the temptations of the court's honors and places. Strafford's "zeal for the royal cause became most obnoxious to the Parliament." The House of Commons impeached him and tried him for treason. Welwood believed that Strafford was doomed when Charles tried to intercede on his behalf. As for the character of

Archbishop Laud, Dr. Welwood concluded that the "indiscreet zeal of a mitred head had got an ascendant over his Master's mind." Nonetheless, Welwood complained that the historical record about Laud's intentions is unreliable: "We have nothing writ of him but what's either panegyric or satire, rather than history." Welwood gathered that what incited the fury of many in Parliament against Laud was the archbishop's "pompous ceremonies [and] theatrical manner of consecrating a new church in London." Welwood argued that Laud must be acquitted of the charges that he inclined to popery, even if some Roman Catholics thought the archbishop was a crypto-papist and offered him a Cardinal's cap. Thus, though "he did everything that was possible to give satisfaction to Parliament," King Charles failed to appease Parliament. According to Welwood, he did, however, mollify the Scots.

Memoirs carefully itemized the rapidly deteriorating situation for the king in London. Welwood interwove the outspoken grievances concerning religion, foreign policy, and Parliamentary rights emanating from the House of Commons with the king's escalating anger at his antagonists' effrontery. Charles objected strenuously to the "roughly penned" Petition and Remonstrance; Welwood implicitly seemed to concur with the king's answer to it, but provided his readers with the opportunity to judge for themselves by including all relevant documents in the appendix. Welwood even dismissed Charles' rash arrival at the House of Commons to demand personally the impeachment of five Members as an unlucky step advised by the king's camarilla. For Welwood, though the king took the first steps toward civil war by raising personal troops, marching to the north, and obtaining ammunition from Holland for his use, Parliament was equally culpable. "Each party blamed the other for beginning this war; and it's not easy to determine which of them began it."

Welwood puzzled over why Charles reneged on a cease-fire tentatively agreed to at Uxbridge in 1645, until he discovered a hitherto unknown letter to the king from the Marquess of Montrose in Scotland. Montrose had been a commander in the first Scottish expedition into England, but gradually he "had repented his former error" and had decided to win Scotland for the king. Charles named him Governor of Scotland, and he returned the favor by winning "three considerable battles." According to Welwood, Montrose sent news to the king that he could count on his speedy delivery of the northern kingdom, and that within a few months he would march into England to Charles' assistance. Delivered to the king just a few hours before he was to have signed the peace warrant, Welwood adjudged the letter so full of assurance as to be irresistible. Hence, Charles refused to sign the treaty. The king's enemies could not have planned it better had they sabotaged the peace negotiations themselves, and that realization made Welwood suspicious. He examined the date the letter was written and noted the time of its royal receipt; he calculated that the letter probably could not have traveled in so few days over the mountainous roads patrolled by armies from the "furthermost north corner of Britain to Oxford" in February. Welwood deduced that if the letter was bona fide and did arrive at the critical moment of decision in the peace process, then Charles' destiny was sealed by the vagaries of timing. The letter, incidentally, is now accepted as authentic by all competent authorities.[13]

Welwood found aspects of Charles I's personality admirable; he was handsome, noble, a loving husband and a devoted father. He had fine taste in the liberal arts and acquired a notable collection of paintings, medals, and sculptures. Welwood examined several of the king's manifestos and declarations, gauging the writing style to be as "able as the most celebrated pens of the time." Despite these positive attributes, Welwood objected to the king's consent to abolition of episcopacy in Scotland, calling it out of character and at odds with his promises at Uxbridge.

An incident in the late 1620s provided Welwood with the opportunity to skewer those opposed to taking up arms in defense of one's creed, Jacobite sermonizers whose insistence on passive obedience infuriated Welwood. For over a decade he had berated men like the Reverend March who professed that religious rebellion was "inconsistent with the principles of the Church of England." Welwood believed that Charles I supported subjects defending their religion and liberties by force of arms, as evident in his military assistance to the Huguenot residents of La Rochelle. The English king sent Buckingham there to help the besieged Protestants resist a governmental crackdown orchestrated by Cardinal Richelieu, Louis XIII's chief minister. According to a communiqué thought by Welwood to be in the Duke's own hand,

Buckingham informed the Rochellers that "no private matter has obliged my Master to make war against the French king, but merely the defense of the Protestant church." Welwood admitted that he lingered over this episode "because it is easy to draw a parallel betwixt this case of King Charles' assisting subjects against their King in the defense of their religion and liberties, and that of another Prince's doing the same upon a late occasion." Buckingham, Welwood neglected to mention, lost the battle for La Rochelle and half his men as well.

But Charles I is the protagonist of *Memoirs*, and Welwood returned to the catalog of misadventures which bedeviled his regime and played on his immoderate desire for power. A forged letter to the Earl of Rothes, purporting to be from twelve leading English nobles, tricked the Scots into invading England in 1646. Rothes later met one of the signatories to the counterfeit invitation, and found to his chagrin that the letter had been a fake. By reciting this episode twice in his narrative, Welwood exculpated the Scots for their impetuous aggression against England and illustrated how Charles I was a victim of perfidious machinations. Dr. Welwood used the occasion as another example of when "Providence seems to play with human affairs and influences the fate of kingdoms." According to Welwood, kismet figured in everyone's calculations during those unsettled times. Even the king was unnerved by an occurrence that seemed to preordain his destruction. Welwood divulged that when Charles was at the library in Oxford during the Civil War, he probed his destiny by a popular fortune-telling test. The challenge involved opening Virgil's *Aeneid* at random to see what the passage augured about the future. The section Charles picked was Dido's ominous imprecation against Aeneas, and Welwood offered his readers John Dryden's translation of the pronouncement of doom, foretelling disaster and death for Charles. His execution in 1649 plunged the royal house of Stuart into total eclipse for twelve years.

Dr. Welwood concluded that King Charles I "deserved a better fate, and he suffered for the faults of others, rather than errors of his own." Oliver Cromwell, by contrast, "invaded and betrayed the liberties of his country and acted a more tyrannical and arbitrary part than all the kings of England together had done since the Norman Conquest." Welwood conceded that Cromwell was a great man, but his memory was forever sullied by kingly blood on his hands. Welwood struggled to categorize Cromwell, who was a gentleman by birth, "though nothing of a scholar," and always wore a coat of mail under his clothes. Dr. Welwood remained unconvinced about the sincerity of Cromwell's spiritual agenda, calling it a "mask of religion" behind which he could "wheedle, which he knew nicely how to do when his affairs required it." Cromwell may have effected great success with foreign governments, but Welwood felt that his performance was rooted in self-aggrandizement rather than patriotism. Cromwell was not satisfied with the title of Lord Protector, thought Welwood, but aimed to be king. Welwood found it ironic that Cromwell died peaceably in bed, surrounded by his friends and family. Maybe Providence was working its magic again, mused Welwood. For just

> as the Ides of March were equally fortunate and fatal to Julius Caesar, another famous invader of the liberties of his country, so was the third of September to Oliver Cromwell; for on that day he was born; on that day he fought the three great battles of Marston Morro, Worcester, and Dunbar; and on that day he died.

Memoirs profiled a generally successful Charles II, restored to the throne after an endless series of post-Cromwellian schemes reminded the nation of "its true and ancient basis." Welwood described the first years of his reign as a continual jubilee, but Englishmen so rejoiced over his return that they neglected to safeguard their liberties and to remain vigilant against their enemies. Parliament voted the king lavish sums, "more money towards the expense of his pleasures than all his predecessors of the Norman Race had obtained before towards the charges of their wars." The legislature might have continued its profligate appropriations if it were not for discovery in 1678 of the Popish plot, "among the darkest scenes of our English history" and the next tidbit of that history Dr. Welwood chose to address. He accepted the truth of a Popish plot in England; he noted that "there has always been [a plot] since the Reformation." Given the threat to liberty that the succession of a Catholic posed, Welwood countenanced the exclusion of the Duke of York as "the only way to prevent ruin." Not wanting to hazard his throne, Charles II himself was almost persuaded by his favorite mistress to abandon his brother and, as Welwood remembered that Henry VIII had tried to do, arrange an alternative head for the crown. At least uncovering the plot awakened most of the nation out of its deep nineteen-year lethargy, wrote Welwood. Even then, a "certain set of men began a second time to adopt into our religion a Mahometan principle under the names of passive obedience and non-resistance," yet another Welwood insult aimed at the Reverend March and his kind. Dr. Welwood did not explain why he thought passive obedience was a Muslim tenet.

Dr. Welwood depicted Charles II as a man with harsh features, "difficult to trace with a pencil," yet exhibiting a noble mien. Welwood did not condemn the king when he called him a "votary to love," but revealed that Charles was not very fussy about his mistresses. In a candid aside, Welwood recorded that the king "seldom possessed of their first favors, yet would sacrifice all to please them." Charles had not a jealous bone in his body, but was witty, fun-loving, and patient. Welwood observed the king's fondness for science and mechanics, especially for building and working ships. Dr. Welwood, hardly disinterested on the subject of medicine, scolded Charles II for encouraging too many quacks and charlatans to set up business in England. Nevertheless, Welwood recognized that the king consulted only licensed physicians when he himself was ill, implicitly absolving the king's brother of the rumored complicity in his death.[14]

Dr. Welwood's medical training afforded him express insight and professional interest in the circumstances surrounding the last illness of Charles II. Welwood weighed the information he had about the king's vitality and the circumstances of his death to determine if there might have been treachery, as some opponents of James II insinuated. Although Charles enjoyed robust health and took care to watch his diet and to exercise, he died before age sixty, something Welwood found unusual. Most of the doctors attending the king pronounced his death a natural one from apoplexy, but Welwood puzzled over the absence of any appropriate warning signs that Charles had been stricken. Rather than a headache, Welwood noted that the king complained of severe stomach and intestinal distress "before a fit took him." In the throes of "distemper," Charles was bled; he revived temporarily and then died. At the autopsy, no one observed the stomach and bowels, which Welwood found suspicious, but all present murmured about the offensive smell emanating from the king's body, hardly typical of "apoplectical distemper." Perhaps the king was a victim, as gossips suggested, of an assassination attempt which prevented him from naming the Duke of Monmouth as his successor instead of James. Even Dr. Thomas Short, a Caroline royal physician and Roman Catholic convert, told his friends that Charles "had foul play done him."

But James Welwood wanted to find the truth, and so he laid out the arguments against the monarch's murder. First, Welwood remarked on the exuberant nature of Charles' life and on his excessive drinking habits in later years. Next, Welwood counted at least two previous occasions when the king was racked with fits which resembled those from which he died. Charles even mentioned his afflictions to those who had not witnessed the episodes. During his fatal attack, he could not speak, a condition common in apoplexy. Finally, Dr. Welwood delineated a suppuration on the king's leg which was allowed to dry up against the wishes of the court doctors and turned into a painful tumor that had not healed when he died. Most importantly for Welwood, the king communicated no suspicion at any time during his sickness that he might have been poisoned and when his body was opened for autopsy, no indication of poison could be seen.

James Welwood devoted 147 pages of his *Memoirs* to the first ninety-seven of the hundred years surveyed. He then spent the next 104 pages dissecting the three years when James II ruled England. As king, James II proved to be a Catholic radical and French pawn, deserving of the loss of his subjects' love and allegiance. At the same time, Welwood characterized the monarch as a man to be pitied. James' reign began auspiciously, and his first speeches were worthy of a Trajan or an Antoninus, high praise indeed from Welwood. But according to Welwood, the king stumbled when he subverted the English constitution and its specific prohibition of Catholics in government offices since the Test Act of 1673. James' insistence on Catholic judges, counsellors, and placemen reminded his subjects of their legitimate fears of popery; Welwood reckoned that a Protestant kingdom ruled by a Roman Catholic king was unstable and self-contradictory.

Ironically, James II did not have the support from the papacy that he and those who opposed him might have assumed. Innocent XI feared an omnipotent France more than the occasional Protestant, Welwood recapitulated, and so treated James' ambassador to Rome rather coolly.

More fervid was the welcome for the ambassador from the Jesuits, who entertained Roger Palmer, Earl of Castlemain, in their seminary and lionized him and his master. Welwood suggested that the Jesuits may have devised the strategy to insinuate Catholicism into England on the pretext of *politique* toleration. Fortunately, the Church of England saw through the contrivance and demurred because pro-Catholic toleration violated the Test Act. Next, as Welwood related it, James tried to dispense with the law, as Charles II had asserted that kings had the right to do; the king carefully secured support from mercenary pens and from the courts. James II had judicial *carte blanche* to use the dispensing power and to waive penal laws at his discretion, opening the floodgates to Catholic preferment throughout England. According to Welwood, Jesuit schools, Romish bishops, Catholic judges and sheriffs, and a new court of Inquisition soon followed. Welwood objected most strenuously to the Commission for Ecclesiastical Affairs which suspended the Bishop of London and moved against the President and Fellows of Magdalen College in Oxford for their defiance. Fortified by their collective courage, other opponents of James' policies came forward, and although Welwood insisted that they were reluctant to intrude, the Prince and Princess of Orange watched anxiously to see if the situation might right itself.

That left Scotland "for the Romish Party to act their designs in," leaving that nation miserable with its liberty lost at the king's mere declaration. Dr. Welwood asserted that foreign states openly commiserated with the Scots, and even Catholics abroad believed it in their interest to have England "as an arbiter of Christendom, especially at a time when they saw they most needed it." Welwood charted the convergence of England's fortunes with those of continental states terrified by the power of France. Stepping forward to champion those common interests was William of Orange, whose ancestry and life Welwood recapitulated with words of praise for a leader who "did all...for the common safety of Europe." Welwood attributed such heroism generally to the House of Nassau, a dynasty that has "fought for liberty, the noblest cause and the greatest stake that mortals can contend for." Welwood abruptly ended his history at the moment of decision for Prince William, suggesting that a sequel for the years after the Glorious Revolution ought to be compiled by someone "of more leisure and capacity to write it."

Welwood knew there might be controversy attending publication of the work: "I can hardly expect that [the memoirs] should please in an age like this, that is fond only of what is writ for and against a party." Yet, he took an obviously partisan stand in his idealized portrait of William, who "did all for the common safety of Europe." The book enjoyed great popularity, going through six editions in Welwood's own lifetime. The style, content, and political bias of *Memoirs* suited it perfectly to the generation of Whigs who benefitted from the revolution. In the preface to the 1718 printing, published anew for the Hanoverian Whigs, Welwood complained about the poor production values of an earlier impression, replete with errata and inferior paper. He continued to evince surprise at the enthusiastic reception afforded his work. Owing, no doubt, to the deaths of James Stuart in France and King William in England within six months of one another, Welwood generally eschewed highly-charged political rhetoric after 1702 despite renewed hostilities with Louis XIV. By then, most Englishmen were tired of war, taxes, and the Dutch. Given the shrinking popularity of William's legacies and the rise of the Tories during the reign of Queen Anne, Welwood found it prudent to segue to a more pacifistic format for his energetic pen. Although Anne did not explicitly endorse traditional Tory ideology, the doctrines of divine hereditary right and non-resistance regained their old predominance. The new *History of the Great Rebellion and the Civil Wars in England* was published to Tory acclaim in 1702. Modeled on Thucydides, it had been written by the Earl of Clarendon, Charles II's chancellor and the maternal grandfather of Queens Mary and Anne. Anticipated as a High Tory manifesto, it was published posthumously just after Anne's accession and the establishment of a government which included by Clarendon's son, the Earl of Rochester. Disputes over the accuracy of the Welwood versus Clarendon interpretations further exacerbated party bickering. Among the cognoscenti, the battle of these books and affined partisan preferences seemed to eclipse daily life. Not since the Civil War had the ruling class been so acutely split over politics, and social contacts between Whigs and Tories became infrequent as each maintained their own clubs, coffee houses, and theaters.

Yet Welwood persevered with his writing. In 1705 he published *A Compleat History of Europe for the Year 1705*, an almanac that he expected to update annually but did not. Almanacs were enormously popular in the Augustan Age; more than half a million copies of different kinds of almanacs were sold every year in Great Britain as a whole, far in excess of any other kind of book including the Bible.[15] Despite its supposedly apolitical concept, Welwood's almanac had a definite Whiggish tang. In the preface Dr. Welwood remarked that "it does not require the greatest penetration in the world to distinguish which of the contending parties was in the right" during the past year. Welwood articulated his endorsement of the War of the Spanish Succession, a war planned by William III against France's re-demonized Sun King. As Welwood saw it, England, led by "the most renowned Duke of Marlborough," commanded "its serene allies" against France, a country bent on enslaving its neighbors under a universal monarchy. The doctor's words were strong, partisan, and still decidedly anti-French: "There will always be a degenerate race of men in the world, whom no hellebore can cure."[16]

Though purporting to be a history of Europe in 1705, Welwood's emphasis is almost exclusively British. Included in the eclectic yearbook is a list of peers, the names of members of the House of Commons by district, an itemizing of Scottish nobles and Irish lords, and the household officers of Queen Anne. Dr. Welwood reported who were the four physicians to the queen and that they received £400 annually plus 10 shillings per day in board wages.[17] The apothecary to the royal household was William Jones who was paid £500, while two apothecaries to the queen, Daniel Malthus and James Chase, got £300 per annum plus board wages of over £127. Anne's surgeon was Charles Bernard, paid £335 with board wages of £140; the household surgeon was Thomas Gardiner, who was compensated £280 for his services.[18] Additionally, in his useful compendium Welwood named the royal chaplains, the horseguards, the deans and professors of Oxford and Cambridge colleges, and the governors of the Bank of England.

Welwood found scholarly gloss even safer, though perhaps less profitable, than compiling a year-end annual. His contributions, however miscellaneous, to the literary world were produced consistently over time. In 1709 Welwood composed a preface to a posthumous printing of Sir Bulstrode Whitelocke's manuscript on early English history. The preface, written at Welwood's home in the York Buildings, was addressed to the editors, confirming for them the authenticity of the folio and touting Whitelocke as "perfectly well qualified for an historian." Whitelocke's history of England from Charles I through the Restoration was already published and widely read. Welwood celebrated that earlier opus as "a lasting monument to his fidelity and exactness, and when he relates any matter or transaction of his own knowledge, he may be entirely depended upon." The doctor remarked on Whitelocke's "short and nervous manner and florid declaratory style," as superior to lengthy, dry tomes; to a fancier of the classics like Welwood, Whitelocke was "an English Florus." Whitelocke's work on Saxon times was singled out by Welwood as particularly felicitous, since he had utilized prior histories written by monks but presented it in a clearer, more exact chronological order. Welwood modestly concluded that "if I may pretend to have any judgment of history, this is the best epitome of its kind."[19]

This edition included a short life of Whitelocke and a bibliography by William Penn, Governor of Pennsylvania. Welwood's association with Penn on this publication is fascinating given their previous mutual disdain. Penn was a Jacobite, out of favor during the reign of William and Mary, and no friend of Bishop Burnet. While Burnet was at The Hague, it was Penn, acting as James' agent, who tried to persuade William to endorse repeal of the Test Act. Burnet particularly objected when Penn tried to convert him to that position and left posterity with an unflattering portrait of the famous Quaker. No doubt Dr. Welwood accepted Burnet's assessment on the Test Act, but Penn was sincerely committed to religious toleration and political compassion. It is likely that their collaboration on the Whitelocke history had some specific meaning, given events of that year.

In December 1709 Henry Sacheverell, a preacher of High Church and Tory views, delivered two inflammatory sermons against the Glorious Revolution from the pulpit of the newly completed St. Paul's cathedral.[20] 40,000 copies of the harangue were printed and distributed throughout the city. The immediate reaction to his verbal fire and brimstone typified the malaise that had stricken the Church of England and the British political system. Discouraged that the accession of

Queen Anne had not brought an end to the menace of toleration, High Churchmen like Sacheverell thought that Whiggish accommodation of Dissenters threatened the very fabric of society.[21] Naturally, the Tory party encouraged these clerics to proclaim their outrage from any platform. With rumors rife in 1709 that the latitudinarian Whigs intended to grant greater liberties to Dissenters, attacks began to mount on "iniquitous moderates," who Sacheverell said were no better than Guy Fawkes.

For his incendiary words at St. Paul's, Sacheverell was impeached by the Whig government and suspended from preaching for three years. His defense for damning the Whigs rested on the arguments Welwood had heard too many times of passive obedience to the rightful king and the illegitimacy of the revolution that ousted James. The prosecution contended that the king derived his authority from Parliament and that its will overrode any divine right he might claim. Pro-Sacheverell riots involving thousands of protesters erupted throughout London in March 1710, spilling down the Strand past Welwood's house to Westminster. In the elections soon after, the Whigs were defeated, Sacheverell's sentence was suspended, and he obtained appointment to a country parish. The Tories increased their majority even more in 1713. Dr. Welwood recoiled from these developments; he was close friends with several key governmental ministers who lost their posts. His party and his temperate stand on religion had been repudiated by the mob. Out of self-protection, he immersed himself deeper in the activities of his professional organization and in his scholarly writing. In this regard, Welwood agreed with Daniel Defoe, who argued that "the gentleman by education" is far superior to the "gentleman by birth."

Welwood immediately brought his next publication to fruition. Like most Augustan Age men of honor, Dr. Welwood found inspiration in the classics of ancient Greece and Rome. Every cultivated human being began study with the two classical languages and a common stock of antique learning. Sustaining this commitment to antiquity was an almost universal belief in the practical value of the classics to the life and work of the governing classes. Throughout Dr. Welwood's writing life, his loyalty to the ideals of Greco-Roman civilization was clear. From the letters exchanged with Vicar March through *Mercurius*

Reformatus and *Memoirs*, Welwood demonstrated familiarity with untranslated historical works from Herodotus to Procopius, although most of the major authors were available in English by 1700.[22] Dr. Welwood believed in the efficacy of even the minor classics for all to read; therefore, it was fitting for him to translate a lesser-known work into English. In 1710 he translated Xenophon's *The Banquet* (or *Symposium*) from the ancient Greek and prefaced it with a 115-page essay dedicated to Lady Jean Douglas, a daughter of James Douglas, 2nd Duke of Queensberry and Duke of Dover, and Lady Mary Boyle. The duke, an avowed Episcopalian, had been an ardent Whig and was the first Scotsman to declare for William of Orange. The duchess had died in 1709, and Welwood showed his romantic side when he wrote to Lady Jean:

> I shall not think a few hours I have stole from the business of my profession have been ill employed in making you a present of this kind. You had a mother who possessed all [the virtues of Socrates] as far as was consistent with the delicacy of her sex and temper—-for if I believed in the transmigration of souls, I should have thought here had once been the soul of Socrates."[23]

The essay contained information about the doctrine and death of the great teacher. Welwood acknowledged his love for Socrates' goal of dispassionate justice, and argued that Socrates must have been a monotheist in view of "his devotion to the true and one God of whom the Athenians had no notion." He asserted that Socrates has been unfairly maligned as a sodomite because ignoble critics of the philosopher have "narrow souls incapable of wonderful friendship."[24] Welwood finished his preface with an exhortation to "imitate this great pattern of natural religion, universal charity [and] good nature," hoping that "whatever my performance in this translation...all notions of virtue are not yet extinct among us."[25]

Given the admiration for Socrates evident in that introduction, Welwood wanted to make Xenophon's view of the great teacher more widely known in England. Xenophon had been a disciple of Socrates before leaving Athens to fight as one of the Ten Thousand in the service of Cyrus the Younger of Persia. Upon his return to Greece he became enamored of Spartan discipline and in 394 B.C. actually fought against the Athenians at Coronea. When Athens banished him, Xenophon retired to a Spartan estate where he wrote extensively about his wartime experiences (*Anabasis*) and about Socrates. Unlike Plato's philosophical portrait of the great teacher, Xenophon sketched the practical and prudent aspects of Socrates' character. According to *The Banquet*, Socrates was chiefly interested in helping his students become good. Based on Welwood's own conviction that personal liberty is essential to truth-finding and to leading the good life, he thought Socrates was timelessly relevant to the English. Perhaps Welwood even had the Tories in mind when he described the contempt Socrates felt for the privileged elite: "an enemy to covetousness and a resolute condemner of riches."

While studying Xenophon, Welwood was certainly reminiscing about the late William III, whose exploits recalled Xenophon's axiom that a prince ought to be the soul of his army. In an issue of *Mercurius Reformatus* published shortly after the Battle of the Boyne, Welwood had written that Xenophon, "that learned soldier," depicted "something of an emanation that flows from the soul of a hero [and] communicates itself to those about them."[26] Welwood found inspiration in antiquity which helped him assay contemporary events, and insights from his own era which gave renascent meaning to the wisdom of the ancients. Moreover, despite Xenophon's penchant for Sparta, *The Banquet* provided additional understanding of Socratic thought and a complementary perspective to that of Plato. Welwood was justifiably pleased with his service to a growing reading public untrained in Greek but enthused about classical works as a wellspring of moral virtue and courage. He had the book printed and distributed by two publishers in disparate London neighborhoods: John Barnes at the Crown in Pall Mall and Andrew Bell at the Cross-keys and Bible in Cornhill.

Welwood's next project had meaning for him on several levels. In 1718 he authored a thirty-eight page preface to an English-verse posthumous translation of Lucan by Nicholas Rowe. An ardent Whig and, as a protege of Chief-Justice Treby, holder of several governmental posts, Rowe acted as under-secretary of state for Scotland from 1708-1711 after praising the union of the two kingdoms. With the accession of George I, Rowe was named poet laureate at the age of forty. Besides verse, he had written successful plays and edited an important compilation of Shakespeare's works which divided the plays into acts and scenes. Welwood knew Rowe personally, portraying him as graceful and well-made, his face regular and of a manly beauty. Rowe was just the sort of literati whom Welwood admired, and his politics conveniently dovetailed with the doctor's as well.

Besides his fondness for Nicholas Rowe, Welwood would have been drawn naturally to Lucan and *Pharsalia*, as he was to many of the classics of Rome. *Mercurius Reformatus* was sprinkled with quotations from Plutarch, Cicero, and Tacitus. Although Welwood modestly posited that such work was "out of my sphere," he sketched a biographical account of Lucan and skillfully discussed the literary and historical value of that epic Latin poem.[27] Welwood held that Lucan ran afoul of the tyrannical Nero when he competed with and defeated the emperor in a rhetoric contest, and not because Lucan or his uncle Seneca, Nero's tutor, were guilty of crimes or involved in conspiracies. Lucan was much admired in the Augustan Age in England for the vigorous beauty and grandeur of *Pharsalia*, a recasting of the civil war between Julius Caesar and Pompey; that Lucan was a young martyr to the tyrannical Nero only burnished his reputation among England's Whigs.

Welwood called *Pharsalia* an imperfect work, and chastised Lucan for treating Caesar harshly, although even here Welwood thought the despotic Nero exerted malevolent influence. Whatever geographic and astronomical lapses *Pharsalia* contains Welwood excused as poetic license, and Lucan's problematical, obscure style he attributed to the poet's youth and immaturity. Nevertheless, *Pharsalia* remained for Welwood an important piece of the historical and literary record, and he praised Rowe for producing the translation.

In spite of his wide interests and insatiable need to comment, Dr. Welwood's bibliography lacks two themes: books about health, medicine, or science, and observations on Scotland. Although he himself was not an active scientist, several men in Welwood's circle of friends and acquaintances published medical and scientific tomes. Dr. Welwood only revealed his professional expertise in scattered passages in *Memoirs* and in a preface to a pamphlet which contributed modestly to a discussion on seventeenth-century quackery. Identifying himself as a Fellow of the Royal College of Physicians, Welwood wrote an epistolary introduction to the tract concerning the "cure" of a girl named Mary Maillard who had a deformed hip. Written in 1693 and published the following year by Welwood's regular political printer, Richard Baldwin, the booklet included a letter from Welwood to the "Lady Mayoress" Ashurst, wife of London's Lord Mayor, Sir William Ashurst. Welwood honored her not only because of her husband's office but also because Ashurst was a Presbyterian who defended the rights of nonconformists and dissenters in the City, a stance Welwood applauded. The letter recounts the miraculous straightening of the youngster's leg after she read the Bible. Keeping a professional distance from the inexplicable part of the case, Welwood noted that the testimony of all concerned was clear and consistent. Mary Maillard had been lame for thirteen years, and then suddenly she was not. Welwood speculated that the hip had been dislocated outward, noting that Mary still limped a bit, and that the leg in question was visibly shorter than the other.[28] Dr. Welwood wrote nothing else of a medical nature in his long publishing career.

Likewise, notably absent from Welwood's published avowals after the 1690s is mention of his native Scotland. There are a few paragraphs in *Memoirs* that deal with Caroline Scotland, but no references at all to anything there after 1688. Welwood was on record earlier in *Mercurius Reformatus* supporting Union with England, but in the interval between his newspaper endorsement of William's plan to unite the kingdoms and the actual treaty negotiations which led to Union, many disturbing occurrences had transpired. Scottish Episcopalians continued to oppose King William on dynastic grounds, and many Presbyterians thought him ambivalent in his attitude towards their interests. The massacre at Glencoe had defamed his reputation in the Highlands, and legitimate disenchantment with the Dutch prince and his London-based advisers stretched to the commercially-minded Lowlands. Particularly distressing was the effect on Scottish overseas trade of the English Navigation Act and the virtual monopolies established by the English East India and Africa Companies. When Scottish merchants found their enterprises blocked by privileged English competitors, they created a lobby supported by Scots living in England like Welwood and in 1693 succeeded in obtaining royal protection for Scottish companies pursuing a variety of interests. William Paterson, a Dumfriesshire native and founder of the Bank of

England, argued that Scotland must do more. He personally coaxed the Parliament in Edinburgh to establish the Company of Scotland Trading to Africa and the Indies in June 1695. Designed to redress the balance and give Scottish merchants a better prospect, the Company aimed to gain control of the narrow isthmus of Darien, the link between North and South America. Scotland would finally have its own colony, a strategic one located midway to India. Half of the subscriptions to the Company's £600,000 capital base were to be raised in Scotland, and the rest from England and elsewhere.

Paterson's influence extended to London where £300,000 was quickly raised from individuals and syndicates, but the bloom of this initial excitement faded when the East India Company swayed King William to make his opposition to the scheme public. English investors withdrew, other European speculators refrained under pressure from William, and ultimately most of the money came from Scots. Consequently, the nation's cash resources depended on Darien's success. Not surprisingly, in view of his monarch's adversarial stance, Dr. James Welwood did not invest in the Darien Company, but he knew many of its Scottish financiers. Included in the list of subscribers were Sir Thomas Burnet, Welwood's longtime Edinburgh friend; Dr. Thomas Dalrymple, a royal physician; the towns of St. Andrews and Dumfries; James Douglas, Duke of Queensberry, and father of *The Banquet* dedicatee, Lady Jean; the incorporated surgeons of Edinburgh; Sir Robert Sibbald, a founder of the Royal College of Physicians in Edinburgh; and Robert Welwood, Dr. Welwood's wealthy merchant cousin.[29]

In July 1698, three ships laden with wigs, Bibles, and 1200 emigrants sailed for the new colony, to be called New Caledonia. Unfortunately, the malarial marshes already belonged to Spain with whom William was seeking to ally, and the colonists' appeals for help to the English settlement at Jamaica went unanswered. Two subsequent Scottish expeditions to New Caledonia met a similar outcome, ravaged by disease, starvation, and Spaniards. The Darien scheme had cost two thousand Scottish lives and the £300,000. As far as most Scots were concerned, responsibility for the debacle lay with William of Orange and the English. By the time that Queen Anne ascended the throne in 1702, Scottish enmity for England had reached new heights.

Given that background, and the indifference of most Englishmen to the vagaries of Scottish politics, the probability for fusion of the two kingdoms seemed slight. Nonetheless, some Scots believed that their country's only hope of economic survival lay in making a deal with their southern neighbors, a deal which would give them some trading privileges. They knew that Anne, despite prodigious efforts, had no direct heir, enabling them to use the threat of a second Stuart restoration to their advantage. The English Act of Settlement in 1701 traced the line of succession to a German cousin, the Electress Sophie of Hanover, granddaughter of James I through the female line. However, the act did not apply to Scotland. As long as the northern kingdom remained a separate country with the possibility of a separate king, the Catholic Stuarts might endanger what Bishop Burnet called "the backdoor" to England. The Edinburgh Parliament tried to use the English fear of the Catholic Stuarts to obtain leverage for equal trading rights and liberty of religion. England responded with the Alien Act of 1705, which declared that Scotsmen were to be treated like aliens unless Scotland accepted the Hanoverian succession. Subsequent incidents heightened tensions, and the two kingdoms seemed close to war. Instead, within a few months, an agreement between England and Scotland was achieved by skillful negotiation, creating the new state of "Great Britain."

Even contemporaries seemed nonplused at the feat. Both sides, however, had something significant to gain from consolidation. With Union, England removed the alarming and unacceptable possibility of a Scotland with an independent foreign policy allying with France. The Scots had pro-Union motivation, too. The terms of the Alien Act made Scotsmen painfully aware of their continued economic vulnerability and commercial weakness. The Court of Exchequer had laid down the English law of nationality affecting alien immigrants in *Calvin's Case* in 1608. Scots born after James I's accession and the union of crowns were considered subjects in England, though they were not always treated as such. Lawyers and jurists found substantial latitude for dissension about the essence and application of the principle of nationality based on place of birth. Hence, since the legal status of Scots long-resident in England was uncertain, the Alien Act alarmed the expatriate community and compelled that group to add its modicum of influence in favor of Union to that being exerted by the English Parliament.[30] Additionally, though the threat of the Stuarts returning to Scotland appeared to give nationalists there a bargaining tool, in reality the accession of a Catholic monarch to the throne of Scotland would bring civil war and certain English invasion. A merger of convenience, therefore, made sense to both countries.

Queen Anne's Commissioner, the young Duke of Argyll, traveled to Edinburgh and convinced the Scottish Parliament to authorize negotiations for a Treaty of Union. Thirty-one delegates from Scotland met in London with an equal number of English representatives, but the Scots' desires for a federal arrangement that would permit the retention of a Scottish Parliament were thwarted when the English refused the concept.[31] Instead, a compromise was reached by which the Scots would send sixteen peers and forty-five members to the English Parliament, far short of the representation their population warranted, but appropriate for their lowly economic status as far as England was concerned. The treaty recognized Scottish law as distinct from that of England and Wales, but no provision was made for the use of Scots Gaelic during legal proceedings.[32] Partly in compensation for the Darien shareholders, Scotland was awarded a monetary bonus of nearly £400,000, known as the Equivalent, for its acceptance of the Hanoverian succession.

What would James Welwood have said in 1707 and after about Union? He was no longer writing political analysis, and with the death of King William in 1702 the inspiration for his commentary was gone from the scene. Nevertheless, we can draw some conclusions by examining his earlier writings and the work of his colleagues at the time of Union. Daniel Defoe, whose Whig pamphlets in the 1690s were sometimes attributed to James Welwood, and vice versa, was hired by Anne's government to write anonymously for the pro-Union campaign. He called the concordance a marriage of policy, not of affection, for though Queen Anne's ministers effected legal unity, religious unity was impossible. That was fine with James Welwood. Scotland had clung to its national Kirk through all challenges, and at least could preserve that institution under the Union of 1707.[33] A Bill of Security affirmed that the Church of Scotland was inviolate. Writing in *Mercurius Reformatus*, Welwood had emphasized the importance of

Presbyterianism to the Scots, because of all churches it "seems to be most fitted to the genius and education of that people." At the same time, Welwood insisted that a moderate and well-stated Presbyterian government in the Scottish Kirk should never threaten a moderate Church of England. The alternative to religious accommodation throughout the new Great Britain would have been unsuitable and irrational to Welwood. When they have had episcopacy established by law, he wrote,

> [the] presbyterians have been made to groan under the sorest oppression, and when presbytery has again succeeded in place of episcopacy, it has also struck upon the same rock that broke the former....No people are so poor and so unhappy as in those places where persecution is set on, upon the account of difference in religion.[34]

The year 1707 surely marked a sea-change for Scotland, but it was part of a European-wide trend in the eighteenth century toward governmental unification based on natural frontiers and geographic proximity. In the early phases of Union, most Scots perceived only its marginal relevance to their lives, while the wealthy assuaged their feelings of national loss with hopes for greater opportunity.

Scottish Presbyterians after 1707 tried to construct a new understanding of "Scotland," borrowing language and concepts from various sources, including traditional Calvinist theology, civic humanism, and their perception of natural law. They hoped to demonstrate that Scotland could be virtuous, prosperous, strong and free as a British province.[35]

However, not everyone north of the border was sanguine about the Union; some reaction in Scotland was swift and hostile. Die-hard Jacobites rejected the treaty and soldiers had to be called in to keep the peace in Edinburgh and Glasgow. Military intimidation by English cavalry succeeded in dissipating Scottish opposition, while the Edinburgh Parliament voted itself out of existence. Scotland was simply no longer sovereign. After 1707 the Jacobite cause became increasingly enmeshed with anti-Unionism; this factor alone would have persuaded Welwood that he was correct to endorse fusing the two kingdoms. Of course, since Union had been initially suggested by William III and continuously supported by the Whigs, Welwood favored it. Negotiations for consolidation received impetus with the War of the Spanish Succession, a war planned by William, and the threat war posed to the territorial integrity and religious liberty of Holland and Britain. James Welwood would have certainly promoted the Act of Union because it removed the northern kingdom and former "auld" ally of the French as a possible base for Catholic incursions while unifying the whole island against the rest of Europe. Louis XIV's backing of a Jacobite invasion in 1708 proved the wisdom of amalgamation. Welwood doubtless applauded the final lines of Nicholas Rowe's play *Royal Convert*, which congratulated Queen Anne for presiding over consummation of the Act of Union. After 1707 the question of the legal isolation of the Scots was moot (with rebellious reminders to the contrary notwithstanding), and the borders of Britain were henceforth marked out by the sea.

Although some Scotsmen lost the center of their political lives when that nation blended with England, Dr. Welwood had already accustomed himself to taking part in the common affairs of Great Britain. In many ways Welwood's incorporation into English life predates the Act of Union and presages the new "invented" British nation whose advent has been described by historian Linda Colley. What factors permitted Welwood to shuck his Scottishness without undue difficulty? Certainly the centrality of Protestantism to religious life drew England and Scotland together from the years of the Reformation; they shared the same King James version of the Bible. Moreover, Welwood clearly associated Protestantism, in whatever guise, as necessary to liberty. Opposition to Roman Catholicism, represented by the institution of the papacy and by the nation of France, was a constant in his life; it impelled his politics and his ensuing changes of address from Scotland to France to England. He had seen firsthand the dangers to liberty posed by the Catholic Louis XIV, had nurtured his anti-Catholic, anti-French convictions at The Hague, and had counted the growing numbers of Huguenot refugees fleeing to Britain after religious toleration was revoked in their home country. For Welwood with his interest in European news, plenty of other examples abounded in Spain, in some German states, and in Austria, which proved the enduring threat of Catholic persecution to Protestants.

But was Providence the only cause of Britain's salvation? In the seventeenth century new ideas about the origins of government circulated among Whigs, proffering a contractual scenario for the beginning of the state. The direct influence of writers like John Locke on the revolutionary settlement may have been inconsequential, but contractualist pamphlets did try to subvert any claims about divine right made on the Stuarts' behalf. For Welwood, however, philosophy mattered less than practical politics.[36] James II had governed badly and dictatorially, had threatened Protestantism and liberty, and had imperiled national sovereignty and security. Welwood admired kingship, but he could not respect James. William of Orange, on the other hand, saved Protestantism and its corollary, personal freedom. The preference for one monarch over another had been a simple one, and, as it turned out for Welwood, brilliantly correct. Choice and Providence complemented one another; action on behalf of liberty "was attended with...irresistible strokes of the Divine Watchfulness and Care...at every turning of the tide, every change of the wind, and every storm at sea."[37] After 1688 England was thoroughly Protestant, even more Protestant than Scotland with its pockets of Highland and Lowland Catholics; the English Parliament insisted on liberties for its citizens, liberties grounded in independence of conscience. Maybe more importantly, England offered physicians greater promise of professional and financial success. No wonder that England had drawn Welwood like a magnet and that in *Memoirs* he was able to refer to *our* English history and *our* Anglican religion.

Comfortable as a Briton, but still proud of his Scottish origins, James Welwood had made a name for himself in London as a journalist, memoirist, translator, and essayist. In fact, Welwood's writings had made him far better known than his work as a doctor. Opened to him was a network of other intellectuals and antiquaries, giving him an unusual breadth of friends and acquaintances in early eighteenth-century London. He had risen from humble beginnings, used his intelligence to secure a professional livelihood, and could now enjoy the rewards of his efforts. Wealth alone did not smooth the way for Welwood's upward mobility, but the combination of his education, his appreciation of culture, and his accumulation of status symbols all assisted in his entree to the circles frequented by the gentry. Nevertheless, his position as a court physician was integral to his political identity, and his association with other doctors added cachet to his reputation. Once again, by tracing Welwood's life we can glimpse yet another facet of the Augustan Era.

The Medical Scene

*J*ust as James Welwood the writer played an important role in the complex, fractured world of Augustan Age politics, so did Dr. James Welwood find himself embroiled in the equally complex, fractured world of Augustan Age medicine. Repercussions from the "scientific revolution" produced conflict between the old-fashioned gentlemen physicians of the Oxbridge establishment trained in the principles of Galen and the ambitious, utilitarian products of the latest experimental continental curricula. Die-hard Galenists railed against change, while doctors prepared in new ways insisted upon it. There were many Englishmen who believed that the dignified character of a physician depended on his familiarity with literature, and on that score the courses of study at Leiden, Utrecht, and even Padua were found wanting. Besides differences over theory, jurisdictional fault lines in health care separated university-trained physicians from the more practically-trained surgeons and apothecaries, who were in turn superior to the myriad unlicensed, unregulated men and women that most people turned to when sick. The complications of this many-runged ladder of medical rank debilitated the efforts of traditional physicians to maintain supremacy in the battle for both respect and customers. Ironically, James Welwood, a fellow and officer of the elite Royal College of Physicians of London, inadvertently contributed to the successes of its challengers.

There were discrete, specialized categories of health care even in the seventeenth century. Three organized and regulated groups of men provided services to the sick. Physicians, university-educated and expensive, theorized about illness and cures. However, the actual administration of drugs, the setting of bones, and the performance of operations was handled by a surgeon. Arising from the Barber-Surgeons guild, the surgeons of Welwood's time had advanced enough in status to challenge the authority of physicians and deserved to be regarded as more than tradesmen. Anatomical lessons for physicians during Welwood's day were given at the Surgeon's Hall. Surgeons had to apprentice for years before receiving admittance to the company and often had bedside training superior to philosophers of medicine. Many physicians were still acquiring degrees based almost exclusively on book-learning, without having participated in any anatomical dissections. Physicians were vulnerable to criticism on another level, too. While many doctors had fled London during the plague epidemic of 1665, surgeons had remained to tend to the dying. Moreover, military surgeons had acquired invaluable experience during wartime, and their return to civilian society was an important stimulus to the medical profession. The increase in the number of London hospitals during the Augustan Age was also crucial to the development of surgical skills and training. Though still paid less than a physician, a surgeon could expect to see that wage gap shrink as his prowess grew. During the Augustan Age, many surgeons publicly impugned the preeminence of physicians and ridiculed their therapies. Daniel Turner, a surgeon to Queen Anne, derided the use of quicksilver by Welwood's friend and colleague, Dr. Hans Sloane.[1] During an autopsy Turner reported that he found a half-pound of mercury in the intestines of a man treated by Sloane.

The apothecaries constituted the third leg of the regulated medical tripod in seventeenth-century England. The remedies prescribed by physicians were made by apothecaries, themselves newly risen in prestige from grocers of old. Like the surgeons, the apothecaries boasted of more personal care for patients and argued their right to prescribe since no one knew medicaments better than they. Many of them implied in circulars that they were better suited to diagnose illness than physicians trained in anachronistic approaches, and ever since Nicholas Culpeper had translated the *Pharmacopoeia Londinensis* into English, knowledge of a doctor's Latin was unnecessary in making medicines. The apothecaries doubtlessly wanted some of the privileges of physicians when they petitioned the House of Commons to be relieved, as members of the College already were, of all parish duties; the Company of Apothecaries pressed for exemption from service in ward offices and on juries. The College of Physicians was thus rightfully concerned about loss of its members' prerogative and income to both surgeons and apothecaries.[2]

Additionally, the Fellows were worried about the number of "irregular" practitioners in London, unlicensed charlatans who violated the canon of medical ethics and worked cheaply among the poor. Traditionally-trained doctors viewed the proliferation of quacksalvers as the regrettable and inevitable product of speculative medicine. If people believed that anyone could recognize the symptoms of a particular malady, and that a specific panacea would always alleviate it, then anyone could dispense those cures on any street corner. As Culpeper himself commented, "all the nation are already physicians," and he envisioned an informed lay public enlightened enough to practice mainly preventive medicine and to cure uncomplicated maladies. Employing that premise, face-to-face meetings between physicians and patients became unnecessary; advertisements in newspapers and handbills enabled anyone to attract customers to alternative medicine and to make some easy money. Dr. Welwood's own newspaper contained many such ads, such as one for "Extract of Licoras," which was promised as a cure for colds, coughs, and consumption. The July 24, 1690 issue touted liquid snuff for headaches and epilepsy or incomparable pain water for only *6d* a bottle. Another commercial in *Mercurius* offered a "cure for lunaticks," an oil to be massaged into the head only; it alleviated melancholy as well as madness. In January 1688 the College sent a letter to all bishops about mountebanks and their unlawful practice, but the Fellows denied that they sought a monopoly on healing. Nevertheless, the College beadle was instructed to record the names of quacks and to bring the culprits before the College's Board of Censors for inspection. The Fellows reiterated that the College was simply exercising the trust placed in it by the monarchy, though they did not always concur with their sovereign's judgment. In 1693 the Fellows refused to grant a license to Cornelius Tilborg, previously a royal physician to Charles II, prosecuted him for practicing without their approval, and fined him £50. Despite an earlier association with the discredited Stuarts and the College's disdain, William III awarded Tilborg credentials to sell his antidote against poison, orvietan, from a stage in any city or town. Perhaps Dr. Welwood influenced the king's approbation, having seen Tilborg's medicine show himself in Scotland.[3]

This, then, was the schism in Augustan Age medicine, rent by theoretical and jurisdictional combat. The professional activities of Dr. James Welwood tended to blur the distinctions so keenly recognized by his contemporaries. During the frenetic 1690s, while maintaining his own practice and serving the state on several medical commissions, Welwood participated in the fellowship of the College and simultaneously tended to the needs of the joint sovereigns. Welwood often styled himself publicly as doctor to William and Mary, and was touted as such on more than one occasion by his medical colleagues. Surely there was reason to assume that the king and queen needed several physicians on their staff since the king was asthmatic and subject to frequent fevers, and the queen suffered from a chronic, worrisome eye condition; moreover, she had experienced two miscarriages in Holland. William and Mary kept several courts and two official households, complicating further matters of court medicine, and making attendance on the king and queen occasionally inconvenient to a doctor without court lodgings.

Royal medical appointments, middle-level household offices, fell to the king; he chose a "first" physician (at £400 per annum), a "serjeant surgeon" (at £396 13*s* 4*d* per annum), three "physicians-in-ordinary" in descending order of payment from second to fourth (£300, £250, and £200 per annum respectively), and a personal apothecary (£500 per annum including all supplies). Mary's medical household included at least two physicians and an apothecary. There was also a physician (eliminated in 1690), a surgeon, and an apothecary to the royal household at large. The monarchs' special patronage indicated a preference for innovative curers, and their pick of physicians encouraged clinical medicine at the expense of the College of Physicians. Their choices invariably produced jealousy within the medical community and confronted appointees with the twin dangers of political and medical missteps.[4]

Welwood was never first physician, but he did become a physician-in-ordinary to the monarchs. Even here, Welwood had a connection to a person who might serve his own advancement. First physician John Hutton, a fellow Scot trained in continental medicine, had risen to prominence like Welwood by dint of his talent and good political sense. He shared Welwood's good luck, for he came to the attention of the future Queen Mary in Holland when she took a fall from a horse, and rose to become Physician General to William's forces in the Netherlands; he was withal involved in William's spy network in England before 1688. Hutton spearheaded an effort to improve the military medical system in Britain and accompanied William to the siege of Limerick and the Battle of the Boyne. Incidentally, being principal physician to the royal couple did not necessarily bring riches or even a dependable paycheck; Hutton's estate was still trying to collect back salaries of nearly £1000 in 1717.[5]

Welwood was first designated as physician extraordinary, or occasional doctor not on a fixed retainer, in March 1690; a month later a warrant from the Lord Chamberlain named him physician to the person.[6] Mary probably influenced most of the original royal appointments, and many of the monarchs' designees were trained, like Welwood, outside Oxford and Cambridge. Welwood certainly attended the queen's household and befriended her. He was already somewhat known to the Dutch king from his sojourn at The Hague while still a medical student. Moreover, Welwood's newspaper, *Mercurius Reformatus*, made astute references in January 1690 to the health of soldiers fighting in Ireland and the possibility of pestilence among them. Welwood judged that while he was persuaded by reports that fevers were endemic throughout Europe that winter, no plague racked William's Irish forces. With Bishop Burnet's recommendation of him as loyal and hard-working, and because of his own reputation as a reliable Williamite, Dr. James Welwood got his first administrative appointment in January 1691 as superintendent of the surgeons in the fleet.[7] Welwood's politics, not his professional skills, brought him royal medical assignments under William and Mary. Nevertheless, most of those appointments related in some fashion to his expertise caring for the sick, and that proficiency was not as easy for the government to come by as one might think.

Evidently, Welwood did his job as superintendent well, justifying his patrons' faith in him and epitomizing the true Williamite reformer. A newsletter dated just a few days after his selection remarks that as the fleet was already fitting out, Welwood was "busy looking after the medicaments and placing fit and able persons to officiate in that great work."[8] He became a member of the six-man Commission for the Sick, Wounded, and Prisoners of War in early spring 1691. Through it, Welwood came to appreciate the peculiar needs of military medicine, especially its reliance on the standardization and regularization of diagnosis and treatment. While traditional civilian doctors may have had the luxury of individualizing patient diagnosis and delegating actual treatment to a surgeon or apothecary, military medicine of necessity combined surgery and treatment directed toward the rapid recovery of a sizable clientele. It was a system that favored empirical theories and pharmaceutical specifics.

The Commission for the Sick and Wounded that Welwood joined had been the object of some criticism in the recent past. Plymouth surgeon James Yonge complained in 1689 of such "bad treatment and ill-usage from the sea commissioners" that he quit working for the army.[9] However, under William III, this commission became a principal vehicle through which reform of military medicine took place and a key expression of the government's understanding that future recruitment depended on care of past and present soldiers and sailors. No appointee would match Welwood's energetic devotion to the king's objectives.

Given an initial fund of £2000 in April 1690, the commission soon depleted that amount when circumstances made clear how desperate was the plight of veterans in some communities. A month later, after several residents of Rochester brought proof that they had quartered the sick and wounded there at a cost to themselves of £1100, the commissioners recommended they be paid forthwith, over and above the money already appropriated to the commission. In fact, the commissioners frequently received dire news about conditions existing and anticipated; they often had to act quickly as unexpected vessels arrived with sick and wounded men at ports incapable of handling their needs. Dr. Welwood complained personally to the mayor of Dartmouth in August 1691 over deteriorating circumstances at the Royal Naval College there; his criticisms were forwarded to the Admiralty. Welwood and his fellow commissioners were informed that same month that neither sick soldiers nor their surgeons at the hospital in Chester had any provisions. To supply the needs of their charges, the commissioners could resort to creative bookkeeping and outright confiscation. In September 1691 they shifted some money apportioned for the housing of veterans at the Royal Hospital in Chelsea to the needs of some foreign prisoners of war. Later that month they requisitioned sheets, beds, and bedding from the matrons at Hounslow Heath Hospital.

Amidst the inevitable confusion of wartime, Dr. Welwood could be depended on when questions about individual citizens called for precise accountability. Notwithstanding Nottingham's misgivings about Welwood's overly zealous publications, the secretary of state knew upon whom to rely for information about individual prisoners and their whereabouts. In a June 1692 letter, Nottingham assured William Blathwayt that Dr. Welwood guaranteed Blathwayt's captured servants had been safely released and would be on the next ship arriving from Calais.[10]

Welwood and his associates on the commission often had to deal with the potentially explosive social conditions created by war. When Irish prisoners bivouacked in London's Soho Square in September of that year, the commissioners had them removed to the Jesuit College at the Savoy chapel near the Thames. Foreign prisoners of war received an allowance from the king to sustain them depending on their rank: twelve pence per day was the going rate for officers, sixpence daily for the rest. Accordingly, the commission acknowledged the needs of hundreds of Irish detained at Marshalsea prison and at Ostend by ordering such payments made. Due to the obvious inadequacy of its original allocation to the commission, the Treasury in June 1691 asked for an estimate of what was then owed by the commissioners and what would carry them through the next six months. They were invited to tally what had already been received from the Admiralty Lords. Sometimes, however, the soldiers and sailors themselves would be taxed for medical services, such as when the commission ordered the Postmaster General to withhold a shilling per month from each seaman's pay. According to their instructions, sixpence should be divided out for a military medical chest kept at Chatham, site of the

Royal Naval Dockyards, tuppence for a surgeon, and a groat (a silver four pence piece) to the chaplain.[11]

Besides his many duties as a Commissioner for the Sick and Wounded, in May 1691 Welwood simultaneously became the principal physician for the forts at Deptford, Greenwich, Gravesend, and elsewhere along the Thames. At Deptford, the government apportioned twelve pence each day for a man's quarters and 6s.8d. for his cure; in London by contrast, the whole charge was only tuppence per day, and some argued that the men were better taken care of in the city.[12] Welwood was empowered by warrant to appoint two added physicians as his deputies for £60 yearly each. While a post like this had formerly been poorly paid with matching levels of performance, the Navy Board now wanted regular, reliable physicians and surgeons to watch over the medical care of the forces. As a paladin in the vanguard of reform, James Welwood took his responsibilities seriously, supervising medical preparations, care of the sick and wounded, and the qualifications of personnel. He was probably distressed over any criticisms about the Thames forts, even when he was not directly answerable for their cause. In September 1692 the Earl of Ranelagh heard grievances from residents in Lewisham, Greenwich, and Deptford concerning the obstreperous behavior of the Earl of Argyll's regiment quartered there. The complainants demanded damages of £34.[13]

Welwood's experience with humane treatment of military men and his championing the fair treatment of captives served him in a 1694 incident concerning the exchange of prisoners. Evidently, in April of that year many English prisoners were stranded at Dunkirk and Calais, waiting to be returned home on the ship which was ready to sail. However, Welwood raised some objection to its master, a man named Thomas Woosters. Although Woosters was vouched for by the army officer charged with hiring him, Major William Churchill, the commissioners asked for subsequent direction from the Duke of Shrewsbury, successor to Nottingham as one of two secretaries of state. No ensuing action on this matter was recorded, but it may be that Welwood was acting on the king's behest in causing trouble at that particular moment for any Churchill. William III had suffered a serious falling out with the patriarch of the Churchill family, John, then Earl of Marlborough, over the monarch's stingy financial allotment to Princess

Anne and her entourage, an entourage that included Marlborough's wife. Marlborough even resorted to communicating secretly with the exiled James II, which, when discovered in 1692, cost him royal favor until Anne's accession a decade later. Perhaps Welwood used the *Eagle* episode to embarrass the Churchills and call doubt upon their endorsements; more than likely, Major Churchill was a scoundrel.

In a system endemic with petty graft, Welwood's name was often mentioned by Samuel Baston, Clerk to the Commissioners for the Sick and Wounded, as its most honest member. Baston brought an official complaint to the Admiralty in 1694 charging several members of the commission with malfeasance and peculation. Besides owing him money dating back to 1691, Baston charged that the commissioners failed to deal with credible reports of corruption in 1692 and 1693 in the transport of prisoners of war. At the center of the scandal was Major William Churchill and his partner, Mr. Masters. This time other ships and other commanders were involved in unauthorized commerce utilizing military vessels; the ever-serious Welwood interrogated the suspects before the full Board and to Baston at least their guilt was well established. In fact, Baston reported that Churchill confessed to the Admiralty, but extenuated the crime by claiming that he and Masters were spies in the Secret Service. But Secretary of State Trenchard, who had recently reorganized the intelligence system at the French ports, denied knowing any of the parties and railed that his name had been scandalously used. Nevertheless, the commissioners failed to bring charges against Churchill or the men in his employ.

Baston likewise called into doubt the reliability of the commissioners' certification of drugs for the army. Rhubarb was one of the most common purgatives and diuretics in the Galenic pharmacy, valued for its gentleness in "strengthening the intestines." Walter Harris, a famous associate of Dr. Welwood's at the Royal College of Physicians, even recommended rhubarb for cleansing feverish children of vicious humors.[14] Baston complained that poor-quality rhubarb had been purchased and approved by the Commissioners for the Sick and Wounded to be ground up and used in treating distemper cases, but even an apothecary's apprentice knew that the rhubarb in question was inferior and ineffective. However, Baston did not rely on the word of a novice in condemning the quality of the medicines they supervised. He procured the opinion of the President of the Royal College of Physicians that the rhubarb "had no more virtue than so much powder of rotten post." Implying that something beyond error was involved, Baston asserted that if impure drugs like this could pass inspection by physicians and commissioners alike, "then God and the consciences of those concerned only knows what other bad medicines have been issued in this manner, for the lucre of gain, and how many men have perished thereby."[15]

Baston charged the commissioners with looking the other way when their agent in Plymouth was bribed by Irish prisoners who subsequently escaped their captivity. This same agent, a man named George Dickinson, abused French prisoners by flagrantly cheating them out of their allowance of victuals. To explore the veracity of this latter charge, Dr. Welwood traveled to Plymouth and personally weighed the provisions allotted the Frenchmen by Dickinson at the hospital there. Instead of the four-pound pieces of meat due them, Welwood found that the prisoners were being shorted by half. Upon his return to London, Welwood submitted that Dickinson be fired, but other commissioners again balked, arguing that no one else could be found to serve in his stead. Baston swore that Dickinson's financial accounts were spurious, but that the commissioners removed those accounts from his supervision to be inspected by others. Further, the industrious Dr. Welwood uncovered forgery at the commission, too. Apparently, one of the commissioner's clerks without authorization scrawled the signatures of the other commissioners from time to time on miscellaneous papers. Welwood found several instances of his own signature affixed to papers he did not remember signing. Baston reported that Dr. Welwood was so agitated, he stormed out of the Boardroom.[16]

Ultimately, the Lords of the Admiralty found four of the commissioners responsible for gross mismanagement and breach of trust, but the accused were able to forestall any punishment and stop the report from coming to William directly by appealing to be tried before the king's council. The king acquiesced to the commissioners' petition by permitting an appeal from the Admiralty decision, and ordered that the matter be examined in greater detail by a committee of the council. William never had the Admiralty report read to him, and he left for Flanders shortly thereafter. In the king's absence, the council reheard the charges and questioned the parties involved, but although a concurring judgment was rendered, the commissioners procured a stay of execution for an unlimited time.[17] To Baston's chagrin, emissaries of the commissioners "employed for that purpose, proclaimed in all public places that they were acquitted like worthy honest gentlemen." The four commissioners had managed to turn civic perception of their stay of execution into an acquittal! Untouched by the law and by the king's desire for ethical governmental service, the accused commissioners then turned on Baston; to defend himself he published his account of the whole affair in April 1695. In it, Baston exempted only Dr. Welwood from any blame in this nefarious business and commended him for seriousness of purpose. More than any other Commissioner for the Sick and Wounded, James Welwood loyally pursued the king's desire for reform through honesty in appointive office; he became a Williamite emblem of virtue and dedication to duty.

In spite of Welwood's toil for the government, the doctor found remuneration slow and bonuses non-existent. He did receive some pay for his work as a commissioner, part of the appropriations recorded in the Treasury Books, but encountered official resistance to his claims that money was due him for overseeing medical care in the citadels along the Thames. In June 1694, Shrewsbury brought to the attention of the Lords of the Admiralty the fact of Welwood's 1691 appointment as principal physician to Deptford, Greenwich, Gravesend, and other river strongholds. Since then, Welwood had received no compensation, not even a travel allowance or expense account. The good doctor must have complained to the queen, who had a personal interest in Greenwich, having recently dedicated a hospital there for disabled seamen. Shrewsbury went on: "Her Majesty, thinking it fit he should be considered for his attendance in that service, commands you to take the same into consideration and report to her...." The Admiralty was to estimate what should be paid to a chief physician, caring for the sick and wounded at several sites, and what comparable allowances physicians in other ports enjoyed.[18] On July 12 the Admiralty Lords wrote back to Shrewsbury that they had considered Welwood's case, and that he did have a valid warrant to be the forts' physician, but only for ordinary traveling charges to Deptford once a week and the other places as needed. There was no salary for him involved. Physicians established in other ports were paid £200 per year, but the Lords agreed that the Thames forts did not need a resident doctor. Welwood's labor for the government was hardly bringing him the honest income and perquisites he might have expected. Even so, Welwood avoided the taint of financial misprision so commonplace during this age of expectation. Many ministers, soldiers, and bureaucrats were caught with their hands in the public till, but Welwood assiduously avoided any scandal or corruption. In May 1695, a month after Baston's complaints were published, more accusations of jobbery which had validity were brought against the Commissioners for the Sick and Wounded. They were charged with authorizing two extra vessels from France, supposedly filled with prisoners, but which in fact contained wine, currants, and other comestibles. Clearly, a trading cartel of some sort had been established with Nantes and other ports, but Welwood was again able to demonstrate convincingly that he had no association with the ignominious scheme.[19] He was undoubtedly disgusted at the greed which left war veterans stranded in France, while a few feasted illicitly at the public trough.

Nevertheless, the appointment of men of Welwood's caliber illumines a segment of William III's administrative plan to alter the medical infrastructure of the military, bringing change to medical staffs used in wartime, to the organization of medical services, and to military medicine. Inevitably, William's reforms affected many medical practitioners.[20] In particular, by modifying the path to medical training, these reforms buttressed the standing of empirical, "practical" medicine at the expense of traditional, learned physicians. The military wanted simple and effective cures for specific diseases that could be applied to any soldier or sailor, but traditional physicians resisted quick diagnoses and easy treatments even during wartime emergencies. The king himself encouraged endeavors to find new therapies for military medical problems: remedies that usually involved on-site battlefield application and sometimes hypothetical medicine, curatives that erudite physicians labeled quackery. Therefore, through his appointive service during William's wars with France, James Welwood unintentionally promoted challenges to conventional medicine and to establishment doctors.

As a continentally-trained physician with several years seasoning, Welwood would have seemed a natural choice for administrative and supervisory duties. There was much work to be done, not only in providing for wounded soldiers and sailors in combat situations, but also in caring for ill and disabled veterans at home. One of Welwood's chief responsibilities was recruitment of physicians and surgeons for military expeditions. Usually each regiment and ship had a surgeon and a surgeon's mate to care for the sick and wounded, but during wartime more medical personnel were needed. The government initially turned for help to London's medical establishment, the Royal College of Physicians to which Welwood belonged. The Admiralty tried to get the College to nominate doctors for all the new available posts, and for a while junior members and licentiates had their names put forth. Those who took the jobs tended to be medical novices in need of advancing their careers. But the Admiralty and the College had a falling out and the nominations stopped being solicited.

The government's problems with the College were three-fold: authority, philosophy, and finance. The College intended to maintain precedence over its rival medical corporations, the Barber-Surgeons' Company and the Society of Apothecaries, believing that only educated doctors could control practitioners they regarded as hardly better than craftsmen. Notwithstanding, the College's place in the medical hierarchy was jeopardized by its attitude toward the kinds of medical treatment favored by the military. Disputes over the College's nominations for vacancies at various medical posts soured relations between the government and the Fellows; eventually, the Admiralty chose its own physicians without consulting the College at all. The quarrel deepened over the issue of medications suitable to supply military campaigns, with the College concerned about the wholesomeness of drugs while the Admiralty pressed for specific medicines; the officers of the College and the Lords of the Admiralty spoke at cross-purposes about different matters. Once again, the Admiralty ultimately pursued its own vision of medicine, outfitting its expeditions with drugs the College opposed. Financial concerns underlay the College's disagreements with William's reforming strategies, for the Fellows feared diminution of their monetary advantage, individually and collectively, over the rest of the medical community. They had valid reason for worry as the College lost its right to supply the army and navy with drugs. Dr. James Welwood had a foot in both camps: he served

William's reforming agenda in a variety of capacities while he actively participated in the traditional medical establishment.

In December 1690, the same year as John Hutton, Dr. Welwood became a Fellow of the Royal College of Physicians, probably because of his connections with the crown and his friendship with Bishop Burnet. According to the Annals of the College, President Walter Charlton welcomed Welwood warmly to the members' Warwick Lane headquarters as "regis et reginae communis medicus" with an introduction citing the new Fellow's ingenuity, character, and erudition.[21] Being categorized as a royal doctor gave Welwood prestige, for in tending to the monarch's body, he tended to the nation's. Charlton himself was a gentleman-scholar and member of the Royal Society interested in philosophy and nature. He praised Welwood's "judicious spirit of hard work" that led him toward difficult knowledge. Welwood valued membership in his profession's vanguard and the friendships that he made in the College. In spite of its troubles, the College was the greatest London institution of postgraduate medical studies, offering anatomy and pathology lectures to its members. Although Welwood did not hold office in the College until his later years, he was an active Fellow during the College's most turbulent era.

Members of the College, the only licensed physicians in the metropolitan area, were organized into Fellows and candidates; additionally, there were nonvoting honorary Fellows and licentiates in the association. To obtain a license to practice, one had to undergo a three-part Latin examination in physiology, pathology, and therapy. Because of the College's restricted membership and control of licensing, the ratio of lawful doctors to Londoners was startling, about 1 to every 4,000 residents, making a medical marketplace of enormous opportunity. Historically conservative, the College had long avoided political controversy whenever possible. In 1660, hoping to curry favor with the Stuarts, it had welcomed Charles II back to England, likening him to a phoenix. The Restoration had advanced the careers of some doctors over others, and the Annals record the complaints of candidates of long-standing leapfrogged by new men of the king's choice. The Fellows had erupted in a chorus of disapproval when Charles raised the charlatan Tilborg to the status of royal physician in 1682.[22] To generate money for the College, honorary Fellows, many suggested by Charles

II, were admitted upon payment of £20, later £100. Though some of the Fellows grumbled that the king ought not intrude in their professional association, the College had acquiesced when he reconfirmed its ancient privileges. In appreciation the king exempted the College from some of the usual civic responsibilities associated with the guilds. The Fellows did not have to provide men for the night watch or provide arms to the city.

The College continued its compliant relationship with the crown in the 1680s, reporting on suspected Papists in their midst when asked and sending a congratulatory letter to James II upon his accession in 1685. Nevertheless, the College was not held in universal esteem within the City, primarily because of the institution's perceived arrogance and pretensions. Especially aggrieved were London's other healers, of whom there were nearly 3,000 in the 1680s.[23] In October 1685, a *quo warranto* was issued against the College charter, part of James' general plan to confirm his control of London's corporations by challenging their privileges. He sanctioned a comprehensive yet hierarchically-controlled pattern of medical practice in the capital, one which circumscribed the opportunity for many to practice medicine. Rather than fight confiscation, the College delivered the charter up to the king, effectively surrendering its previous rights. The new king wanted to pack the College with men of his choosing, and Thomas Witherley, former physician to Charles II and President of the College during James' reign, suggested increasing membership from forty to eighty Fellows. Given the need to include all London physicians who were fit to be Fellows, this was real reform, even if flavored with political purpose. Significantly, when a new College charter was granted in 1687, twenty-nine novice members were noted. The College did insist, however, on some sort of doctorate for honorary Fellows, and the king blackballed four existing Fellows for political offenses.

Although the Royal College of Physicians continued its domination of the medical world after the issuance of its new charter, the Annals suggest that the physicians were anxious about losing control and patients to surgeons, apothecaries, and irregular medical practitioners. There was still bias evident against continentally-trained physicians, surely more than at mid-century when half the Fellows were foreign graduates. During the period 1681-1700, the era of Welwood's entry into the College, thirty-five of the Fellows held their medical degrees from Oxford or Cambridge; only eighteen Fellows had graduated from foreign institutions.[24] In 1694 a College committee proposed double fees for Fellows whose degrees were not from Oxbridge. Moreover, many of the College doctors disdained the honors and attention bestowed on the Royal Society, founded shortly after the Restoration and charged with promoting the new philosophy of experimentation. With their emphasis on empiricism, the Society's "virtuosi," as they rather immodestly called themselves, exasperated traditional physicians. Some of the College's younger doctors, especially those trained in investigative research, joined the rival organization and encouraged its work.

Besides the theoretical and philosophical squabbles that beset the College in the seventeenth century, jurisdictional disputes plagued the Fellows during Welwood's time. Just as French physicians zealously kept control over the profession through the university faculties, London doctors had been exclusively licensed and monitored by the Royal College of Physicians. Henry VIII had granted the College its first charter in 1518, ostensibly to improve the professionalism of doctors, but in addition to give control of caring for the sick to university-educated physicians. By the terms of the College's charter, no physician was permitted to practice within seven miles of the City unless he had been elected a Fellow or held the College's license. The College also safeguarded the quality of medicaments within London. Among the College's officers was a Board of Censors, Fellows whose task it was to burn impure drugs in the grocers' and apothecaries' quarters.

The Royal College could punish transgressions within the medical community, as is demonstrated by its investigation of the celebrated man-midwife, Hugh Chamberlen. The last in a long line of Huguenot *accoucheurs,* Chamberlen had been one of Charles II's physicians-in-ordinary and had written on the efficacy of Jesuits' bark, quinine from Peru, for recurrent fevers. In early 1689 he was charged by the College with malpractice in the case of Phoebe Wilmer. Chamberlen had dosed her, six months pregnant, with a farrago of vomitories and purgatives besides cupping and bleeding her eight ounces on three separate occasions. Phoebe Wilmer miscarried and died. The College found

Chamberlen guilty of malpractice and fined him £10, which he paid. It is conceivable that the Fellows actually wanted to punish Chamberlen for another infraction of establishment prerogatives. Like his father and grandfather before him, Hugh Chamberlen had recently petitioned the Lord Chancellor for a patent relating to midwifery. The College counter-proposed that it would assume control from the bishops who ordinarily approved midwives for their moral qualification rather than for their technical skills. Though the plans of one midwife during the reign of James II to set up a birthing school as part of a foundling hospital were not carried to fruition, in December 1689 the College did permit the licensing of a midwife after examination. At any rate, the Fellows harbored no permanent hard feelings towards Hugh Chamberlen; he became a member of the College five years later.

Guarding the mysteries of the profession was another totem for the College to maintain. John Radcliffe, a curmudgeonly but successful royal doctor and member of the College, was fined by his colleagues for not writing his cases up in Latin. The forty shilling penalty did not deter him from putting prescriptions into English, for he believed that medicine ought to be intelligible to the unwell. Unbowed when the College dismissed him, he became London's wealthiest physician and left his fortune to build the famous Radcliffe Camera at Oxford University.

Fearing a diminution of its authority after the Glorious Revolution, the Royal College of Physicians sought assurances that its stamp of approval was still needed on all drugs within London. One of its officers reported to the Fellows that certain drugs and medicines intended for the army and navy were being prepared by a commission under the direction of Dr. John Hutton. In January 1691 the College petitioned Dr. Hutton, then principal physician to William and Mary, to maintain its right to inspect all such drugs. Hutton, who had been with William at the Battle of the Boyne the previous summer, pledged to help the College maintain its privileges. He assured the Fellows that the king was only concerned with the efficacy of the medicines. Consequently, the College compiled a catalogue of medicines the next year to be available for treatment of the 5,000 men assigned to the West Indies; the entries range from aqua to vin, alsliaeae to ubar.

But the College was still pricklish about its prerogatives, always citing the statutes of three Parliaments to support its medical monopoly. When in December 1692 a letter arrived from the Lords of the Admiralty asking the College to nominate three or four physicians from whom the Lords might choose one to take care of the sick and wounded in the fleet at Portsmouth, the College retorted that it should be able to nominate the one fellow. The College named the only medical member of the Kit-Kat Club, Dr. Samuel Garth, but hedged its hauteur with the caveat that no other Fellows could be spared at that time.

The College created some of its own problems by keeping the number of approved physicians preposterously small in a burgeoning metropolis. Fellows and licentiates numbered 136 in 1695 within a city of more than half a million inhabitants; by 1719 there were only seventy-eight properly validated physicians in the capital, and they often kept their patients at arm's length or beyond. By Welwood's time, many practitioners no longer visited the indisposed in their homes but met them in coffeehouses or private rooms. Some never saw their patients at all, sending surgical emissaries to examine sufferers and report back with observable symptoms. No wonder that open defiance of the College's control was widespread when monarchs turned to unlicensed doctors.[25] Even bishops began to reassert their traditional prerogative of licensing physicians in order to relieve the pressing need for medical men in their dioceses, men who might deign to administer directly to the infirm.

Just as the reputation of physicians suffered from their own apparent pride, so did the status of the College decline over its attempts to curtail the success of foreign doctors who engaged in conjectural medicine, doctors like Johannes Groenevelt, a licentiate whose methods irked the College censors. In the mid-1690s Groenevelt, one of many Dutch doctors who came to England after the Glorious Revolution, was charged with malpractice by a female patient supported by the College censors and committed to Newgate prison for prescribing large doses of cantharides taken with camphor. The charges produced a split in the ranks of the Fellows and made Groenevelt a sympathetic figure in London. Found not guilty of malpractice by the Court of King's Bench, he brought a countersuit with the Society of Apothecaries against the College and, although the College temporarily had its right to police physicians reaffirmed, its reputation was demolished.[26]

The Fellows did try to repair some of the institution's image problems by voting in 1695 to open a dispensary for the sick poor adjacent to the College in Warwick Lane. Fifty-three of the Fellows contributed 20*s.* to fund the project. Ostensibly founded for humanitarian motives, the dispensary enabled the College to challenge the disbursing monopoly of the apothecaries. Opponents charged that the dispensary, finally opened in 1698, was merely a device for making money through the very same quackish promises of good medicine at low cost which the physicians had lambasted; satirists derided the bickering London medical community. Soon two dispensary branches opened, undercutting the apothecaries' prices even more. To commemorate the event, Samuel Garth wrote a best-selling poem, *The Dispensary*, which ridiculed the objections of the apothecaries. The already convoluted war among the varied practitioners of medicine recurved between dispensarians and anti-dispensarians, the apothecaries notable among the latter.

Therefore, it is somewhat fitting that the ultimate challenge to the preeminence of London doctors came, not from the surgeons, but from the apothecaries. In 1704 the London Society of Apothecaries won a famous victory in the highest court in the land over the Royal College of Physicians, a success which put them on a par with the doctors. William Rose, a veteran master apothecary in the City, prescribed medicines for unhealthy people and charged them inflated prices for the drugs. He did so, like other apothecaries, because he could not legally charge for consultation. But Rose charged too much, in the opinion of a patient, who took his complaint to the Royal College of Physicians, which in turn brought charges before the Court of King's Bench for unlicensed practice. Pamphleteers, hired by the Fellows to support their side, rejected the right of apothecaries to practice, mainly on social grounds. When that court found against Rose, the Society of Apothecaries appealed the case to the House of Lords on a writ of error, and in March 1704 the peers, England's highest appellate tribunal, declared for Rose. The decision in the *Rose Case* proved that publicity and politics had dovetailed against the College.[27] The decision was a historic one, for it meant that practicing apothecaries could treat the indisposed. Before long the number of apothecary shops in London had tripled, making all too real the College's fear of competition. All of the internecine bickering had taken its toll on the College, whose members panicked in disarray. Their new charter included emphasis on professional dignity, suitable apparel, and the ethics of consultation.

Picayune matters continued to haunt the Fellows of the College during the reign of Queen Anne despite the near-collapse of their professional leadership. The Annals are filled with reports of unpaid dues, fraudulent balloting, indecorous deportment, and other grievances. Several of the members complained about new statutes that kept many bona fide practitioners out of the College; some of the objectionable statutes were repealed.[28] However, there does appear to be some softening of the College's position toward medical physics in particular and empiricism in general. Many physicians, some of them members of the College, exploited a variety of theories in their patient analyses, mixing Galenic with newer chemical and mechanical ones. The Fellows may have been attempting to appear more philosophically progressive and less ambivalent about change; they may also have been trying to square their institution's position vis-à-vis the Royal Society.[29]

James Welwood became a particularly active member of the Royal College of Physicians during the reign of George I, perhaps because Whig politics were dominant once again. He was elected a censor in 1722, making him one of four Fellows charged with inquiring about practitioners, questioning patients, judging new medicines, and then reporting regularly to the President.[30] Now acknowledged a doyen in his profession, Welwood replaced Richard Blackmore later that year as one of the eight Electors of the College, an inner executive circle which functioned like a nominating committee.[31] After Dr. Welwood's death, Henry Plumptre, physician at St. Thomas' Hospital, supplanted Welwood as Elector at the Royal College of Physicians in May 1727.

Unlike several of his professional colleagues, Welwood left few medical records or lists of favorite remedies for us to examine. Eponymous preparations abound in seventeenth-century therapy, such as Scot's Pills (aloes, jalap, gamboge, and anise), Goddard's Drops (raw silk), and Dr. Lower's tincture (senna, anise, coriander, raisins, and aqua vitae) for colic. Samuel Haworth, an extralicentiate of the College who called himself a student of the plague, sold tablets from his London shop. He would not divulge the ingredients. Most doctors had favored unpatented remedies which they either jealously guarded or shared with inquiring colleagues. For instance, Francis Glisson suggested that rachitic patients avoid fish and other cold foods while taking a decoction of rhubarb and raven's liver. For ague his cure was snails, pounded and boiled in milk, to which was added cut-up earthworms, sugar, and candied eryngo (sea holly). For smallpox he prescribed powdered violet, wood-sorrel, and root of the pestilence-wort (butter-burr) diluted in wine.[32] John Pechey, a fellow of the College and author of a famous herbal, called for plantain seeds in broth to prevent miscarriage and raspberry syrup before delivery; he advised the leaves of the wayfaring tree for loose teeth and birch juice for pimples. Richard Lower, among the wealthiest of London physicians, prepared a brew of fennel, parsley water, horseradish, turpentine, and syrup of marsh-mallow for patients with painful urination; for heartburn the ingredients included chalk, crabs' eyes, and oil of nutmeg in milk and water. For "shrunken sinews," he advised that while sitting by a fire, one rub on strained balm made from twelve young swallows and strawberry leaves boiled in fresh butter.[33]

George Bate, physician to Charles II, left a remarkable gallimaufry of medical recipes to Dr. William Salmon who added a few of his own concoctions when the 1,000-page *Pharmacopoeia Bateana* was published in 1694. It contained functional instructions on making various medicinal waters and what each was for. Some of the waters were multipurpose; Salmon claimed that aqua chaybeara (a potpourri of white wine, strawberry juice, sperma cete, and mummy) cured hemorrhoids, ulcers in the urinary tract, and the "green sickness" in virgins. Instructions and ingredients were often highly specific; Salmon maintained that oil of hazelwood is only effective when the hazelwood in question has been cut down in September. He insisted that the royal cathartic, an electuary of green ginger, red roses, and oil of cinnamon, is best administered as a purge for gouty patients.[34]

John Radcliffe, the College Fellow fined for writing his prescriptions in English, published six hundred pages of prescriptions and observations. Though a royal doctor to Queen Anne, Radcliffe intended his corrective mixtures to be of general service to all physicians, surgeons, and apothecaries, as well as to their patients. He must have divined a market for such a recipe book; the first edition sold 1600 copies in six months. Included are formulas for diuretic wine, nephretic pills, cephalic snuff, hysteric electuary, anodyne plasters, volatile julep, and powdered myrrh pessaries to be used only by married women. One could choose from among restoratives made from strawberries and cherries, chocolate and cinnamon, or marrow and prune broth.[35]

Irrespective of their rivalries, doctors often consulted with one another and suggested courses of therapy. Hans Sloane inquired of William III's doctor, William Briggs, what he ought to do about a melancholy patient given to regular nighttime fits. Similarly, he asked for help in a case involving a stubborn cough that even laudanum wouldn't cure. Dr. Ferdinando Mendez wrote to Sloane in 1721 asking for the name of "an honest and dexterous bonesetter" and thanking Sloane for sending a patient to him. Andrew Balfour, one of the founders of the Royal College of Physicians in Edinburgh, asked Charles Scarborough, an original fellow of the Royal Society, how to treat Lord Lauderdale, who, after taking Balfour's prescribed emetics, still suffered from severe bellyache.[36]

The College had its own pharmacopoeia, first published in 1618, with new editions in 1650 and 1677. In its earliest incarnation, the compendium contains directions for lozenges made of dried vipers, powders of precious stones, oil of ants, and 932 compounds with the names of their Greek and Arabian originators attached. The pharmacopoeia of 1650 contains cochineal, moss from the skull of a victim of violent death, and Gascoyne's powder, a compound of bezoar, amber, pearls, crabs' eyes and coral. In the 1677 update, the names of the Greeks and Arabs disappear, showing that their influence had waned, while burnt alum, digitalis, steel tonics, human urine, and Irish whiskey make their appearance for the first time. Among the unusual entries are bee-glue, cock's-comb, cuttlefish, isinglass, human perspiration, the saliva of a fasting man, wood-lice, and the Wormian bone from the skull of an executed criminal.[37]

Surgeons and apothecaries had their manuals and recipe books, too. Charles II's surgeon-in-ordinary, John Browne, found celebrity in the medical community for his work on tumors. Using Galenic assumptions, he examined the metaphysical causes of tumors and determined which veins to bleed, how to purge, and what to apply to the poisoned organ. When all else fails, he wrote, apply live pigeons to the parts affected. He considered erisypelas a tumor requiring plentiful bleeding and a rhubarb electuary; for cancer, unguent of frogs or oil of nightshade was recommended; for pestilential buboes, oysters should extract the venom.[38] In a coded journal, apothecary Nicolas LeFevre advocated a combination of tobacco in milk for asthma and amber for hysteria. The most complete record of the pharmaceutical needs of the court can be found in the 500-page daybook of royal apothecary James Chase, which lists what mixtures he prepared. Druggist to the crown for over thirty years, he frequently readied purgatives, vomitories, laudanum for pain, and blends to ward off everything from melancholy to intestinal worms. Chase itemized thirty-five categories of common medications including eleven different waters and the patients for whom they were brewed. Among the Chase alteratives were "tachama-hacca," a gum used extensively as a diuretic; "urina hom san," an emulsion that contained the urine of a healthy man used as an enema; and powdered pearl dissolved in treacle syrup to strengthen the heart.[39] Queen Anne used "hiera picra," a laxative composed of aloes and canella or cinnamon bark; a facial cerate made of calamine, wax, and olive oil; ground millipedes in butter for sore throat; and a camphor-clove salve for toothache. At her doctors' urging in 1702 and 1703, she soaked in the mineral waters at Bath spa, where she was cupped and bled.[40]

Medicaments from the New World entered the market in Welwood's lifetime including ipecacuanha, a remedy for dysentery; antimony cups made from Mexican wood for tumors and wounds; and Jesuits' bark as a treatment for malarial fevers. No other drug affected the medical profession as did the bark, and its impact on medicine has been compared to that of gunpowder on war.[41] Malaria was one of the most familiar yet serious ailments in Augustan Britain. Each spring, despite improvements in public sanitation and the drainage of swamps, outbreaks of intermittent fever (or ague) debilitated and killed residents of southeast England. Jesuits' bark, called cinchona by natives of the Peruvian mountains, had specific anti-febrile aspects; quinine, a bitter alkaloid in the bark, became a cornerstone of innovative medicine. Use of the bark challenged a fundamental Galenic belief in the natural fermenting action of the blood, making established heroic measures unnecessary. Besides objections raised by traditionalists to Jesuits' bark as a specific cure for recurrent fever, many doctors dismissed it on account of its politically-charged name. Because cinchona was associated with the Roman Catholic order and was first dispensed through the Pharmacy of the Collegio Romano, it was suspect in Protestant countries.

The man in England most closely associated with Jesuits' bark was Robert Talbor, an Essex apothecary who billed himself as a pyretiatro (or feverologist) with a secret remedy. Talbor successfully treated Charles II, who made him a physician-in-ordinary in 1672, ordered the Royal College of Physicians not to interfere with the man's lucrative practice, and knighted him in 1677. The great doctor, Thomas Sydenham, claimed to have arrived at a bark-based cure for ague independently, but Talbor's book, *The English Remedy*, was published posthumously in London in 1682. Anyone could read Talbor's suggestions about ways of ingesting the bark in powdered form, usually mixed with anise and parsley and steeped in claret, but he cautioned it not be taken in combination with other drugs. Infuriating the Galenists, Talbor warned that it is "a mistake in physick to make a hodge podge of a great many ingredients."[42] Though primarily associated with fever cases, cinchona was used in seventeenth-century Britain to stimulate the patient's appetite; physicians also prescribed it to prevent hemorrhage and diarrhea, for which it is completely unsuited. Talbor was aware of the possible deleterious side-effects of quinine, and he catalogued convulsions, seizures, and constipation as probable consequences.[43]

The application of drugs like Jesuits' bark exacerbated the theoretical and jurisdictional antagonisms within the medical establishment, while elevating the importance of surgeons and apothecaries. The Keeper of the Apothecaries' Garden in Chelsea attempted to grow the fever-bark tree in 1685. Eventually, College physicians incorporated cinchona into their own pharmacies. Dr. Radcliffe mixed powdered bark with black-cherry water and peony syrup to be quaffed for fever every three hours. Hans Sloane, who preferred mercury for patients with intestinal distress, confirmed the efficacy of Peruvian bark for intermittent fevers regardless of reports of blindness in four of his patients. He exchanged letters with another royal doctor, Peter Barwick, about recommending powdered cinchona to Queen Mary in 1689. In 1712 College President Charles Goodall, a known defender against medical impostors, championed the cortex of the cinchona tree while ridiculing standard heroic measures usually prescribed for fevers. He attributed the bark's side-effects including nausea and vertigo to the fever itself. In a 1718 manual, another fellow of the College and the Royal Society, John Woodward, while opposing Sloane's employment of metals in treatment, praised the bark, too.[44] By the beginning of the Georgian era, several mainstream physicians authored treatises which extolled the medicinal properties of cinchona against pernicious malaria.

In the midst of the dizzying choices available to the medical community, when all else failed, many believed that the royal touch could cure disease. Sovereigns in England had for generations laid hands on their subjects who suffered from the King's Evil, scrofulous lesions associated with tuberculosis. The credulous envisioned the malady actually entering the monarch's body, where God's will worked to suppress it. During his reign Charles II touched 100,000 victims of the disease according to his surgeon, John Browne; even before the Restoration Charles exercised the royal gift on healing on the continent. Reflecting the transitional nature of medicine at the close of the seventeenth century, Browne wrote that "there are great and divine favors transmitted through sacred majesty" to heal those afflicted with scurvy, rickets, and strumas, diseases that emanate from the sins of the people.45 James II touched, too, and the crowds that assembled whenever a day of healing was announced were enormous. During one of his progresses, 800 persons gathered in the choir of Chester Cathedral, seeking a miracle from the regnant thaumaturge, although the number of supplicants rose and fell depending on the king's popularity. Some came for the pieces of gold the monarch hung around their necks, but the royal surgeons screened out the healthy from those who really needed the cure.

William III found the rite disgusting as well as absurd, but his refusal to touch subverted his popularity, diminishing whatever mystique his monarchy held for the common people. He touched on only one occasion, blessing the patient by saying "God give you better health and more sense." The Whig historian Macaulay credited William with "too much sense to be duped, and too much honesty to bear a part in what he knew to be an imposture."[46] Jacobites murmured that an impious usurper would not want to try his hand at a magical ceremony only legitimate sovereigns could perform. As a Williamite and a continentally-schooled physician, Dr. James Welwood surely spurned such unscientific and superstitious practices; his own newspaper supported an alternative to the royal touch. An advertisement in *Mercurius Reformatus* (August 14, 1689) vaunted the safe purgative pills of Thomas Kirleus, described therein as a physician to Charles II. The pills could cure an interesting array of ailments including leprosy, venereal disease, and the king's evil for a mere one shilling. Welwood evidently preferred association with quacks than with the charisma of inherited monarchy. But magic is a powerful weapon, and Queen Anne, beset herself with medical woes, immediately reinstituted the regal ritual. She allayed some of her own fear of contagion by distributing touchpieces called "angels" in lieu of actual physical contact and had her chief surgeon screen applicants for touching when she visited Bath in the fall of 1702.

Though modern readers may scoff at their ancestors' reliance on thaumaturgy, even mainstream cures imposed on sick people startle our sensibilities. Based on Galen's teaching that bodily humors controlled health, classical physicians sought to balance those humors and restore the patient's unique well-being. Too much of one humor could only be rectified by reducing it to acceptable levels. Excess blood required bleeding, sometimes to the point of fainting or syncope; surplus phlegm or bile of either the yellow or the black variety called for a vigorous purge. A humoral deficit could best be addressed with complex medicines, compound pills, and herbal drinks, known to have restorative and forfending properties. Blood depletion, thought to be the cause of aging, could be retarded with a better diet, fresh air, and potent medications. Many prescriptions contained a variety of ingredients in the hope that one or more of them might be effectual. Most doctors developed a repertory of concoctions for various ailments, but others specialized in treating certain diseases or certain kinds of patients. Traditional physicians believed that disease could transmogrify over time, further underscoring the uniqueness of treatment. Empiricists, on the other hand, thought of disease as a specific entity to be cured by a specific countermeasure and not as some protean physiological instability distinct in each person.[47] Although Dr. Welwood was continentally-trained and might be expected to employ the medical techniques of the empiricists, the evidence about his prescriptives hints at a characteristic pragmatic mix of old and new with a slight Galenic flavor to the pharmacy. In medicine, as in everything else, he took the middle ground.

Despite the absence of Welwood's recipe books or records of his private cures, some conclusions can be drawn about his preferred remedies. Moreover, there are indications that his medical advice was taken seriously by friends and family, particularly by his in-laws and fellow Williamites, the Molesworths.48 When Viscount Robert Molesworth wrote to his wife in 1706 concerning her anxiety about their son Richard, then ill on the continent, he invoked the name of Welwood. The good doctor knew the attending physician treating the Molesworths' son, then aide-de-camp to the Duke of Marlborough, and reassured them that Dr. Ogle "will not fail making use of Jesuits' bark and blistering plasters."49 In Welwood's assumptions about efficacious therapies is a discernable mix of medical philosophies; Jesuits' bark for the specific treatment of recurrent fever and blistering for humoral balance. Like many of Welwood's friends, Molesworth was both politically active and intellectually accomplished. Irish-born, he sat in both Dublin and Westminster Parliaments, and was a member of the Irish privy council until 1713. Like Welwood, he was a widely-read author; his 1694 pamphlet, Account of Denmark, sold 6,000 copies in three editions. He translated Hotman's Franco-Gallia (1711) and promoted modern agricultural techniques. Robert Molesworth had seven sons and four daughters including the poet, Mary Monck.

Another missive between the elder Molesworths, dated 1721, discusses the efficacy of Robert's "old glyster (clyster)...for the wind colic. Yesterday I made use of it with good success by way of preventive, for when my body is brimful of wind, it will not receive a glyster." Seemingly, more was needed than the usual enema, for Dr. Welwood prescribed that the viscount drink "strong white wine with an ounce of bruised mustard seed infused in it, a glass twice a day, cold." However, Lord Molesworth's health did not improve and he had periodic painful bouts of gravel, stone, and strangury. A friend, Daniel Pulteney, wrote to John Molesworth in February 1725 that Dr. Welwood had been positive for years that it was an ulcer in the old man's bladder but that "these distempers are seldom cured, though there are intervals of ease; it is but too plain, in more instances than this, that physicians only guess, and as often mistake as hit right." Robert Molesworth died in May of that year.

The viscount's eldest son, John, was a commissioner of trade and plantations, and undertook many diplomatic missions. Polly Molesworth sent a note to him at Leiden in October 1719, informing him that a friend of theirs was very weak after childbirth but that Dr. Welwood, believing her consumptive, had ordered the patient "to go into the country and drink asses' milk." Dr. Welwood knew of the salubrious effects of asses' milk from various dispensatories, like the *Pharmacopoeia Londinensis*. Under *assinus* is recorded:

> The milk is alexipharmick [poison antidote], nourishes and cleanses; it helps in consumptions, diseases of the stomach and lungs, impostumes and exulcerations of the reins [kidneys], stone in the bladder and gout; it loosens the belly, provokes urine and the terms. Outwardly it is costinetick [cosmetic], softens the gums, and eases arthritic pains; give inwardly from half a pint to a pint.[50]

Some continental pharmacopoeias included asses' milk in their list of simples and Welwood would have been familiar with a treatise by Friedrich Hoffman celebrating the "extraordinary virtues" of asses' milk in the cure of various diseases. Even in Georgian days, asses' milk was customarily prescribed as a tonic for weak constitutions; it was thought to be lighter and easier to digest than cow's milk.

Welwood was not alone in his preference for the countryside. Most health advice books printed in his lifetime regarded rural life as the norm; urban living was an artificial divergence that invited ancillary health risks. Many Galenists connected high population density and suffocating air with ill health, but almost anyone could claim practical expertise about health and the environment, drawing upon personal experience and traditional knowledge.[51]

Welwood's advice about health care sometimes extended beyond conventional diagnoses. In 1722 his son-in-law, Walter Molesworth, informed brother John Molesworth, then plenipotentiary in Turin, that Welwood warned about taking leave in Italy during the summer. The doctor recommended visiting Naples only in the winter. In the same missive, Walter lamented that his wife, Welwood's daughter, had been "sent out to Twittenham for the air and asses' milk." John Molesworth evidently inherited his father's intestinal troubles, for a letter from George Malcolm in May 1724 suggests that much discussion about his stomach, bowels, bladder and spleen had taken place in London. While in Italy John Molesworth had taken the waters at Pisa and Lucca on recommendation of his doctors, but evidently without relief. He had then traveled to Aix. Dr. Welwood told Molesworth to avoid "purging by irritation" because fevers resulted from such evacuations. Instead, perhaps resulting from his experiences on the wartime commission for the sick, Welwood recommended chewing rhubarb, about two grains shaved very thin, four or five times a day for about a month. "The rhubarb will strengthen your stomach, help digestion, correct these grumblings in the bowels, strengthen the hemoroidl (sic) vessels." Welwood also prescribed drinking and soaking in the baths at Aix to overcome the effects of "astringents unseasonably used." All of this was to be topped off by a nourishing chaser of asses' milk, a constant fixture in Welwood's pharmacopoeia. Unfortunately, John Molesworth died a few months after his father in 1726.

James Welwood had devoted most of his energies during the reign of Queen Anne to his classical writings and to his professional life. Whig fortunes reached a nadir in the last years of Anne's rule, and the Tories forced a conclusion in 1713 to the War of the Spanish Succession, planned by William III and carried on by Queen Anne. But the Whigs were the sponsors of legislation that provided for a smooth royal succession, which they had wisely anticipated during the joint monarchs' government. If both the Stuart sisters died without issue, the crown would pass to their Germanic cousins in Hanover. Though Anne tried mightily, enduring seventeen pregnancies before she was thirty-five years old, her only surviving child succumbed to scarlet fever in 1700. Therefore, when Queen Anne passed away in 1714, Georg Ludwig, the Elector of Hanover, became King of England. For their political myopia and reluctance to welcome the heir apparent, the Tories were excluded from ministerial office for fifty years. Once again, the Whigs and Dr. Welwood enjoyed kingly favor and court privilege as George I, the man whose accession they helped arrange, ascended the throne.

CHAPTER SEVEN

Dr. Welwood and Mrs. Howard

*D*uring the reign of George I an unlikely but affectionate nexus was established between septuagenarian Dr. James Welwood and Henrietta Howard, a royal courtesan half his age. Their acquaintance probably came about through his daughter, Elizabeth, a contemporary and correspondent of the woman, but they may have known of one another anyway because the circle of celebrity and social acceptability in Augustan Age London was small. Whatever its origin, the amity and sincerity of their relationship appears indisputable. The senescent doctor played a principal part in the woman's effort to shed or at least to silence her belligerent, cuckolded husband so that she might remain the mistress to the Prince of Wales. Though he was no stranger to political controversy himself, the ancient physician was a respected and righteous family man. Nevertheless, in the last year of his long life he provided useful support and advice to a royal paramour who abandoned her family to further her own fortunes.

Welwood's personal life had been steady and conventional. His marriage to Barbara Armor had produced three daughters, but the first Mrs. Welwood died sometime around 1700. James Welwood had three minor children to care for; he needed a wife and they needed a mother. At the age of fifty-one, he made a good match in 1703 with Elizabeth Tregonwell Seymour, daughter of Dorset gentry and widow of Henry

Seymour, younger son of the Speaker of the House of Commons. Coincidentally, it had been Edmund Ludlow's published letter to the Speaker which had upset Queen Mary and initiated Welwood's foray into the history of the Stuarts. Her authorized chronicler had married into the critics' camp!

Welwood's household had expanded considerably with his wedding to Elizabeth. The thirty-something bride had two children by Seymour, a son and daughter. She also brought £1000 to the marriage, and in a pre-nuptial agreement, the couple anticipated the possibility of more children. They had carefully planned how their respective monies might finance a country estate and house large enough for a bigger family.

James Welwood had come a long way from his days as a poor scholarship student at St. Andrews. Two of his daughters married advantageously. Welwood's eldest daughter, Mary, became the second wife in 1716 of Scotsman James Maxwell of Barncleugh, Irongray. Their daughter, Barbara, would one day return to Annandale with her husband, James Johnstone, and give birth to a son, Wellwood. Dr. Welwood's youngest daughter, Elizabeth, married into the aforementioned Molesworth family and remained in London. Dr. Welwood was particularly attached to his grandson and namesake, James Molesworth. Jane Welwood, his middle daughter, remained unmarried and at home with her father. Although there was some estrangement later from his stepson, Edward Seymour, relations among the other blended-family members were happy and loving. Dr. Welwood's manservant, William Lacy, and Mrs. Welwood's maid, Martha Wilson, lived with the couple for decades.

London during the Augustan Age effervesced with activity and growth. Welwood's own newspaper had advertised books in the 1690s about the city including *Angliae Metropolis*, an analysis of the conditions in London, its history, and its notable buildings. By 1700 the London conurbation, consisting of the old walled city plus its satellite communities of Westminster, Southwark, and East London, surpassed Paris to become the largest city in western Europe with a population of over 500,000. Daniel Defoe estimated that by the 1720s a million and a half souls called the metropolis home; more conservative calculations acknowledge over a million residents.[1] Immigration infused cosmopolitan London with a constant flow of newcomers, perhaps 8,000 net immigrants per year during the Augustan Age. Their contributions to London's economy were impressive. The influx of Huguenot textile workers made the English silk industry a major rival to the French. But unlike the ambitious apprentices who came to London in previous generations, many in the new wave of immigrants were poor and destitute, crowded into the small tenements of poor parishes. Despite his later reputation as a stalwart admirer of the capital, Dr. Samuel Johnson attained his first renown with a complaint against the city, in which he inquired whether anyone "would leave, unbrib'd, Hibernia's land, or change the rocks of Scotland for the Strand?"[2]

In fact, Dr. Welwood himself did live comfortably in the York Buildings near the Strand and close to the river, part of the urban development in the West End that emphasized the growing social segregation within greater London. In the 1680s property speculator Dr. Nicholas Barbon had developed the site, where the Duke of Buckingham's York House had stood, adjacent to a waterworks in Villiers Street. The Commission for the Sick and Wounded had met in the York Buildings when Dr. Welwood served on it, so Welwood was familiar with the neighborhood. Welwood probably moved to that location shortly after his second marriage, but he was certainly there by 1709 when he inscribed the placename on his Whitelocke preface.

Welwood's house was conveniently located off the Strand midway between the western limits of incorporated London, where the Royal College of Physicians was situated, and the seat of government in Westminster. In his prime he could walk from the York Buildings to Whitehall and St. James' Palace, to Dorman Newman's shop in the Poultry, or to the College in Warwick Lane; in his dotage he could commute by hired hackney coach. Dr. Welwood's neighbors — civil servants, government contractors, military officers, and professionals — depended on their proximity to Whitehall Palace or for the cachet of a good address. Barbon's developments typically formed around squares of courtyards and gardens. The four-story townhouses made of brick or stone did not front directly on a cluttered street, but on a peaceful green. Though in a suburb of the City, Welwood's community was crowded: a 1695 survey numbered more than 3600 houses in Welwood's parish and more than 400 houses in his ward. Average rents then within the parish ranged from £20-£40, making it among the most expensive neighborhoods. The Strand area bustled with business and residential life, a perfect urban mix of activity uses; coffee houses, including Graecian's, a favorite of Dr. Welwood's, dotted the area. Although the waterworks supplied 2,500 London houses, Christopher Wren had judged it clean and quiet enough for the community when he approved its construction as Surveyor-General. At the turn of the century, an octagonal tower of 70 feet had been added and the company used steam power to supply a reservoir at Marylebone. This, then, was the vista Welwood overlooked each day.[3]

Dr. Welwood was proud of his house and its furnishings, and his home saw frequent company. He had a significant collection of artwork, portraits, engravings and the like, which decorated the lower floors. Welwood owned enough pictures that he bequeathed any five that she might choose to his widow, the rest staying with the house for his principal beneficiary, his daughter Jane. Large numbers of ambitious professionals, especially physicians like Welwood, commissioned por-traits of family members painted in the fashionable half-length "Kit-Kat" size, so-called because more than forty eminent members of the famed Whig club had their likenesses drawn by Godfrey Kneller in that style. The painted subjects look rather melancholy because that was the cultural mode in portraiture. The appearance of public severity intentionally demonstrated the intellectual and civic excellence of this small group of clever and powerful people who lived between Whitehall and the City. Kneller charged £50 for a full-length picture, less for a smaller canvas, and although most of the background work was done by assistants, Kneller painted the subject's face. In art as in everything else, Whigs and Tories differed; the Tories patronized Swedish painter Michael Dahl.[4]

Like many London doctors, James Welwood was content with one capacious townhouse and did not feel the urge to set himself up as a country squire. Having no sons may have influenced his decision to eschew landowning instead of more easily divisible assets. During his later years Welwood became an active parishioner at St. Martin's-in-the-Fields, the Anglican church just around the corner from his home. The foundation stone for the rectangular basilica was laid in March 1721 and construction continued until 1726. A coal tax was passed in 1711 to finance fifty new churches in London after the Great Fire, but only twelve completely new churches were built. St. Martin's was erected by contributions from its membership, generous enough to purchase a remarkable 215 feet-high steeple. As a member of the affluent congregation, Welwood contributed handsomely to the project. So whatever the religious persuasion of his youth, Welwood certainly attended mainstream Church of England services in his later London years; in fact the vicar of St. Martin's while Welwood was among the congregation became Archbishop of Canterbury. One wonders what the spirit of John Welwood would have made of his brother's compliance with prelates.

Surely Welwood expected to enjoy the final chapter of his life in peace and relative contentment, communicating with politically agreeable souls, translating the occasional ancient text, and exchanging books with fellow bibliophiles. He wrote often to a friend and fellow physician in Newcastle, Dr. Cage, mainly about politics and international affairs in the same manner as he had presented the news of the day to the readers of *Mercurius Reformatus*. Among his close associates in London were Lawrence Echard and Hans Sloane. Echard, chaplain to William Wake, the Archbishop of Canterbury, shared Welwood's fondness for history and the classics; he wrote a multi-volume history of England that stretched from Julius Caesar to George I. Without independent means, Echard confessed, common authors like himself had difficulty maintaining their integrity and telling the truth. Like Welwood, Echard damned James II as a Catholicizing absolutist and hailed King William as the nation's savior, but Echard chose to praise Tory leaders and accept their explanation that James had forfeited his throne by desertion. Echard's compliments to the Tories differentiated his books from his competitors and show the range of Whig writing. Nevertheless, he was strongly influenced by Dr. Welwood's *Memoirs* and borrowed extensively from Welwood's analysis of the early Stuarts.[5] Echard's history remained enormously popular through several editions despite criticisms that the author was too credulous with his sources, especially Clarendon's history. For instance, he included a report of Oliver Cromwell's interview with the devil on the morning of the battle of Worcester.

Though nearly twenty years Welwood's junior, Echard suffered from serious ill health that brought him to London in 1722 where George I bestowed on him the revenues of two manors in Suffolk. Although they differed on many political questions, Echard and Welwood became close comrades when the former penned a work on the Glorious Revolution which included a review of the Stuarts. A member of the Society of Antiquaries that met weekly at the Bear Tavern in the Strand, Echard published a spate of books on subjects as diverse as the comedies of Terence and Plautus to the geography of the Netherlands. His books were translated into French, Italian, and Spanish. Though Welwood did not participate in the Society's affairs and was never a member, Echard and he were remarkably alike in their intellectual pursuits.

Hans Sloane, another crony of Welwood and fellow Whig, is remembered as president of both the Royal College of Physicians and the Royal Society. Like Welwood, Sloane claimed Scottish heritage, his father having been head of a colony settled in Ulster by James I. Like Welwood, he had gotten his medical degree in 1684 in France, at Orange, in a tiny principality in the south not subject to the French king, from which the Princes of Orange derived their name and which did not persecute Protestants. He, too, had seen the effects of Louis XIV's religious encroachments when the king forbade the levying on Catholics of a tithe to support the university and the resultant threat of the school's closure. When the delinquent salaries of the professors and pastors there were paid by the Princess of Orange, Sloane, like Welwood, became a devoted admirer of the future queen.

Hans Sloane joined the Royal College of Physicians in 1687 and spent the Revolution of 1688 in Jamaica, having accompanied the Duke of Albemarle as attending physician. Sloane typified the interests of the amateur natural historian and accumulated a significant collection of Caribbean flora and fauna. Parliament eventually purchased Sloane's curiosities and souvenirs, which he insisted be kept together, for £20,000 as the foundation for what would become the British Museum. His library was justly celebrated, containing more than 50,000 volumes and over 4100 manuscripts. During Welwood's lifetime Sloane's library tempted the old doctor to borrow books including one about his cherished Fifeshire.[6] Like Welwood, Sloane authored only one medical publication, a piece on sore eyes, but he was often consulted by Queen Anne, who like her sister suffered from that affliction. He later became physician-general to the army, and first physician to King George II. Abstemious in his habits, Sloane lived to be ninety-two, and when he died he left his botanical garden in Chelsea to the London apothecaries. He and Welwood clearly had much in common; the fraternity of these two successful medical men seems almost inevitable.

Like many a professional raised up by good fortune and hard work from humble origins, Welwood enjoyed the good life of Augustan England, respected by family and colleagues. He surely counted on a peaceful dotage free from the strife of his youth and middle age. Only a random medical emergency might be expected to disturb Welwood's otherwise placid life, such as when he was called upon to tend to the loser in a duel between Scottish factions in the capital. In July 1716 Welwood was summoned by the Gordon family to attend to fatally-wounded Major Cathcart, pierced through the heart and lungs during a very bloody swordfight in a Kensington field. Dr. Welwood found that the other duelist, Alexander Gordon, was dying from six separate wounds. Since the families were known to have opposing political views, the fairness of the fight became an issue and Welwood had to testify at the coroner's inquest the following day.[7] Dr. Welwood, incidentally, having put down his political pen, had nothing at all to say about the issue that split those Scottish families, the 1715 Jacobite uprising in Scotland on behalf of James Edward Stuart, the ill-fated "warming pan baby." He would have opposed the revolt in the sternest terms and approved the eventual transplanting of vanquished rebels by the London government. This was surely a topic Welwood would have discussed thoroughly with his circle of Scottish compatriots in London.

Despite the deadly duel episode, for the most part, Welwood's life in early Georgian London was calm, predictable, and in keeping with the gravity of his profession. But then he got enmeshed in the personal lives of Henrietta Howard, her husband, Charles, and her lover, the Prince of Wales. Seventy-five year-old Dr. James Welwood became a go-between during the final marital crisis of the Howards, delivering letters to all points of the royal triangle, and acting as a trustee for Mrs. Howard. During one fateful year, which was to be his last, Welwood personally interceded in the nasty Howard domestic upheaval and separation.

The intersection of the lives of Dr. Welwood and Mrs. Howard is fascinating, brief, and quizzical. There was no intertwining of interests, no history of fraternal connections, no evidence of mutual bond of background, education or place. The implausible friendship of Dr. Welwood and Mrs. Howard was evident only at the end of his life and at the middle of hers. James Welwood was elderly, university-trained, and a member of his profession's most prestigious circle. Henrietta Howard was half his age, and her sole claim to fame was being Prince George Augustus' mistress. Dr. Welwood was opinionated about politics, while Mrs. Howard so assiduously avoided partisan bickering that she became known as "the Swiss," and her apartments "the Cantons."[8]

Neither politics nor possibility of gain appear to have motivated Welwood, but at a time in his life when it would have been wiser to shun stressful situations, the doctor served as peacemaker among irreconcilable parties. In addition, Welwood was a devoted family man, whose relationships with spouse and offspring were profound and lifelong. Indeed, it was probably his devotion to the memory of his youngest daughter, Elizabeth, a confidante of Mrs. Howard, that propelled him into such turbulent circumstances. For her part, Mrs. Howard forsook husband and child to enjoy the life of a courtesan, and to establish separate residence from them even after royal ardor had cooled. Finally, Welwood's life was characterized by serious vocation, avocation and public service. The motif of Henrietta Howard's life was one of affable opportunism and self-promotion. They were the unlikeliest of friends.

Henrietta Hobart Howard, later the Countess of Suffolk, was the eldest daughter of Henry Hobart, a Norfolk ne'er-do-well who was killed in a duel while Henrietta was still a girl. As with other celebrated women, the actual date of Henrietta's birth is a matter of some dispute. She may have been born as early as 1681 or as late as 1688.[9] Henrietta certainly told acquaintances that she, like her good friend Alexander Pope, was born in the year of the Glorious Revolution, and that she had married very young. Youthfulness in a woman, then as now, was valued more than maturity.

Women in the Augustan Age were defined by their gender, by their relationship to a man, and by their social class. The motif of Henrietta's life was her desire for financial security and social significance, but there were few ways in early modern England by which a woman might attain those goals. There were even fewer options for females of the gentry because they were valued principally for their dowries and reproductive abilities. Education, the route to success pursued by Welwood and other professional men, was of little monetary value to Henrietta since respectable careers were not open to women. Since the Protestant Reformation, upward mobility in an order of nuns, an attractive alternative for many intelligent females to an unhappy arranged marriage, was precluded. At any rate, Henrietta Hobart was neither studious nor devout. Earning a living was possible, of course, and many women of Henrietta's class supported themselves by writing, painting, and other genteel pursuits.[10] But Henrietta Hobart had few apparent marketable talents and aspired to a sumptuous lifestyle.

The only real option for her seemed to be attachment to a wealthy man, either as a wife or a mistress. Marriage was naturally preferred since it conveyed respectability and permanence, but marriage to someone like her father was unacceptable to Henrietta. She desired the cachet of aristocracy because she expected it to bring riches. Likewise, she would have hoped for someone with a town house to complement his country estate; most women in Augustan England embraced urban life as a deliverance from the boredom and restrictions of the country-side.[11] However, the stresses of marrying any unsuitable man were terrible for a woman in Henrietta's time, especially since death or desertion was the only escape.

A sexual revolution in England accompanied the Stuart Restoration, partly in reaction to Puritanism and partly in recognition of freedom of expression. Frank and hedonistic eroticism deeply affected the upper classes which practiced a libertinism characterized by adultery and illegitimacy.[12] The higher the level of society, the greater the promiscuity. Extra-marital liaisons increased among the court aristocracy, were popularized in a new literary genre, and spread slowly to the rural elite. Upper-class girls, especially those married to incompatible husbands, were bombarded with invitations to adultery by married and unmarried men of their own social status. Kings and princes were particularly generous to their ladies, even those of less-than-gentle rank, as the last of the Stuart men had shown. Charles II had supported a remarkable series of women and their offspring, providing for them at court or at lavish country mansions built for their pleasure; even the dour William III had kept a royal mistress.

Rejection of matrimonial chastity as "the clog of all pleasure, the luggage of life," continued into the eighteenth century. The magazine *Town and Country* featured a prominent gentleman and his mistress in each monthly edition, turning the women into quasi-respectable celebrities. Young Henrietta Hobart knew that many powerful aristocrats, even outwardly uxorious ones, had mistresses who were rewarded handsomely.

Nevertheless, in 1706, hoping to significantly raise her social status, Henrietta married Charles Howard, third son of the Earl of Suffolk. From its inception the marriage disappointed her. Howard had no patrimony, and although Henrietta had a dowry of £6000, she soon learned how quickly money could be squandered. At the time of their marriage, £2000 of her dowry was settled on Henrietta's husband and soon dissipated in drink. The Howards' only child, Henry, was born in 1707. Forced by financial need to anticipate the Hanoverian succession and to ingratiate themselves with the future ruling family, the Howards moved to Germany and into the social circle of the prospective royalty.

Due to their rather moderate financial standing, the extravagant entertaining necessary to capture the notice of the Electress Sophie and her son was stressful. Henrietta told more than one companion that she had to sell her beautiful hair to pay for dinners and soirees meant to ingratiate the English couple with potential ministers and patrons. Surprisingly, their strategy worked, for soon Henrietta became a darling of the aged Sophie and her grandson's wife, Caroline of Ansbach. Moreover, Sophie encouraged camaraderie between Henrietta and her grandson, George, insisting that Mrs. Howard could teach the future king English.[13] According to Countess Mary Cowper, Lady of the Bedchamber to Caroline, promises of reward were made before the Howards left for London in 1713, where they racked up such debts that they occasionally used the name "Smith" to make purchases on credit.[14] Eventually, the promises were redeemed as both Howards received appointments in 1714 when Queen Anne died, preceded seven weeks in death by the eighty-four year old Electress, and the House of Hanover moved to England. Mr. Howard became Groom of the

Bedchamber to King George I and Mrs. Howard was named a woman of the Bedchamber to Caroline, Princess of Wales.

In spite of their collective good fortune, Henrietta disliked her marriage. Like many women of the Augustan Age, she doubted the efficacy of the institution. In a 1716 reflection on the marital state, curiously omitted from John Wilson Croker's edition of her letters, she bemoaned her fate and that of other women: "I know many miserable wives from man's tyranny and power as I know unhappy and ridiculous husbands only made so by much indulgence; nay do I know one single instance where great tenderness is attended with submission to a woman's will."[15] Perhaps Henrietta was persuaded that married life was less than satisfactory by the myriad of unhappy unions about which she knew. It certainly seemed that marital discontent reached epidemic proportions among the elite, and, of course, the only people she knew were of the upper classes. She might have found more spousal contentment prevalent among the middle classes. On the other hand, noble mistresses, like the romantic heroines of the chivalric troubadours in the Middle Ages, were often treated very well. An open breach between the Howards was apparent by 1717.

For whatever reason, Henrietta Howard became the mistress of George, the Prince of Wales. Two catalytic events may have propelled her into his arms. The first was the spectacular estrangement of George I and the Prince in 1717 over a question of familial prerogative in the naming of a godfather to the newest royal grandson. Already mutually disdainful and jealous of each other's political bases, their quarrel escalated beyond reason, and the Waleses were forced to leave the palace. Henrietta accompanied them to their new apartments in Leicester House and to a livelier political galaxy to rival that of the king. Her husband stayed on at St. James' with the king's entourage. Mrs. Howard's friend, Horace Walpole, called Howard "worthless and contemptible," but it was Henrietta who did not take her young son with her. Later documents suggest that the boy remained with his father and became permanently estranged from his mother.[16]

Mrs. Howard emerged as one of the most admired women at the alternative court, sought out by office-seekers and literati alike who appreciated her connections, personality, and discretion. Horace Walpole asserted that Tories Lord Bolingbroke secretly and Jonathan

Swift openly had cultivated Henrietta's approbation for political purposes, though he concurred with the opinion that her influence on the Cabinet was negligible. Lord Peterborough, a roué old enough to be her grandfather, pursued her unsuccessfully, writing her adolescent verse. She was not a beauty; contemporaries thought her face plain and her figure fleshy. The great wit Lord Chesterfield called her a "specimen of [George's] bad taste and strong stomach." But, according to Lord Hervey, who was married to another of Caroline's attendants, Henrietta was "civil to everybody, friendly to man, and unjust to none."[17] Swift, while in her favor, described Henrietta as "an excellent companion for men of the best accomplishments who have nothing to ask." Alexander Pope sought her company and wrote:

> I know a thing that's most uncommon.
> > (Envy be silent and attend!)
> I know a remarkable woman,
> > Handsome and witty, yet a friend.
> Not warped by passion, aw'd by rumour,
> > Not grave through pride, or gay through folly,
> And an equal mixture of good humour,
> > And sensible soft melancholy.[18]

Mrs. Howard's liaison with the Prince commenced from their common residence at Leicester House.

The second factor in making Mrs. Howard mistress *en titre* was the failure of the Prince's attempted flirtation with Mary Bellenden, maid of honor to the Princess and Henrietta's friend. In 1720 Miss Bellenden, considered the most attractive woman in the Leicester House faction, secretly married John Campbell, 2nd Duke of Argyll. The Prince was humiliated by this rejection, and turned to the dependable Mrs. Howard. She quickly accepted the role. There was nothing degrading or shocking in her new status, for prominent wives were as freely unfaithful as their husbands. Female adultery in high circles was estimated a fashionable vice rather than a crime.

A final factor nudging the Prince in the direction of Mrs. Howard was the apparent approval of Princess Caroline in her husband's choice of a lover. Caroline never lost her controlling influence with the Prince and was able to establish a *modus vivendi* with Mrs. Howard that lasted until 1734. Horace Walpole recalled that the Princess reveled in employing Mrs. Howard "in the most servile offices about her person." Prince George once criticized the way that Mrs. Howard dressed Caroline, snatching a scarf from around the Princess' neck and complaining that "because you have an ugly neck yourself, you love to hide [hers]."[19] Caroline understood, no doubt, that things could have been worse, and even expressed regret at Henrietta's ultimate fall from royal esteem. Other mistresses might not be so agreeable and moderate in their demands or so apolitical either!

Among the friends with whom Henrietta Howard corresponded was Dr. Welwood's daughter, Elizabeth Welwood Molesworth. She was the wife of Captain Walter Molesworth, a veteran of the Spanish war and fifth son of Viscount Molesworth. According to Croker, the match was "a stolen one" which Henrietta protected.[20] Affectionate letters were exchanged between the women including two in 1720 which mention the soaring value of South Sea Company stock. When George I became king there were three great financial corporations in London— the Bank of England, the East India Company and the South Sea Company. All three had received their privileges by making loans to the government and by taking over portions of the national debt. Tory leader Robert Harley chartered the South Sea Company in 1711 to compete with the Whig-founded Bank of England and to procure political support as he negotiated an end to the War of the Spanish Succession. Holders of unfunded government debt had to exchange their securities for company stock. Promoters promised that the company would benefit from an Anglo-Spanish provision in the Treaty of Utrecht. According to the peace terms ending the war, England received the asiento, a monopoly on the slave trade into Spanish ports in South America and the South Seas. Though less profitable than anticipated, the Company held the rights to that monopoly and stock prices rose.

Walter Molesworth charted the progress of the speculative venture; in a 1719 letter to his brother on the Continent, he reported that an acquaintance told him of a £500 investment made the previous year that was now selling for £9,000. "Would to God we had all of us had the money and luck to have done the same."[21] As for the Molesworths, "our lottery is now drawing, wherein we [Betty and I] have six tickets among us." Offering its own stock in exchange for government bonds, in early 1720 the Company proposed to assume responsibility for the entire national debt, a transaction which it assumed would be lucrative for the shareholders. The government accepted the proposal and stock prices skyrocketed from £128½ in January to £1000 in August.[22] In April 1720, Mrs. Molesworth wrote that Mrs. Howard, who had earlier invested in the company, must be happy over the meteoric rise of the shares, and noted that Mr. Molesworth, now himself a shareholder, had "celebrated drunkenly with his men."[23] Writing from Axminster in June, Mrs. Molesworth again congratulated Mrs. Howard on her early stock investment, and wished that she had been as lucky. By her calculations, Mrs. Howard's shares had risen over 500%. "I am almost South Sea mad…and…cannot without regret reflect that for want of a little money, I am forced to let slip an opportunity which is never likely to happen again." But James Welwood had already made some investment in the Company possible for his daughter. Mrs. Molesworth reported in the same letter that Lady Sunderland, Molesworth's cousin, had at last secured a £500 subscription for them, "which money my father laid down for us."[24] No doubt Mrs. Molesworth wished she had considerably more to put into such a sure scheme.

However, the South Sea Bubble burst in September 1720. Banks that could not collect loans on the inflated stock failed and thousands of investors were ruined, including many in government. The Prince and Princess of Wales, royal ladies, and even the king had gambled in South Sea stock. England was thrown into a period of political strife and turmoil. In the midst of the uproar, *The London Journal* published letters from "Cato" that were highly critical of George I's government and ministers. Recent readings of "Cato's Letters" categorize the authors as Country opposition writers who attacked governmental methods and measures they considered detrimental to the political and economic independence of the propertied classes. Country writers argued their case in moral and constitutional terms, suggesting that placemen in the House of Commons and in the army subverted a balanced constitution by embodying the interests of the Court. Furthermore, they vigorously opposed long Parliaments and infrequent elections. Among those connected with the newspaper were Sir John Trenchard, son of William III's Secretary of State; Benjamin Norton Defoe, natural son of the famous Daniel; and Lord Molesworth,

Welwood's in-law. Gossips of the day credited Molesworth, then an outstanding Parliamentary leader of the opposition, with being chief author, and John Molesworth received compliments as "Cato's son" from more than one admirer. However, Walter Molesworth, writing to his brother, claimed that their father "never was the author of any personal or scurrilous reflections" which had angered the government toward him.[25] Nonetheless, the Molesworths' association with a newspaper excoriated by the government must have made Dr. Welwood smile.

Robert Walpole, a Whig minister who himself had lost a considerable amount of money, was called upon to salvage the financial wreckage. While stalling revenge schemes aimed at the Company's directors, Walpole restored and reorganized the Company and through a series of legislative measures forbade future unincorporated joint stock ventures. In 1721 the king appointed Walpole both first lord of the treasury and chancellor of the exchequer; Walpole is usually referred to as the first Prime Minister though he shared power with others in government until 1730. Walpole's ascendancy may have been made possible by the South Sea Bubble, but shareholders were not so fortunate. The playwright John Gay, a close friend to Mrs. Howard, had made £20,000 off an initial investment of £1,000, but ignoring advice to sell, he continued to speculate and lost everything. Those who had invested late, as had the younger Molesworths, lost the most.

Elizabeth Welwood Molesworth died in 1725, but Mrs. Howard maintained contact with her family. Walter Molesworth, now a widower and in need of employment, wrote to Henrietta early in 1727 asking her to help him become the Prince's groom or equerry and that he would then reciprocate with "whatever conditions or provisos you may annex to this favor." Mrs. Howard was evidently insulted by his implication, and said as much to another Welwood daughter, Barbara, because Captain Molesworth later wrote to apologize. He mentioned that his sister-in-law had told him of Henrietta's complaint. In spite of whatever umbrage she took at Molesworth's approach to office-seeking, she did recommend her late friend's husband to the Duke of Argyll.[26] Perhaps Henrietta used her influence for Dr. Welwood's son-in-law because the old physician was then currently serving her need for a respected and venerable go-between.

The already nominal marriage of the Howards began to dissolve in the stresses produced by the family quarrels of the House of Hanover. When Henrietta departed from the royal palace in 1717 to live with the Prince and Princess of Wales, Mr. Howard had demanded that she return and remain under his husbandly supervision. Under "injunction" from George I, who particularly disliked Princess Caroline, Mr. Howard insisted that Henrietta leave the Princess' service. Her polite refusal infuriated Howard; he wrote to her that "(your) unparalleled...behavior to me has twice endangered my mind." He asserted that he was just as determined as she, and threatened to bring the law to bear on his side, since her virtue and reason seemed to have disappeared. Henrietta placed the blame for their separation on Mr. Howard, accusing him of abandoning her and failing to recognize her duty to Her Royal Highness. Since she said she had good reason to fear her husband's temper, she was sure the law would protect her. She insisted she was acting on her own impulses and that her history with Howard convinced her that "it is absolutely necessary to have some regard for my own preservation, though it should not for the present be altogether agreeable to the notions you have conceived."[27]

When a reconciliation of sorts between the king and the Waleses, engineered by Robert Walpole, took place in the spring of 1720, Mr. Howard became more amenable to a financial settlement in lieu of her presence, no doubt apprised of Henrietta's influence with the Prince and other prominent individuals. Henrietta's friends in the Tory literary clique included Swift, Pope, Gay, and Dr. John Arbuthnot, the latter like Welwood a writer and royal physician to Queen Anne. They urged her to avoid any coerced payoff to Howard and sympathized with her during this period of harassment. By 1723 Mr. Howard was aware that the Prince was contributing £12,000 toward the building of a house for Mrs. Howard, conveniently located at Marble Hill in Twickenham, just across the river from the Prince's summer palace at Richmond. Mary Bellenden's husband, the Duke of Argyll, and his brother, Lord Isley, were the trustees of the monies the Prince gave to Mrs. Howard for her villa. But Mr. Howard had procured no settlement for himself by 1726 and, again prodded by an angry George I, he reverted to his demand that Henrietta return to him.[28] The Howards' war of words resumed, and this time a prominent role in the fracas was reserved for old Dr. Welwood.

Charles Howard wanted to pry his wife away from the Waleses by any means. He tried appealing to her maternal responsibility: "if you have any thought of ease to the small posterity of a child you seemed to love, how ungrateful and shocking a part he must share in life." Henrietta, however, would not be moved:

> You mention, Sir, a tender subject indeed, my child. I wish to God he was of a riper age and so be judge between us. I cannot but flatter myself he would have more duty and humanity than to desire to see his mother exposed to misery and want, if not by his father's commands, but yet worse by the influence men in power have over him for the poor precarious expectation of Court favours.[29]

There is, however, no evidence that she wrote to or communicated with her son at any time during the family's disintegration.

Becoming desperate, Mr. Howard then wrote directly to Caroline in April 1726 and mentioned the command of the king that Henrietta "immediately retire from her employment under Your Royal Highness." He noted that he himself had been unsuccessful in his exhortation to Mrs. Howard, and that the situation caused him great distress. A week later Henrietta received word from Howard that the King had "personally directed...(her) removal...and expected her immediate compliance."[30]

Mr. Howard also enlisted the aid of the Lawrence Echard's patron, the Archbishop of Canterbury, in breaking Henrietta's resolve to stay with the royals. William Wake wrote to the Princess urging her to avoid the unpleasant publicity Howard's threatened writ might cause. Wake suggested that the Princess' enemies might be behind the situation, and that the only way to defuse the potential explosion was to send Henrietta away. Henrietta later recalled for her friend Horace Walpole that the letter from the Archbishop was presented with "malicious pleasure" to Henrietta by Caroline herself.[31] There seemed to be good reason for fearing embarrassment from Howard; he had already appeared loudly drunk before the guards in the quadrangle at St. James', demanding vociferously that Henrietta be restored to him.

Even more outrageous was Mr. Howard's accosting Caroline herself

in her quarters and threatening to pull Henrietta from the Princess'
coach if he found her in it. Caroline reported the incident to her friend,
Lord Hervey. She said that she had taunted Mr. Howard to "do it if
he dare," though she admitted being afraid of him because he was
"brutal, indeed a little mad, and seldom quite sober." The Princess
recounted that she thought he might throw her out of the open
interview-room window right then, so she eased towards the door and
safety. When Howard persisted that he would complain to King George
about the matter, the Princess retorted that the King had nothing to
do with her servants.[32]

Mrs. Howard had her allies and intercessors, too. Dr. Welwood
became an important part of the communications network established
by the Howards to put pressure on one another. Both Howards sent
messages via Welwood, and as the haggling over her dowry resumed,
Henrietta named Dr. Welwood and her brother, John Hobart, trustees
of her money.[33] Henrietta often asked Welwood to deliver letters to
her husband and to wait to see his reaction. In early May 1726
Welwood performed such a task for Mrs. Howard, and during a
discussion with her husband, Welwood was shown the Archbishop's
letter to Caroline, as well as letters to Howard from Wake and the
Princess. Howard pointedly remarked to Welwood that the Princess
had no desire to keep Henrietta from her husband, and "that every
disinterested person living, who does not flatter [her], and encourage
this misbehavior in [her], is ashamed to think of [her] treatment of
me."[34] Mr. Howard had Welwood personally transcribe the epistles to
present to Henrietta.

Dr. Welwood did not immediately confront Henrietta with the
documents, but he did report to her that Mr. Howard was highly
incensed at her letters to him. He offered the advice that it did not
seem wise to treat her husband's demands "roughly, which is still his
great complaint. Time may wear out both private and public impres-
sions and being passive sometimes is of great use in the conduct of
life."[35] He promised to "spare no pains to put an end to this affair"
and to continue in her service until the matter was settled to her
satisfaction.

To avoid subsequent wrangles with her estranged husband, Mrs.
Howard left London for Richmond. Safely ensconced away from the

city and bothered by headaches and worsening premature deafness, Henrietta once again turned to Dr. Welwood for assistance, although she never appears to have consulted with Welwood about illness.[36] She appreciated the old man's chivalric efforts:

> I am extremely obliged to you and shall always be ready to ac-
> knowledge that handsome manner with which you show yourself my
> friend. The thanks you refuse convinces me that I am much in-
> debted. Those who are most capable of doing an act of friendship
> are often those who endeavour most to conceal it."[37]

Henrietta confided in Welwood that she thought the time might be auspicious to bring about a financial settlement with her husband. Mrs. Howard proposed that Caroline give Mr. Howard £1,200 per year to let her stay with the Waleses. Caroline rebutted that suggestion with the quip that it was too much to expect her to keep the king's *guenipes* under her roof and to pay them, too![38]

The final extant missive between Mrs. Howard and Welwood from the spring of 1726 informed the old physician that Mr. Howard no longer appeared intent on prosecuting his side of the affair. Henrietta asked Welwood to see him again, to tell Howard how explicitly she trusted Welwood as an intermediary, and to "use all your [influence on] him" to bring the matter to closure. She reiterated her determination "for me ever willingly to live with him or quit this family whose service defends me from ... poverty, want...and ill-treatment."[39]

The rancorous marital bickering between Henrietta and Charles continued for many months, but Welwood did not live to see the denouement of the Howard brouhaha. He died at home April 2, 1727, and Mrs. Howard turned to other friends and acquaintances for advice and assistance as she battled for freedom from her husband. After the accession of George II to the throne in June 1727, Charles Howard accepted a separation settlement of £1200 per annum, funneled from the king through Mrs. Howard's increased allowance.

Though apparently prominent and influential during the first years of the new reign, Mrs. Howard's place in the king's affections soon began to wane. However, as Welwood might have described it, fortune continued to fancy Henrietta. Despite the odds against his succeeding to the family earldom, Charles Howard became Earl of Suffolk in 1731.

Ironically, it was because of Henrietta's new status as Countess of Suffolk that Queen Caroline elevated her to groom of the stole; Henrietta further prospered when her still-estranged husband died in 1733, and in the following year, effectively discarded by the king but with her dignity intact, she retired from court to Marble Hill. Queen Caroline was sorry to see her go, because she always regarded Mrs. Howard as no real threat at all to her own pre-eminence in the king's affections. When George heard of his wife's efforts to persuade his mistress to remain, he reprimanded her, teasing that he did not want an "old, dull, deaf, peevish beast stay to plague" him.[40] In 1735 Henrietta married an old friend, George Berkeley, with whom she enjoyed a happy life until his death in 1747. Though twelve years his senior, Henrietta survived Berkeley by twenty years, still surrounded by admiring and talented people.

In her dotage Henrietta reminisced about the glorious, hectic days when she was a most celebrated woman, loved by a prince but married to a beast. She owed at least some measure of thanks to the avuncular Dr. Welwood, who tried to extricate her from an unpleasantly notorious situation for the sake of her happiness. Politics do not appear to have entered Welwood's considerations, and he was never associated with the Leicester House faction. He refused any tokens of appreciation during his time as go-between, but may have been motivated by the memory of a beloved daughter whom Henrietta had befriended. Whatever the reasons for his activity on her behalf in the imbroglio with her husband, James Welwood had served the Countess of Suffolk well.

Epilogue

Dr. James Welwood had also served his family well, and they mourned his passing. A funeral of sufficient note was held that the College of Heralds recorded its contribution to the event. It was the custom among notable families in Augustan London to set a square tablet bearing the coat of arms of the deceased on the front of his home at the time of his death. These were called hatchments, probably from the word "achievement." Since Dr. Welwood had no ancestral bearings, one had to be conceived by herald painters. They created a sketch of the insignia emblemizing Welwood's family, complete with colors approved by the institution, and combined it for the hatchment in a pattern alongside his wife's arms, Tregonwell of Dorset. The purchase of a coat of arms from the Heralds' College, regulators of heraldry and blazonry since 1483, posthumously gave Dr. Welwood gentle standing recognized in law. In the midst of prayers and candles, Welwood was interred at midnight April 6, 1727, in vault number 2 of St. Martin's-in-the-Fields; six of his physician colleagues carried his coffin to the vault.

James Welwood's will tells a fascinating story of paternal devotion and attention to detail.[1] Prior to the mid-nineteenth century, the proving of wills and the granting of administrations lay with the ecclesiastical courts and some manorial courts. Place of death and size of the estate determined in which court a will would be probated. The Prerogative Court of Canterbury was the metropolitan probate court for the southern province. Situated in London, it had appellate jurisdiction throughout England and sole jurisdiction when the deceased had significant property in two bishoprics. Significant property (*bona notabilia*) was defined as £5 outside London, £10 in the City. The PCC also had authority over the estates of those who had died abroad or at sea in possession of English goods.

Court copies of probated wills and the inventories of estates provided by executors, mandatory until 1782, give important information about the deceased's wealth and intentions. James Welwood's last will and testament was signed and sealed in March 1727, just three weeks before he died. It replaced previous documents, which is not surprising given Welwood's long life, second marriage, and substantial estate. The first part of his will deals with a prenuptial indenture tripartite entered into in 1703 by Welwood and Elizabeth Seymour with two trustees to mutual investment. The contract called for an account to be set up and monitored by the trustees, for the possible purchase of land after the Welwoods' marriage. Welwood contributed £2000, and the widow Seymour £1000. But, perhaps because they had no more children and were comfortable in the York Buildings, the land was never purchased. After twenty years without offspring, they realized that their previous covenant was moot, and so had released one another by deed in 1723 from the terms of the earlier arrangement. Mrs. Welwood retained full disposal rights over the £1000 she had originally provided, with Dr. Welwood receiving the interest from her portion during his lifetime as well as his own £2000. Dr. Welwood named his unmarried daughter Jane as sole executrix and instructed her to pay his debts promptly.

He specified that Mrs. Welwood, his dear wife, was to inherit "all the furniture of and in the floor up one pair of stairs in my house in York Buildings wherein I now live except the pictures which hang in the said floor." He bequeathed her half the plate he owned and five of his pictures "as she shall think proper to choose from." He gave £500 each, "good and lawful money of Great Britain," to his daughter Mary Maxwell and to his son-in-law Walter Molesworth, expressing the wish that these sums be paid within a year of his death. He provided £10 to his servant William Lacy to be paid in six months "as a token of my love to him and his sister for faithful service to me." Lacy was one of three witnesses to Welwood's signature and seal. Jane Welwood got all the rest of the estate including the house and its valuable artwork.

It was rather unusual for a daughter to be named executor of her father's last testament, especially when his wife survived him and when there were sons-in-law available for the task. Urban widows normally served as executrices, particularly those in the capital, perhaps because city couples shared in business enterprises or because fewer men had male kin in town to serve as their executors. Dr. Welwood probably wished to spare his wife the burden of handling this task; older widows were least often named executrix even in cities. Clearly, Welwood was no misogynist, as he chose another female to do the job. Fourteen percent of the men in early modern England who did not choose their wives as executors made the decision to name a woman to that responsibility, but only 6.2% named a daughter.[2] Many men of Welwood's era viewed women incapable of civil, legal, or magisterial functions; indeed, there appears in copious anecdotal evidence an increasing reluctance to recognize women for any sort of trusteeship from 1700 onward. For instance, a man named Mark Brownell in his diary for 1729 noted that he had appointed a new executor, "women not being fit for lawsuits."[3] The active involvement of women in family finance declined as one moved up the social scale, so that although women were deemed important in pastoral econo-mies and in small urban enterprises they were not so regarded among the upper classes or even among the successful professionals like Welwood. Since the executor of an estate had to respond to any demands that the courts might make, James Welwood's choice of his daughter Jane as sole executrix demonstrated both affection and confidence in her abilities.

Elizabeth Seymour Welwood outlived her aged husband by only five years. She had moved away from the bustle of the Strand to a quieter, more fashionable neighborhood near Golden Square in Soho, bringing with her Martha Wilson and William Lacy. Mrs. Welwood's will illumines some of the domestic activity experienced by her side of the family.[4] She remained close to her step-daughter, Jane, and left her £50. However, relations between mother and her only son had been troubled for years as is quietly apparent in her testament. Mrs. Welwood bequeathed £50 and all of her wearing apparel to her maid and only £20 to Edward Seymour. No other mention is made of him in her will. In this respect, like Dr. Welwood, his widow chose to ignore convention and extend preferential favor to a female. Mrs. Welwood's daughter,

Mary, had married Sir Robert Munro and had presented her with three beloved grandchildren—Henry, George, and Elizabeth. From a trust established with the £1000 returned to her by Dr. Welwood, one which appears to have been producing substantial profits, Mrs. Welwood directed that Dame Mary Munro inherit the net estate with payments to be made periodically by the trustees. In other ways the widow's will followed custom; her executors were men and the priority of her secondary recipients reflected the weight of gender and birth order. Mrs. Welwood specified that should her daughter die, then her elder grandson, Henry, would be the chief beneficiary of the trust at age twenty-one; younger grandson George or any other male offspring of the Munros came next in line. If there were no surviving grandsons, then her granddaughter and namesake, Elizabeth, would get the bulk of the trust, but only on the occasion of a marriage consented to by both parents. Mrs. Welwood evidently was not ready to break too many traditions with her bequests. Like the good doctor, Mrs. Welwood was buried in the vault at St. Martin's-in-the-Fields after a funeral provided for in her will. The same heraldic painters who had created a hatchment for her husband devised one for the commemoration of Mrs. Welwood's death in 1732.

However, Dr. James Welwood's legacy was more than material. He was a harbinger of the Whig interpretation of English history, a Protestant and progressive view of the past which "draws lines through certain events, some such line as that which leads through Martin Luther and a long succession of Whigs to modern liberty."[5] The result is the imposition of a definite pattern upon the entire historical time-line and of a design that intersects tidily at the present. This method clearly manifests an axiom of progress: that Protestants and Whigs have been immutable partners climbing the summit to the twentieth century, while Catholics and Tories perennially obstruct that upward crusade. In the Whig interpretation, the ancient British constitution has survived to be enjoyed today, thanks to the ceaseless efforts of generations of Whigs and in spite of the impediments spawned by a series of Tories. The Whig historians who came after Welwood shared his appreciation of the catalytic role played by William of Orange in preserving that constitution. Moreover, because of their cheerful emphasis on the inevitability of progress, Whig historians tended to produce popular books with sweeping narratives, as did Welwood. His *Memoirs of the Most Material Transactions* appeared in a seventh edition in 1749; in 1820 a best-selling new issue, reprinted from the third edition of 1700, influenced the blossoming career of the most celebrated English historian of all time.

Thomas Babington Macaulay composed a prize-winning essay in 1822 which emphasized the dangerous dynamism produced by Manichaean political struggles during England's seventeenth century. With the pendulum of history swinging between anarchy and despotism, the nation was constantly threatened by fear and violence. Deprecating both Puritans and Tories, Macaulay found in the Whigs a moderation reminiscent of the Elizabethan *via media*. Like Welwood, Macaulay's hero was the Prince of Orange. Writing his *History of England* in 1848, the year of revolution, Macaulay praised William III's military achievements as head of the alliance against France: to check Louis XIV was "the single object of the highest calling." Macaulay also trumpeted the domestic accomplishments wrought by the king, particularly William's transformation of the political system. Macaulay credited the king with permanently ending the crippling cycle of indigenous mayhem in England in 1688. He excused the Whigs' anti-Catholicism as a necessary evil; though the Whigs were really latitudinarian, James' papist policies had left them no alternative. Like Welwood, he envisioned the Irish as "aboriginal" and the Act of Union with Scotland as a blessing.[6]

It should come as no surprise that there are many similarities in incidents highlighted and opinions expressed in the publications of James Welwood and the great Whig historian. Macaulay drew upon the writing of James Welwood to document his historical account. He specified Welwood's *Memoirs, Answer to the Late King James' Last Declaration*, and *Reflections upon the Late Horrid Conspiracy* as sources in his text, and referred to nine separate issues of *Mercurius Reformatus* for information in the tumultuous post-revolutionary years.[7] Welwood was a bridge from the Augustan Age to that of the Victorians, a forefather of the Whig interpretation of history.

One characteristic of Welwood and the other Augustan Age writers that Macaulay did not emulate was their fondness for the ancients. Macaulay criticized many of the Greek and Roman historians whom

Welwood specifically admired: Herodotus, Xenophon, Plutarch, and Livy. As did the Whig historians who followed him, Macaulay projected his times onto the past and vice versa. His own Whiggery led him to champion the Reform Bill of 1832, the passage of which the historian called an enlargement of the "Glorious Revolution."

Lord Macaulay's grand-nephew and biographer was George Macaulay Trevelyan, self-professed legatee of the Whig tradition. Like his great-uncle, Trevelyan expected that history also be considered literature; his stylish books blended theoretical shrewdness and romanticism without much recourse to the archives. Trevelyan did not cite Welwood's history in his 1904 *England under the Stuarts*, but relied on the books of Echard, Whitelocke, William Penn, and Bishop Burnet. Trevelyan quoted Burnet at length and called his view of natural rights "far ahead of his contemporaries," certainly more enlightened than the Tories, whom Trevelyan charged with hating the idea of Christian goodwill.[8] Like Welwood, Trevelyan regarded the evolution of religious toleration as the most meaningful achievement of seventeenth century Englishmen. He wrote:

> At a time, when the Continent was falling prey to despots, the English under the Stuarts had achieved their remarkable emancipation from monarchical tyranny by an act of national will; in an age of bigotry, their own divisions had forced them into religious toleration against their real wish.[9]

In *The English Revolution* (1938) Trevelyan suggested a new baptism for the heroic affair; he thought it ought to be called the "Sensible Revolution," not because it lacked glory, but because it was bloodless.

Sir J. H. Plumb, author of *The Growth of Political Stability* (1967), was Trevelyan's pupil. Plumb's works, like his mentor's, emphasize English political life, towering personalities, and the history of progress. Plumb's biographer has asserted that "by defending the utility of the study of history in the conventional sense, Plumb did not merely justify his own career and writings, but he also placed himself in the Whig tradition."[10] J. P. Kenyon, one of Plumb's protégés and now himself a venerable historical doyen, completed the chain when he wrote in an article about James II's deposition that "as is often the case, Macaulay had it exactly right."[11] A writer of popular history influenced by the

Whig interpretation was Sir Winston Churchill, demonstrating that this view of the past is not exclusively reserved to academics. In conclusion, one of Welwood's most enduring though unrecognized legacies was inspiring the scholarly lineage of Macaulay, Trevelyan, Plumb, and Kenyon, who in turn trained the current crop of traditional British historians and biographers.

Additionally, Welwood's other publications had both staying power and influence. His translation of Xenophon's *Banquet* remains the English-language standard to this day, often included in anthologies of the historian's works. His valuable exchange of letters with Vicar March define in lucid terms the allegiance controversy. The elegant but readable style of *Mercurius Reformatus* influenced Richard Steele's famous Whiggish periodical, *The Tatler* (1709-1711), and especially its successor, *The Spectator* (1711-1712), which Steele wrote with Joseph Addison. Addison's graceful prose engaged his readers' reason, and like Welwood, his political purpose was grounded in a solid education in the classics. The periodicals of Steele and Addison in turn helped to shape public opinion, giving great impetus to the growth of newswriting and journalism.

Despite the persistence of Welwood's written heritage and the availability of his published works, memory of the man began to fade by the end of the eighteenth century. It is lamentable that as the reputation of Welwood became dependent on vignettes recorded in antiquarian chronicles, Whig historians enamored with heroic narratives jettisoned his oeuvre as a source. Men of the second-tier of fame simply disappeared from sweeping sagas devoted to the few great politicos, medicos, or literati of his day, although Welwood contributed something to all three categories of celebrity. His name did resurface in the middle of the nineteenth century as part of a compilation of the membership in the Royal College of Physicians. The usually reliable William Munk had more questions than answers about Welwood in his entry in *Roll of the Royal College of Physicians of London*, published in 1861. Although Munk noted that Welwood was interested in political history, he was not entirely certain of the spelling of the doctor's name, suggesting that it may have been Velvud, and that he might have been a Danish cousin of James I's queen.[12] Moreover, Munk was not positive that Welwood had a medical degree at all, but if he did, Munk recorded it may have been from Padua. Moreover, Munk asserted without documentation that Welwood was a physician to William and Mary.

Dr. James Welwood was omitted completely from the first editions of the *Dictionary of National Biography*, but when his life was included in later editions, the details given were at best speculative, at worst horribly wrong. The first *D.N.B.* article about Welwood, authored by medical historian Norman Moore in 1891, gauged the doctor's birth as between 1650 and 1655, spelled his name as Wellwood, and labeled Robert of Touch and Jean Livingstone his parents. Moore also incorrectly identified Welwood's Scottish alma mater as Glasgow and his medical degree from Leiden. According to a mistaken Moore, Welwood returned to England with William of Orange; Welwood's family is never mentioned. A corrected sketch of Welwood's life by E. S. de Beer first appeared in 1932 in the *Bulletin for the Institute of Historical Research*, but another generation would have to wait for that correction to be widely available in a 1966 *D.N.B.* supplement.[13] De Beer properly determined the date of Welwood's birth, his parentage, and schools, although he did misunderstand the date of Welwood's undergraduate degree at St. Andrews.

James Welwood's place as a political writer and physician in Augustan England got a boost from the efforts of Donald Wing in 1945 to continue the cataloguing efforts of A.W. Pollard and G.R. Redgrave. Pollard and Redgrave inventoried early English books published between 1475 and 1640; Wing did the same for the period 1641-1700.[14] University Microfilms in conjunction with the British Library subsequently began microfilming early English books and newspapers from nearly the entire Tudor-Stuart era (1475-1700). Now, through interlibrary loan facilities, more than five thousand pieces can be obtained easily, including almost all of Welwood's writing along with the work of his fellow Whig polemicists and his Jacobite counterparts. The index to the Wing collection by subject as well as by author is particularly helpful to scholars. Welwood has also joined the pantheon of authors included in *English Historical Documents*, a popular sourcebook of excerpts from important commentators. Passages taken from *Memoirs of the Most Material Transactions* describe Charles II and the Duke of Monmouth.[15]

After James Welwood's death, the Welwood family continued to prosper in Britain, particularly the Scottish cousins who married into various influential families. Two generations later a daughter of the Welwoods of Garvock married a Maconochie; their son by means of entail assumed the name and arms of Welwood. Nineteenth-century Welwoods can be found among members of the Scottish Bench, in the Bengal Lancers, and as recipients of the Order of the British Empire. Most appropriately, in one of those twists only fate can accomplish, a twentieth-century Welwood descendant, Laurence Maconochie-Welwood, married Lady Elizabeth Henrietta Howard, youngest daughter of the 10th Earl of Carlisle.[16] Perhaps the ghosts of Dr. Welwood and the Countess of Suffolk made that happen.

Notes

Introduction

1. Dorothy Porter and Roy Porter, eds., *Doctors, Politics and Society: Historical Essays* (Amsterdam: Rodopi, 1993), 1-2.

2. So-called for the literati's fascination with the classics of the Rome of Augustus, the period from 1680-1730 has long been identified by scholars as a unit of historical cohesion spanning the Stuart-Hanover dynastic watershed.

3. Henry VIII created the Royal College of Physicians in 1518. In 1540 the London Guild of Surgeons united with the Barbers to form a joint livery company that lasted until 1745, when the Surgeons established a separate corporation. The Royal College of Surgeons received its first royal charter in 1800.

4. See F. W. Bateson, ed., *The Cambridge Bibliography of English Literature*, 2 (Cambridge: Cambridge University Press, 1966): 705, 763, 870.

5. James Welwood, *Mercurius Reformatus*, October 10, 1691.

6. Frank Sulloway, quoted in Robert S. Boynton, "The Birth of an Idea," *New Yorker* 7 October 1996, 72. Incidentally, Sulloway's thesis, that later-born children rebel against parental traditions, would seem to fit James Welwood, although Welwood "rebelled" by becoming a moderate member of the establishment. See Frank Sulloway, *Born to Rebel* (New York: Pantheon, 1996).

7. For Augustan Age anti-Catholicism, see John Miller, *Popery and Politics* (Cambridge: Cambridge University Press, 1973). Although some

Caroline Catholics may have behaved provocatively and Englishmen had understandable misgivings about the religious preferences of the Stuart monarchs, J. P. Kenyon calls the Protestant reaction of the late 1670s "paranoia." John Kenyon, *The Popish Plot* (New York: Penguin, 1974), 9.

Chapter One: Tumultuous Beginnings

1. Knox's successor, Andrew Melville, claimed that the Kirk should direct affairs of state and called James "God's silly vassal" to his face.

2. For more insight on the Scottish religious question, see F. N. McCoy, *Robert Baillie and the Second Scots Reformation* (Berkeley: University of California Press, 1974) or J. H. S. Burleigh, *A Church History of Scotland* (London: Oxford University Press, 1960).

3. James Welwood, *Appendix to Mercurius Reformatus* (London: Richard Baldwin, 1692), 3.

4. The Dunfermline parish valuations ranged from a low of £7 for one John Adie to a high of £2878 for Lord Yester. See Robert Sibbald, *History, Ancient and Modern, of the Sheriffdoms of Fife and Kinross*, rev. ed. (London: J. Watson, 1803), 440, 444, 454, 468. Dr. Sibbald, a charter fellow of the Royal College of Physicians of Edinburgh and member of the Royal College of Physicians in London, certainly knew James Welwood.

5. The author is indebted to Dr. Norman Reid, Keeper of the Manuscripts at the University of St. Andrews Library, for information contained in the minutes of the St. Andrews Presbytery meeting of 26 January 1643.

6. T. C. Smout, "Education and Poor Relief," *History of the Scottish People 1560-1830* (New York: Charles Scribner's Sons, 1969), 88-90.

7. Daniel Defoe, *A Tour through the Whole Island of Great Britain*, 2 vols. (London: Dent, 1962), 2: 315.

8. For more information on the general horrors of the witch-craze phenomenon see Brian P. Levack, *The Witch-Hunt in Early Modern Europe*, 2nd ed. (New York: Longman, 1995) and H.R. Trevor-Roper, *The European Witch-Craze* (New York: Harper and Row, 1969). Both authors connect witch-hunts with the religious struggles that pitted Christians against one another. Protestants or Catholics, when in the majority, attempted to stamp out the obdurate minority. For the Scottish witch-hunts see Christina Larner, *Enemies of God* (Baltimore: Johns Hopkins University Press, 1981).

9. William McDowall, *History of the Burgh of Dumfries* (Yorkshire: E.P. Publishers, 1972), 405-407.

10. Larner, 107. Known as "waking" or "watching" the witch, sleep deprivation became a routine method of extracting confessions.

11. See the remarks to the reader in Andrew Welwood, *Meditations Representing a Glimpse of Glory* (Boston: Rogers and Fowle, 1744), ix; Hew Scott, *Fasti Ecclesiae Scoticanae: Succession of Ministers in the Parish Churches of Scotland*, 3 Vols. (Edinburgh: William Paterson, 1867), 2: 661-62. The minister married a second time, siring another daughter.

12. Defoe, 590.

13. Searching for the Devil's Mark was an established tradition in Scottish witch-hunts. King James VI (later James I of England) recommended this procedure to determine if a suspect had made a pact with Satan. See Brian Levack, "The Great Scottish Witch Hunt of 1661-1662", *Journal of British Studies* 20 (1980): 99.

14. Larner, 91. Witchcraft was overwhelmingly a woman's crime; it was almost the only woman's crime of this period in Scotland.

15. McDowall, 430-433.

16. Quoted in Patrick Walker, *Six Saints of the Covenant*, 2 Vols. (London: Hodder and Stoughton, 1901), 1: 202-205. Welwood closed his letter with greetings from his wife to "you and the two lads."

17. Dr. James Welwood also had a sister, Helen, and a half-sister, Mary. Genealogical information on the various branches of the Welwood family can be found in Peter Chalmers, *Historical and Statistical Account of Dunfermline*, 2 Vols. (Edinburgh: William Blackwood and Sons, 1859), 2: 440-459.

18. Andrew Welwood, 270. The book contains Andrew Welwood's final letters to his family, as well as"The Dying Saint's Song," reprinted in its entirety on pages 243-249.

19. Like Andrew Welwood's *Meditations*, Guthrie's sermons found a later audience in America where they were printed as *The Christian's Great Interest* by H. Ranlet in 1796 at Exeter, New Hampshire, and sold at his bookstore.

20. Andrew Welwood, 250-273.

21. See Patrick Walker's chapter on him in *Six Saints of the Covenant*.

22. Quoted in Patrick Walker, 210. Walker was a vehement Presbyterian apologist who saw Sharp's murder as justified (217).

23. Andrew Veitch, *Richard Cameron* (London: Pickering and Inglis, 1923), 59.

24. See John D. Comrie, *History of Scottish Medicine*, 2 Vols. (London: Bailliere, Tindall and Cox, 1932), 1:228. It is also possible that opting for medicine was a way for James Welwood to rebel against his father's and brothers' life choices and to secure his own niche in the family. See Frank Sulloway, *Born to Rebel* (New York: Pantheon, 1996), 95-100.

25. Included on any list of prominent St. Andrews graduates in Welwood's era would be the Scottish supporter of the Royalist cause in the Civil War, James Graham, Earl of Montrose; Archibald Campbell, Earl of Argyll, leader in Scotland of the Monmouth Rebellion in 1685; John Maitland, Duke of Lauderdale and the effective leader of Scotland for most of the reign of Charles II; John Claverhouse, scourge of the Covenanters and supporter of James II; Sir George Mackenzie, founder of the Advocates' Library; and Sir Robert Moray, first President of the Royal Society set up by Charles II in London. Douglas Young, *St. Andrews: Town and Gown, Royal and Ancient* (London: Cassell, 1969), 191.

26. The best history of the University is Ronald G. Cant, *University of St. Andrews* (Edinburgh: Scottish Academy Press, 1970), although it is mainly constitutional in scope. One might also consult R. H. Campbell and A. S. Skinner, *The Origin and Nature of the Scottish Enlightenment* (Edinburgh: John Donald, 1982) for a general view of the intellectual state of Scotland in Welwood's era.

27. Comrie, 2: 374-375.

28. James B. Salmond, ed., *Veterum Laudes* (Edinburgh: Oliver and Boyd, 1950), 82-87.

29. See Joseph Levine, *Dr. Woodward's Shield* (Ithaca, NY: Cornell University Press, 1977) and *The Battle of the Books* (Ithaca, NY: Cornell University Press, 1991).

30. See Hugh Kearney, *Scholars and Gentlemen: Universities and Society in Pre-Industrial Britain 1500-1700* (Ithaca: Cornell University Press, 1970). Kearney asserts that, because it lacked an urban base, only St. Andrews was still influenced by the social ideal of the gentleman after the Stuart Restoration.

31. See Ronald G. Cant, "The Origins of the Enlightenment in Scotland: the Universities" and Christine M. Shepherd, "Newtonianism in Scottish Universities in the Seventeenth Century", in *The Origins and Nature of the Scottish Enlightenment*, ed. R. H. Campbell and Andrew S.

Skinner (Edinburgh: John Donald, 1982). At least one prominent historian asserts that Calvinist societies became enlightened only when they broke from Calvinist traditions. H. R. Trevor-Roper, "Religious Origins of the Enlightenment," *Religion, the Reformation and Social Change*, 2nd ed. (London: Macmillan, 1972), 207-209.

32. According to Dr. Norman Reid, Keeper of the Manuscripts at the University of St. Andrews Library, the entry on Welwood in the revised *Dictionary of National Biography* is wrong to credit him with a Bachelor of Arts degree in 1668, probably resulting from a misreading of the matriculation entry.

33. Another Test Act (1678) excluded Roman Catholics except the Duke of York from Parliament. Despite the deleterious effects of imposing a religious test on candidates for secular office in England, the original Test Act was not repealed until 1829.

34. John Wilson Croker, ed., *Letters of the Countess of Suffolk and the Honorable George Berkeley*, 2 Vols. (London: J. Murray, 1824), 1:51. Croker, a prominent Tory politician as well as a successful editor of Boswell's *Life of Johnson*, was secretary of the Admiralty from 1810-1830. Welwood, *Appendix to Mercurius Reformatus*, 14.

35. The party epithets were crafted in derision: Whig was a pejorative designation for a Scottish Presbyterian rebel in the Civil War period and Tory derived from the Irish word for outlaw.

36. Hubert Fenwick, *The Auld Alliance* (Kineton, Warwickshire: Roundwood Press, 1971), 89-90.

37. Cameron graduated M.A. from St. Salvator's in 1665, preached in the late 1670s in Annandale, and consorted with Scottish exiles in Holland in 1679, but there is no evidence of a Welwood connection.

38. See Harold J. Cook, *The Decline of the Old Medical Regime in Stuart London* (Ithaca NY: Cornell University Press, 1986).

Chapter Two: Educational Controversies

1. Lynn Avery Hunt, *Revolution and Urban Politics in Provincial France* (Stanford CA: Stanford University Press, 1978), 9-11. See also Philip Benedict, ed., *Cities and Social Change in Early Modern France* (London: Unwin Hyman, 1989), 24. Benedict places the population of Reims at 35,000 in 1650 and at 31,000 in 1700. Another text suggests that the town's population slumped precipitously around 1680 and remained stagnant throughout the eighteenth century. Pierre Desportes, ed., *Histoire*

de Reims (Toulouse: Univers de la France et des Pays Francophone, 1983), 220.

2. John Durkan, "The French Connection in the Sixteenth and Early Seventeenth Centuries," in *Scotland and Europe, 1200-1850*, ed. T. C. Smout (Edinburgh: John Donald, 1986), 24.

3. For a French-language history of the medical faculty at Reims, see Andre Jacquinet, *Le Centre Universitaire Medical de Reims: 1550-1967* (Reims: Coulon, 1967). For a critical analysis of the University of Reims, see Laurence Brockliss, *French Higher Education in the Seventeenth and Eighteenth Centuries* (Oxford: Clarendon Press, 1987), 391-443.

4. R. W. Innes Smith, *English-Speaking Students of Medicine at the University of Leyden* (Edinburgh: Oliver and Boyd, 1932), 245. The author speculates that this graduate may indeed be James Welwood, but offers no evidence.

5. For more information on the Royal College of Physicians in Edinburgh, see W. S. Craig, *History of the Royal College of Physicians of Edinburgh* (Oxford: Blackwell Scientific Publication, 1976).

6. *Mercurius Reformatus*, July 4, 1691.

7. Mario Turchetti, "Religious Concord and Political Tolerance in Sixteenth- and Seventeenth-Century France," *Sixteenth Century Journal* 22 (1991): 15-18.

8. The University itself was closed in 1793 during the French Revolution and remained dormant for a century and a half. It was reopened in 1967, but following passage of a reform bill for French higher education was refounded in 1970 as the University of Reims Champagne-Ardennes. The institution today is geographically spread out over four counties and serves 27,000 students.

9. For analysis of the state of English science, see Charles Webster, *The Great Instauration: Science, Medicine and Reform 1626-1660* (New York: Holmes and Meier,1976) and a gentle riposte by John Henry, "The Scientific Revolution in England," in *The Scientific Revolution in National Context* (New York: Cambridge University Press, 1992), 178-209.

10. John Archer, *Everyman His Own Doctor* (London: n.p., 1671), 34.

11. Rattansi Pyarali, "Paracelsus and the Puritan Revolution," *Ambix* 12 (1964): 6fn. For seventeenth-century change in the Royal College of Physicians, see Harold J. Cook, *The Decline of the Old Medical Regime in Stuart London* (Ithaca: Cornell University Press, 1986).

12. Desportes, 216.

13. Durkan specifically mentions the "unswerving" Galenic bias at the universities of Paris and Montpellier. In a lengthy listing of Scottish professors and students at French provincial centers, he altogether omits reference to Reims.

14. Charles Coury, "The Teaching of Medicine in France from the Beginning of the Seventeenth Century," *History of Medical Education*, ed. C. D. O'Malley (Los Angeles: University of California Press, 1970), 122. On the other hand, Coury calls other medical programs (such as Orange, Avignon, Nancy, Nantes, and Angers) discredited or marginal.

15. The same situation bedeviled English doctors during the reign of Charles II. Unlicensed quacksalvers were afforded legal status by the king and were sometimes protected with monopolies granted to administer certain "prescriptions." Apothecary Robert Talbor was awarded the sole right to dispense Jesuits' Bark, a cinchona tree product called quinine today. Leslie Matthews, "Italian Charlatans in England," *Pharmaceutical Historian* 9 (1979): 2-5.

16. Jacquinet, 11-13.

17. Colin Jones, "Médicins du Roi and the French Revolution," in *Medicine at the Courts of Europe 1500-1837*, edited by Vivian Nutton (London: Routledge, 1990), 227. The other French provincial schools besmirched by the nearly scandalous awarding of the *petit ordinaire* were Angers, Cahors, Caen, Valence, Avignon, Pont-à-Mousson, Nancy, and especially Orange, alma mater of famed London physician and collector, Hans Sloane. Coury, 127.

18. According to Pol Gosset, sometimes two theses were required and the degree was never granted *in absentia*. R. W. Innes Smith, *English-Speaking Students of Medicine at the University of Leyden* (Edinburgh: Oliver and Boyd, 1932), xiv.

19. John. J. McCusker, *Money and Exchange in Europe and America, 1600-1715* (Chapel Hill: University of North Carolina Press, 1978), 9. McCusker reports that the French *écu*, the widely used silver coin of the realm, equalled three *livres* and was worth £0.23 in 1651 and in 1702. The *louis d'or* was gold and fetched £0.73 in 1651 and £0.86 in 1702. See also R. Bonney, *The King's Debts: Finance and Politics in France, 1589-1661* (Oxford: 1981).

20. Quoted in Robert G. Frank, "The John Ward Diaries," *Journal of the History of Medicine*, 29 (1974): 162.

21. Coury, 130. Of course, physicians also received income from their practices above faculty salaries.

22. Prior to 1707 and the Act of Union Scotland had its own money of account, denoted as in England in pounds, shillings and pence, but valued differently than English money; £13 Scottish equalled £1 sterling. McCusker, 32.

23. Geoffrey Holmes, *Augustan England: Professions, State and Society 1680-1730* (London: George Allen and Unwin, 1982), 209.

24. A.H.T. Robb-Smith, "Medical Education at Oxford and Cambridge Prior to 1850," *The Evolution of Medical Education in Britain*, ed. F.N.L. Poynter (London: Pitman Medical Publishing Co., 1966), 39.

25. Innes Smith speculates that Welwood may have followed this pattern, citing Robert Wellwood enrolled in 1675 at Leiden and a "Thomas" Wellwood associated with King William in Scotland. Innes Smith, 245.

26. Harold J. Cook, *Trials of an Ordinary Doctor* (Baltimore: Johns Hopkins University Press, 1994), 60-63.

27. Brockliss, 398.

28. Benedict, 24.

29. William Beik, "Louis XIV and the Cities," in *Edo and Paris*, eds. James McClain, *et al* (Ithaca: Cornell University Press, 1994), 76.

30. Martin Lister, *A Journey to Paris in the Year 1698*, edited by Raymond Phineas Stearns (Urbana IL: University of Illinois Press, 1967), 188-189. Dr. Lister, who by the time of his Parisian visit was a colleague of Welwood's, served as a physician to William III and to Queen Anne. In 1698 he attended the Earl of Portland on embassy to the court of France.

31. Coury, 141.

32. La Salpêtriére still functions as one of Paris' most important medical centers. Diana, Princess of Wales, died there in 1997.

33. Marshall Dill, Jr., *Paris in Time* (New York: G. P. Putnam's Sons, 1975), 82-102.

34. For the French references see *Mercurius Reformatus*, September 9, 1690; *An Appendix to Mercurius Reformatus* (London: Richard Baldwin, 1692), 13. Welwood in 1691 identified a Monsieur Pellison as a Parisian acquaintance of "nine years ago" One mention of The Hague "some years ago" came about in the context of an anecdote about William of Orange's love of hunting. *Mercurius Reformatus*, October 9, 1689.

35. Sir Henry M. Imbert-Terry, "Some Memorialists of the Period of the Restoration," in *Essays by Divers Hands: Transactions of the Royal Society of Literature of the United Kingdom*, New Series, Vol. 2, ed. William R. Inge (London: Humphrey Milford, 1922), 75.

36. T. C. Smout, *Scottish Trade on the Eve of Union 1660-1707* (Edinburgh: Oliver and Boyd, 1963), 90-91.

37. John Carswell, *The Descent on England* (New York: John Day, 1969), 28-29.

38. J. P. Kenyon contends that economic instability and dislocation in London exacerbated existing religious hostilities. Chronic unemployment, a recession in 1678, a serious fire in early 1679, and the sudden dissolution of Parliament combined to produce a volatile political environment in the capital. John Kenyon, *The Popish Plot* (New York: Penguin, 1974), 274-275. Oates' fortunes followed the throne; tortured and imprisoned during the reign of James II, he was released and pensioned under William III.

39. Mercurius Reformatus, February 19, 1690; Andrew Lossky, *Louis XIV and the French Monarchy* (New Brunswick, NJ: Rutgers University Press, 1994), 216-218.

40. Georges Boussinesq and Gustave Laurent, *Histoire de Reims*, 2nd ed., 2 Vols. (Reims: Matot-Braine, 1933), 1: 87-146.

41. Pierre Goubert, *Louis XIV and Twenty Million Frenchmen* (New York: Vintage Books, 1966), 155-158.

42. Robin D. Gwynn, *Huguenot Heritage* (London: Routledge and Kegan Paul, 1983), 35-40.

Chapter Three: Welwood and the "Glorious Revolution"

1. Samuel Johnson, the great eighteenth-century lexicographer and himself a Tory, defined "Tory" as one who adheres to the ancient constitution of the state and the apostolic hierarchy of the Church of England, as opposed to a Whig. He defined "Whig" as simply the name of a faction.

2. Kenyon, *The Popish Plot*, 233-234.

3. Historical Manuscripts Commission, *Report on the Manuscripts of the Late Allan George Finch, esq.*, (London: His Majesty's Stationery Office, 1922) 2:281.

4. Five new members were added during this time, including "one who

is duly graduate examined and approved off by ye colledge is a residenter in Edinburgh and payd ye whole deus." W. S. Craig, *History of the Royal College of Physicians of Edinburgh* (Oxford: Blackwell, 1976), 152. For more on the impetus behind the College's founding, see Paul Wood, "The Scientific Revolution in Scotland," in *The Scientific Revolution in National Context*, Roy Porter and Mikulas Teich, eds. (New York: Cambridge University Press, 1992), 263-287.

5. This is not Thomas Burnet, the English cleric (1635-1715), who is remembered for books on fanciful geology and the Flood.

6. James Welwood, *Memoirs of the Most Material Transactions in England* (London: 1700), 172-175.

7. James Welwood, *Appendix to Mercurius Reformatus* (London: Richard Baldwin, 1692), 14.

8. Celia Fiennes, intrepid lady traveler, wrote in 1699 that Newcastle's "shops are good and of distinct trades, not selling many things in one shop as is the custom in most country towns and cities." Celia Fiennes, *Through England on a Side-Saddle in the Time of William and Mary* (London: Field and Tuer, 1888), 177.

9. The author is indebted to Elizabeth Rees, Chief Archivist for Tyne and Wear Archives Service, for a search of the minutes of the Common Council of the City of Newcastle from 1684-1694. Despite his later public feud with Vicar John March, Welwood's name does not appear anywhere in those minutes.

10. Catholics could not vote in local elections until restrictions were lifted in 1797 or in parliamentary elections until the Catholic Emancipation Act of 1829. The effigy of Guy Fawkes, chief conspirator in 1605, is still carried in procession and ritually burned every November 5. See Antonia Fraser, *Faith and Treason: The Story of the Gunpowder Plot* (New York: Doubleday, 1997).

11. Hatred for Father Petre persisted long after the crisis of 1688. Petre was burned in effigy on Guy Fawkes' Day every year in England until the end of Queen Anne's reign.

12. W. A. Speck, "Religion's Role in the Glorious Revolution," *History Today* 38 (July 1988): 31.

13. Roger Howell, Jr., "Newcastle and the Nation: The Seventeenth-Century Experience," in *The Tudor and Stuart Town*, ed. Jonathan Barry (London: Longman, 1990), 290-294.

14. Princess Anne, devastated over the deaths of her own babies and

over two recent miscarriages, may have originated the scheme to discredit her brother's birth. She conveyed the canard to her sister in Holland and maintained her agreement with the story all her life. Edward Gregg, *Queen Anne* (London: Routledge and Kegan Paul, 1980), 54-58. However, the birth of a daughter to James and his wife four years later silenced the lie for everyone else.

15. G. C. Gibbs, "The European Origins of the Glorious Revolution," *Kings in Conflict*, ed. W. A. Maguire (Belfast: Blackstaff Press, 1990), 17.

16. John Miller, "The Glorious Revolution," *Kings in Conflict*, ed. W.A. Maguire (Belfast: Blackstaff Press, 1990), 39.

17. P. M. Horsley, *Eighteenth-Century Newcastle* (Newcastle upon Tyne: Oriel Press, 1971), 8. The statue was later salvaged by the Common Council and cast as new bells for two Newcastle churches.

18. Gibbs, 26.

19. James Welwood, *An Answer to the Late King James' Declaration to All His Pretended Subjects in the Kingdom of England* (London: Dorman Newman, 1689), 19-20.

20. All of the March-Welwood correspondence is contained in James Welwood, *Vindication of the Present Great Revolution in England* (London: Randall Taylor, 1689).

21. On January 30, 1661, Samuel Pepys recorded the first fast day in observance of Charles' execution, and from 1662-1859 by royal mandate a special service solemnized the day of his death. Vernon Staley, "The Commemoration of King Charles the Martyr," in *Liturgical Studies* (London: Longmans, Green, 1907), 66-83.

22. Since John Locke's contractual defense of revolution was not published until 1690, Welwood seems to anticipate the famous *Two Treatises*. Of course, he had the opportunity while in the Netherlands at the same time as Locke to learn of his work. Locke returned to England in 1689 on the same ship as the Princess Mary. At least two influential scholars dismiss Locke as ineffectual in his time. See J. R. Jones, *The Revolution of 1688 in England* (New York: Norton: 1972) and J. P. Kenyon, *Revolution Principles, The Politics of Party 1689-1720* (New York: Cambridge University Press, 1977).

23. James Welwood, *Mercurius Reformatus*, November 13, 1689.

24. Tony Claydon, *William III and the Godly Revolution* (Cambridge: Cambridge University Press, 1996), 7-17. Claydon emphasizes the cadre

of clerics whose Williamite propaganda was directed by Burnet, but laymen like Welwood contributed to the effort, too.

25. For more on Brady, see Philip Hicks, *Neoclassical History and English Culture* (London: Macmillan, 1996), 82-90.

26. Welwood, Appendix, 14.

27. The pamphlet is dated August 1689 and was originally available in London from Dorman Newman.

28. Their name derives from the Latin for James, Jacobus.

29. P. W. J. Riley, *King William and the Scottish Politicians* (Edinburgh: John Donald Publishers, 1979), 1-4.

30. *Mercurius Reformatus*, March 5, 1690.

31. *Mercurius Reformatus*, February 12, 1690. Welwood also denigrated the "wild Irish," probably for their support of James II, and the "monstrous nations of Africa" in earlier issues of the paper.

32. *Mercurius Reformatus*, March 5, 1690; September 24, 1690.

33. William L. Sachse, "The Mob and the Revolution of 1688," *Journal of British Studies* 4 (1964): 23-40. See also Robert Beddard, "Anti-Popery and the London Mob, 1688," *History Today* 38 (July 1988): 36-40.

34. Gary S. DeKrey, "Political Radicalism in London after the Glorious Revolution," *Journal of Modern History* 55 (1983): 591.

35. Lansdowne MSS 841, folios 54-57, British Library.

36. Howell, "Newcastle and the Nation," 296; Leo Gooch, *The Desperate Faction?* (Kingston upon Hull: University of Hull Press, 1995, 14.

Chapter Four: Welwood and Grub Street

1. See Elizabeth Walsh et al, *Yesterday's News: Seventeenth-Century English Broadsides and Newsbooks* (Washington: Folger Library, 1996), an informative pamphlet for a past exhibition at the Folger Shakespeare Library.

2. Tim Harris, *Politics under the Later Stuarts* (London: Longman, 1993), 20-21.

3. Mark Goldie, "The Revolution of 1689 and the Structure of Political Argument," *Bulletin of Research in the Humanities* 83 (1980): 480-484.

4. Lois G. Schwoerer, "Liberty of the Press," in *Liberty Secured? Britain*

before and after 1688, ed. J. R. Jones (Stanford CA: Stanford University Press, 1992), 210.

5. F. W. Bateson, ed., *The Cambridge Bibliography of English Literature*, 2 (Cambridge: Cambridge University Press, 1966): 704-705. Bateson also records a *Mercurius Reformatus* published in Edinburgh from June 1690 to May 1691 which he attributes to the "heir of Andrew Anderson." *Ibid.*, 781. See also Michael Treadwell, "Lists of Master Printers: The Size of the London Printing Trade, 1637-1723," *Aspects of Printing*, ed. Robin Myers and Michael Harris (Gosport: Oxford Polytechnic Press, 1987), 141-170.

6. Despite Welwood's scorn, gentlemen after 1680 entered a wide cross-section of businesses including publishing, which was combined with other trades and professions. Richard Grassby, *The Business Community of Seventeenth-Century England* (Cambridge: Cambridge University Press, 1995), 163.

7. C. John Sommerville, *The News Revolution in England* (New York: Oxford University Press, 1996), 99. Prof. Sommerville has since reported that he "cannot justify [his] statement that Welwood's *Mercurius Reformatus* had government sponsorship [and] cannot even reconstruct how [he] was led to that view." John Sommerville to Elizabeth Lane Furdell, February 20, 1997. He may have been influenced by Mark Goldie's unjust description of Welwood as a hack. See Goldie, 514, and below, fn. 11.

8. Historical Manuscripts Commission, *Report on the Manuscripts of the Late Allen George Finch, esq.*, (London: HMSO, 1922) 2: 281. Daniel Finch, 2nd Earl of Nottingham, was a moderate Tory politician and close confidante of Queen Mary.

9. *Ibid.*, 2: 392-393.

10. *A Modest Enquiry into the Present Disasters* (London: Richard Baldwin, 1690); a Dutch translation was published simultaneously in Amsterdam, and a sequel further connecting the Anglican clergy to a Jacobite conspiracy appeared under the imprint of John Dunton later in the same year. See also Leona Rostenberg, "Richard and Anne Baldwin, Whig Patriot Publishers," *Papers of the Bibliographical Society of America* 47 (1953): 10. Mark Goldie has pointed out that Baldwin's presses were not reserved for Whigs; Tories wrote nine of the twenty-eight tracts he published on the allegiance controversy, yet another reminder of the problems historians face defining and categorizing political groups. Goldie, 493.

11. *Ibid.*, 515.

12. James Welwood, *An Answer to the Late King James' Declaration to All His Pretended Subjects* (London: Richard Baldwin, 1689), 2. There was a second 1689 edition of the work in English (published by Dorman Newman), one in Dutch, *Ein Antwoord op de Declaratie gegeven op't Kasteel te Dublin*, and another in 1693, indicating that it must have been quite popular.

13. *Mercurius Reformatus*, July 25, 1690; September 18, 1691.

14. *Mercurius Reformatus*, September 25, 1689; February 19, 1690; July 18, 1690; September 5, 1690; September 18, 1690; October 1, 1690; September 12, 1691.

15. Quoted in John Philip Kenyon, *The History Men* (Pittsburgh: University of Pittsburgh Press, 1983), 35.

16.Quoted in Daniel Statt, *Foreigners and Englishmen* (Newark, DE: University of Delaware Press, 1991), 188.

17. *Mercurius Reformatus*, November 13, 1689.

18. A series of unsigned letters "from a person in Amsterdam to his friend in London" was published in 1689 in seven volumes by Randall Taylor as *The Dilucidator* and advertised in Welwood's paper. The London recipient could be Welwood himself.

19. See Alison Olson, "Coffee House Lobbying," *History Today* 41 (Jan.1991): 35-42; R. B. Walker, "The Newspaper Press in the Reign of William III," *Historical Journal* 17 (1974): 702; Peter Clark and Paul Slack, *English Towns in Transition 1500-1700* (Oxford: Oxford University Press, 1976) 74; John and Linda Pelzer, "The Coffee Houses of Augustan London," *History Today* 32 (Oct. 1982): 40-48; and Steve Pincus, "Coffee Politicians Does Create," *Journal of Modern History* 67 (1995): 807-835. By custom if not law, women were excluded from the premises.

20. Tacitus was particularly useful to Whiggish writers like Welwood, because he helped them locate the origins of Parliament in the Saxon *witan*. Hence, liberty did not need to be created; it merely needed to be restored. H. Trevor Colbourn, *The Lamp of Experience* (Chapel Hill: University of North Carolina Press, 1965), 7.

21. *Mercurius Reformatus*, November 13, 1689; Sommerville, 14. 22. Keith Thomas, "The Meaning of Literacy in Early Modern England," *The Written Word: Literacy in Transition*, ed. Gerd Bauman (Oxford: Oxford University Press, 1986), 99. Beryl Diamond has applied the Flesch Reading scale to *The Current Intelligence* and to *The London Gazette*, papers comparable to Welwood's. He has determined that both

publications focused on a highly literate category of Londoners, roughly equivalent to those with a ninth or tenth-grade American education today. Standard writing in the United States in the 1990s roughly equates to the seventh-grade level. The author thanks Professor Diamond for use of his unpublished manuscript, "A Lively Presenter of News: Henry Muddiman, *The Current Intelligence* and its Rival, *The London Gazette*."

23. James Welwood, *Weekly Remarks*, April 8, 1691. The copy of the March 25 issue that I perused has a bit of marginalia written in late seventeenth-century hand: "a silly thing to Welwood's Observator."

24. *The Weekly Remarks*, May 4, 1691.

25. For the best discussion of the varieties of Jacobites, see Paul Kleber Monod, *Jacobitism and the English People, 1688-1788* (Cambridge: Cambridge University Press, 1989).

26. By the last years of Queen Anne's reign, the London Tories had absorbed the populist following and rhetoric of the Whigs. Gary S. DeKrey, "Political Radicalism in London after the Glorious Revolution," *Journal of Modern History* 55 (1983): 613. Defoe spoke for many when he complained that "we are the most divided, quarrelsome nation under the sun."

27. Burnet's critical appraisal of William can be found in John Miller, *William and Mary* (London: George Weidenfeld and Nicolson, 1974), 120; Defoe is quoted in Statt, 115.

28. Thomas Babington Macaulay, *History of England*, 3 Vols. (New York: Dutton, 1968), 3: 78.

29. For information on Newman and Baldwin, see H.R. Plomer, et al., *Dictionaries of the Printers and Booksellers Who Were at Work in England, Scotland and Ireland 1557-1775* (Yorkshire: The Bibliographical Society, 1977), 16-17, 137, 217; and Leona Rostenberg, "Richard and Anne Baldwin, Whig Patriot Publishers," *Papers of the Bibliographic Society of America* 47 (1953): 1-42. Plomer quotes John Dunton that Baldwin's business got too big for him to handle, and he botched the expansion of his company into another shop in Fleet Street. Baldwin continued to draw the government's fire; in 1697 he was sued by the King's Printers for printing speeches. *Ibid.*, 17. Baldwin died in 1698.

30. Historical Manuscripts Commission, *7th Report*, Appendix: 206-207; House of Commons Journal, November 9, 21, 27, and 39, 1691.

31. Richard Doebner, ed., *Memoirs of Mary, Queen of England* (London:

David Nutt, 1886), 55; Stephen Baxter, *William III* (New York: Harcourt Brace and World, 1966), 301.

32. *Finch MSS*, 4: 442, 451. Historians are unsure if either James or Louis were aware of the plot, but it is doubtful they would have repudiated it if the conspirators had succeeded. John Miller, *James II* (Sussex: Wayland, 1978), 238.

33. *Reflections upon the Late Horrid Conspiracy Contrived by Some of the French Court to Murther His Majesty in Flanders* (London: Richard Baldwin, 1692). A list of Gallophobic books printed by Baldwin follows the text and includes a translation from the French of a book about Louvois, a work on recent persecutions of the Huguenots in Aquitaine, and a salacious history of the amours of Madam de Maintenon with the French king.

34. Roy Sundstrom, *Sidney Godolphin* (Newark DE: University of Delaware Press, 1992), 43. Since William was in Ireland in 1690 and often in the Netherlands during campaigning season after 1691, the Cabinet developed to coordinate wartime planning and to assist Mary. Mary Ede, *Arts and Society under William and Mary* (London: Stainer and Hill, 1979), 38.

35. Kenneth S. Gallagher has suggested to me that William's supporters would not have objected to mere cosmetic slurs on the prince's proboscis, but that Anderton's reference was to the *commedia dell'arte* with the king cast as the violent male in the English puppet version, Punch and Judy.

36. Quoted in R. B. Walker, "The Press under William III," 696.

37. William Anderton, *True Copy of the paper delivered to the sheriffs of London and Middlesex by Mr. William Anderton* (London: n.s., 1693); Samuel Grascome, *An Appeal of Murther from Certain Unjust Judges* (London: s.n, 1693). For the Anderton case, see Philip Hamburger, "Seditious Libel," *Stanford Law Review* 37 (1985): 714-720.

38. Historical Manuscripts Commission, *Thirteenth Report: The Manuscripts of Sir William Fitzherbert, Bart., and Others*, Appendix, Part 5 (London: Her Majesty's Stationery Office, 1893), 33.

39. *Calendar of State Papers, Domestic Series, of the Reign of William and Mary, 1694-1695* (London: His Majesty's Stationery Office, 1906), 326-327, 498, 506.

40. Dr. Welwood to Dr. Cage, May 29, 1701. Additional MSS 4107, folio 72, British Library.

41. The defendants apparently were pardoned and the government's

hopes of controlling the press foundered in unforseen difficulties. For more on the strategy behind and the results of James' 1693 declaration, see Daniel Szechi, "The Jacobite Revolutionary Settlement, 1689-1696," *English Historical Review* 108 (1993): 610-628.

42. Tracking authorship of Jacobite pamphlets is a difficult chore, but the usual suspects ought to include Charles Leslie, George Hickes, James Ferguson, and Charlwood Lawton.

43. Add. MSS 4107, f. 72. Welwood's opposition to the movement toward High Church policies evident by the end of William's reign is clear in his condemnation of Bishop Francis Atterbury.

Chapter Five: Welwood's Prolific Pen

1. Tony Claydon, *William III and the Godly Revolution* (Cambridge: Cambridge University Press, 1996), 85-86.

2. Welwood later married Seymour's daughter-in-law, demonstrating the few degrees of separation among the Augustan age elite.

3. The Roman Catholic Church practices canonization, acknowledging the saint as an intercessor with God. Anglican commemoration allows for the "saint" to serve as an exemplar. F. L. Cross, ed., *Oxford Dictionary of the Christian Church*, 3d ed. (Oxford: Oxford University Press, 1997). For more on the memorialization of Charles I, see Byron S. Stewart, "The Cult of the Royal Martyr," *Church History* 38 (1969): 175-87. The legend played a role in English politics well into the nineteenth century in the writings of the Young England crusade and in the Oxford and Ritualist movements.

4. Welwood's work appeared before Lord Clarendon's *History of the Rebellion* was published in 1702, soon after Queen Anne (Clarendon's grand-daughter) ascended the throne. Laird Okie asserts that a revival of the cult of Charles I as "Royal Martyr" developed after Anne's accession, but sympathy for the executed king clearly existed in the previous decade. Laird Okie, *Augustan Historical Writing* (Lanham MD: University Press of America, 1991), 21.

5. The British Museum did not open until 1759. There was no Public Record Office or publications of historical documents until the nineteenth century, and England lagged behind other countries in promoting historical study and preserving historical remains.

6. *Mercurius Reformatus*, December 18, 1689; Henry Imbert-Terry, "Some Memorialists of the Period of the Restoration," *Essays by Divers*

Hands: Transactions of the Royal Society of Literature of the United Kingdom, ed. William R. Inge, New Series, 2 (London: Humphrey Milford, 1922): 76-79.

7. Philip Hicks, *Neoclassical History and English Culture: From Clarendon to Hume* (London: Macmillan, 1996), 9-14.

8. Kenyon, *The History Men*, 37. Nevertheless, Kenyon cautioned against relying too much on Burnet, whose history was excised and amended to please his patrons. J. P. Kenyon, *Robert Spencer, Earl of Sunderland* (Westport CT: Greenwood Press, 1958), 102fn.

9. Hicks, 129.

10. Imbert-Terry, 92.

11. James Welwood, *Memoirs of the Most Material Transactions in England for the Last Hundred Years, Preceding the Revolution in 1688*, 2nd ed. (London: Tim Goodwin, 1700).

12. See Linda Levy Peck, *Court Patronage and Corruption in Early Stuart England* (London: Routledge, 1993); Anne Somerset, *Unnatural Murder: Poison at the Court of James I* (London: Weidenfeld and Nicolson, 1997).

13. Imbert-Terry, 78.

14. *Ibid.*, 149.

15. Linda Colley, *Britons* (New Haven: Yale University Press, 1992), 20. Colley mentions an 1682 Aberdeen almanac which sold 50,000 copies in a year.

16. James Welwood, *The Compleat History of Europe...for the Year 1705* (London: n.p., 1705), preface.

17. The physicians-in-ordinary were Drs. Edward Hannes, Thomas Laurence, Martin Lister, and David Hamilton. Famed physician-writer John Arbuthnot was physician-extraordinary. Welwood, *Compleat History*, 43.

18. Royal apothecaries paid for supplies out of their salaries, which accounts for the size of their pay. Sergeant-Surgeon Gardiner's duties included screening applicants for the queen's touch, a semi-magical healing rite long performed by English monarchs on scrofulous subjects.

19. See Welwood's introduction to Bulstrode Whitelocke's *Memorials of the English Affairs, from the Supposed Expedition of Brute to this Island to the End of the Reign of King James the First* (London: E. Curll, 1709). Whitelocke's best-known work picked up the narrative in 1625. *Memorials*

of the English Affairs from the Beginning of the Reign of Charles I to the Happy Restoration of King Charles II was first published in 1682 and was proffered by Whig partisans as the riposte to Clarendon's history. Whitelocke died in 1675.

20. See Geoffrey Holmes, *The Trial of Doctor Sacheverell* (London: Eyre Methuen, 1973).

21. For a discussion of the politics of virtue in Augustan England, see Shelley Burtt, *Virtue Transformed: Political Argument in England, 1688-1740* (Cambridge: Cambridge University Press, 1992).

22. Alexander Pope's verse translation of *The Iliad* appeared in 1715 and *The Odyssey* followed in 1725. Homer made Pope a fortune, £10,000.

23. *Banquet of Xenophon* (London: John Barnes, 1710; Glasgow: 1750), 113. Considering his humble birth, Welwood traveled in noble circles. Lady Jean married Francis, Earl of Dalkeith and Duke of Buccleuch.

24. *Ibid.*, 28, 56.

25. *Ibid.*, 112.

26. *Mercurius Reformatus*, July 25, 1690.

27. Nicholas Rowe, trans., *Lucan's Pharsalia*, with a preface by James Welwood (Chiswick: n.p., 1822).

28. James Welwood, *A True Relation of the Cure of Mary Maillard* (London: Richard Baldwin, 1694), 25.

29. Dr. Welwood's name is not included on the list of Scottish subscribers preserved in the National Library of Scotland or among the London investors in the Corporate Affairs Archives of the Royal Bank of Scotland. See also James Samuel Barbour, *History of William Paterson and the Darien Company* (Edinburgh: William Blackwood and Sons, 1907), Appendix F.

30. Daniel Statt, *Foreigners and Englishmen* (Newark DE: University of Delaware Press, 1995), 32-33.

31. In 1997 a resounding majority of Scots voted for devolution, re-establishment of a Scottish Parliament after 290 years of union with England. The legislature, to be in place by 2000, will have responsibility over domestic law and a limited taxing authority.

32. Though not officially banned, native Gaelic speakers in Scotland cannot plead in their own language in court. The author is grateful to Maureen Meikle at the University of Sunderland for this observation.

33. Hugh Trevor-Roper, *Religion, the Reformation and Social Change*

(London: Macmillan, 1972), 466-467; P. W. J. Riley, *The Union of England and Scotland* (Manchester: Manchester University Press, 1978), 240-241.

34. *Mercurius Reformatus*, March 5, 1690.

35. Colley, *Britons*, 12. See also Arthur Williamson, "Scotland, Antichrist, and the Invention of Great Britain," *New Perspectives on the Politics and Culture of Early Modern Scotland*, ed. John Dwyer, Roger Mason and Alexander Murdoch (Edinburgh: John Donald, 1982).

36. Dr. Welwood can be termed both a catalyst and a product of a new, worldly mindset in which religion no longer dictated thinking, but was one of many things to think about. John Sommerville argues that a more secularized England came about because of an active press which helped to redraw the boundaries between the spiritual and the mundane. For more on the other secularizing factors that came into play, see C. John Sommerville, *The Secularization of Early Modern England* (Oxford: Oxford University Press, 1992).

37. *Reflections upon the Late Horrid Conspiracy Contrived by Some of the French Court to Murther His Majesty in Flanders* (London: Richard Baldwin: 1692), 4.

Chapter Six: The Medical Scene

1. William Munk, *Roll of the College of Physicians*, 2 Vols., (London: Longman, Green, and Roberts, 1861) 2: 35.

2. See Frank H. Ellis, "The Background of the London Dispensary," *Journal of the History of Medicine and Allied Sciences* 20 (1965): 197-212.

3. Leslie G. Matthews, *The Royal Apothecaries* (London: Wellcome Institute, 1967), 102, 137-138.

4. Harold J. Cook, "Living in Revolutionary Times: Medical Change under William and Mary," in *Patronage and Institutions*, ed. Bruce T. Moran (Rochester NY: Boydell Press, 1991), 119-123.

5. Munk, 1: 481.

6. The warrant is cited as LC 3/32 p. 53 in J.C. Sainty and R.O. Bucholz, *Officials of the Royal Household 1660-1837*, Part I: Department of the Lord Chamberlain and Associated Offices (London: University of London, 1997), 183. Welwood was not, as Peter Chalmers suggests, the monarchs' physician in Scotland; that nomination fell to Welwood's old friend, Thomas Burnet. Other Scottish appointments included David Hay, Andrew Balfour, Robert Sibbald, and Thomas Dalrymple. See Peter

Chalmers, *Historical and Statistical Account of Dunfermline* 2 Vols. (Edinburgh: William Blackwood and Sons, 1859), 1: 529; Cook, "Living in Revolutionary Times," 124-128. For a fascinating, unpublished "scrapbook" of information relating to royal medical appointments, see Samuel D. Clippingdale, Medical Court Roll 1, Royal College of Surgeons Library.

7. *Mercurius Reformatus*, January 29, 1690. For the appointment as superintendent of the surgeons in the fleet, see Historical Manuscripts Commission, *Twelfth Report*, App. vii, 313. For the job as principal physician to Deptford fort, see *The Calendar of State Papers, Domestic Series, for the Reign of William and Mary, 1694-1695*, 178-179, 220. For the commissioner for the exchange of prisoners, see *The Calendar of State Papers, Domestic Series, for the Reign of William III, 1695*, 256.

8. Historical Manuscripts Commission, *Twelfth Report*, Appendix, Part 7 of S.H. Fleming, esq. (London: Her Majesty's Stationery Office, 1890), 17(2): 313.

9. James Yonge, *The Journal of James Yonge*, ed. F.N.L. Poynter (Hamden CT: Archon Books, 1963), 203. Yonge specifically named Commissioners Addison, Starkey, and Shepheard as those who treated him badly.

10. Historical Manuscripts Commission, *Report on the Manuscripts of the Late Allan George Finch*, 4 (London: HMSO, 1965), 267.

11. *Calendar of Treasury Books, 1660-1718*, 5(1689-92), (London: His Majesty's Stationery Office, 1931): 402, 413, 846, 915, 1209, 1260, 1296, 1308, 1310, 1492; Historical Manuscripts Commission, *Finch MSS*, 3 (London: HMSO, 1957): 406.

12. Samuel Baston, *Baston's Case Vindicated* (London: n.p., 1695), 18fn. Baston, Clerk of the Commission for the Sick and Wounded, argued that "in every £100 the King paid at Deptford, his majesty paid above £80 thereof in his own wrong."

13. *Calendar of Treasury Books*, 5:1810.

14. John Ruhräh, "Walter Harris, Seventeenth-Century Pediatrist," *Annals of Medical History* 2(1919): 239. See also David Potterton, ed., *Culpeper's Color Herbal* (New York: Sterling Publishing, 1983), 155. Nicholas Culpeper's *Complete Herbal*, published in 1649, was intended to be a poor man's dispensary and was among the most popular books of its kind.

15. Baston, 48fn. Baston investigated the price of good rhubarb, fit for

an apothecary's use, and found it cost twenty-four shillings per pound. Rhubarb bought by the commissioners cost only nine pence per pound.

16. Baston, 8, 10-12, 14, 18.

17. Baston refers to the commissioners obtaining "a *celsit executio,*" thereby avoiding any punishment at all. I believe he erred writing "*celsit,*" the term for a stay of execution is *cesset executio,* close to what Baston thought he heard. Baston, 20.

18. *Calendar of State Papers, Domestic Series, for the Reign of William and Mary, 1694-95,* (London: Eyre and Spottiswoode, 1895), 178-179.

19. *Calendar of State Papers, Domestic Series, for the Reign of William III, 1695* (London: Mackie and Company, 1908), 256.

20. See Harold J. Cook, "Practical Medicine and the British Armed Forces after the 'Glorious Revolution', *Medical History* 34 (1990): 1-26. I am grateful to Professor Cook for his views about Welwood's appointments.

21. Welwood's induction is recorded in Annals of the Royal College of Physicians, Vol. 5, f.125b, Library of the Royal College of Physicians, London. Permission to cite these handwritten archives has been obtained from the College Registrar. Charlton's reference may refer to a Scottish appointment for Welwood. For an index of royal physicians through 1700 see Harold J. Cook, *The Decline of the Old Medical Regime in Stuart London* (Ithaca: Cornell University Press, 1986), 281.

22. See Leslie G. Matthews, "Italian Charlatans in England," *Pharmaceutical Historian* 9 (1979): 2-5.

23. For analysis of the jurisdictional conflict in Augustan medical circles that precipitated great changes within English medicine, see Geoffrey Holmes, *Augustan England: Professions, State and Society 1680-1730* (London: George Allen and Unwin, 1982), 166-235.

24. Rattansi Pyarali, "Paracelsus and the Puritan Revolution," Ambix 12 (1964): 6fn. Pyarali counts 186 members of the Royal College in all categories.

25. Queen Anne often consulted John Shadwell, unlicensed by the college until 1712, but a member of the Royal Society and prosperous anyway.

26. See Harold J. Cook, *Trials of an Ordinary Doctor* (Baltimore: Johns Hopkins University Press, 1994).

27. Pressure to decide for Rose might have come from the church, as a

strong link between the clergy and apothecaries existed in Augustan England. The clergy supplied apothecaries country-wide with more apprentices than any other occupational group. Geoffrey Holmes, *Augustan England* (London: George Allen and Unwin, 1982), 212.

28. Annals of the Royal College of Physicians, Vol. 7, 182-198.

29. Theodore M. Brown, "The College of Physicians and the Acceptance of Iatromechanism in England, 1665-1695," *Bulletin of the History of Medicine* 44 (1970): 28-29.

30. For information on officers of the Royal College of Physicians, see George Clark, *History of the Royal College of Physicians in London*, 2 Vols. (Oxford: 1964), 1: 90-92.

31. Munk, *Roll*, 1:483. Ironically, Blackmore's admission to the College in the great augmentation of 1687 had been seen as demeaning to the institution.

32. Francis Glisson, *Treatise on Rickets* (London: n.p. 1651), passim; Glisson reports one rumor that you could catch rickets from a red-headed wet nurse. Christina Hole, *The English Housewife in the Seventeenth Century* (London: Chatts and Windus, 1953), 86-92.

33. John Pechey, *The Compleat Herbal of Physical Plants* (London, H. Bonwicke, 1694), 149; Richard Lower, *Dr. Lower's Receipts* (London: n.p., 1700), passim.

34. William Salmon, ed., *Pharmacopoeia Bateana* (London: Sam Smith 1694), passim.

35. Edward Strother, ed., *Pharmacopoeia Radcliffeanae* (London: C. Rivington, 1716), 419.

36. SL 123, folio 1; SL 4046, f. 132; SL 4077, f. 15, Sloane Manuscripts, British Library.

37. Fielding Garrison, *Introduction to the History of Medicine*, 4th edition (Philadelphia: W. B. Saunders, 1929), 289.

38. John Browne, *Preternatural Tumours* (London: S. R., 1678), 76, 120, 379.

39. Leslie G. Matthews, "Day Book of the Court Apothecary," *Medical History* 22 (April 1978): 161-173.

40. Queen Anne was also forcefully bled for various afflictions, sometimes even to syncope. For her health and the doctors who treated her, see Elizabeth Lane Furdell, "Medical Personnel at the Court of Queen Anne," *The Historian* 68 (1986): 412-429.

41. Quoted in Garrison, 290. Garrison alleged that cinchona delivered the deathblow to Galenism in medical practice.

42. Robert Talbor, *The English Remedy* (London: J. Wallis, 1682), 29.

43. Robert Talbor, *Pyretologia: A Rational Account of the Causes and Cures of Agues* (London: R. Robinson, 1672), 44.

44. SL 4036, ff. 57-61; SL 123, f. 7; John Woodward, *The State of Physick and of Diseases* (London: T. Horne, 1718), 52.

45. John Browne, *Adenographia* (London, n.p., 1684), 188. See also Elizabeth Lane Furdell, "King's Evil," *Historical Dictionary of Stuart England*, Ronald Fritze and William Robinson, eds. (Westport CT: Greenwood Press, 1996).

46. Thomas Babington Macaulay, *History of England*, 3 Vols. (New York: Dutton, 1968), 3: 78. Macaulay ridiculed the large proportion of the population thinking itself scrofulous, and speculated that the "cure" of those with only slight and transient maladies kept up the vulgar belief." He did repeat the report, however, that the single person whom William touched was cured.

47. Cook, "Living in Revolutionary Times," 113.

48. Robert Molesworth was a writer for *The London Journal* along with fellow Whigs Daniel Defoe, Thomas Gordon, and John Trenchard, another friend of James Welwood. Welwood's daughter, Elizabeth, married Molesworth's son, Walter.

49. The Molesworth letters can be found in Historical Manuscripts Commission, *Report on Manuscripts in Various Collections*, 7 (London: HMSO, 1914): 244, 281, 304, 345, 378, 386.

50. William Salmon, *Pharmacopoeia Londinensis or New London Dispensatory*, 5th ed. (London: J. Dawks, 1696), 198-199.

51. Andrew Wear, "Health and the Environment in Early Modern England," *Medicine and Society*, (Cambridge: Cambridge University Press, 1992), 131-133.

Chapter Seven: Doctor Welwood and Mrs. Howard

1. Peter Clark and Paul Slack, *English Towns in Transition* (Oxford: Oxford University Press, 1976), 62; Daniel Defoe, *A Tour through the Whole Island of Great Britain* (London: Penguin, 1978), 294, 700.

2. Quoted in A. R. Humphreys, *The Augustan World* (New York: Harper and Row, 1954), 6.

3. For an economic assessment of Welwood's neighborhood, see Gregg Carr, *Residence and Social Status: The Development of Seventeenth-Century London* (New York: Garland, 1990), 150.

As for the waterworks, in the 1720s the company unwisely ventured into land speculation and insurance, making its finances precarious and litigable. One of its investments was in forfeited Scottish estates bought after the 1715 rebellion.

4. For portraiture and its civic value, see John Murdoch, "Painting: from Astraea to Augustus," in *Cambridge Cultural History of Britain*, Vol. 4, ed. Boris Ford (Cambridge: Cambridge University Press, 1992), 234-265; Mary Ede, *Arts and Society in England under William and Mary* (London: Stainer and Bell, 1979), 100-105.

5. Laird Okie, *Augustan Historical Writing* (Lanham, MD: University Press of America, 1991), 37. See also Deborah Stephan, "Laurence Echard, Whig Historian," *Historical Journal* 32 (1989): 843-866.

6. Sloane MSS 4062, f.3, British Library.

7. Historical Manuscripts Commission, *Report on the Laing Manuscripts*, 2 (London: HMSO, 1925): 186-188.

8. *Letters of the Countess of Suffolk and the Honorable George Berkeley*, 2 Vols., ed. John Wilson Croker (London: 1824) 1: 82.

9. J. M. Rigg's brief sketch in *The Dictionary of National Biography* gives her dates as 1681-1767, making her 86 when she died. A contemporary obituary in *Gentlemen's Magazine* supports the 1681 birthdate, but later historians and antiquarians have disagreed. Lewis Melville refuted the Rigg entry, insisting that the marriage of Henrietta's parents took place in 1684. John Lord Hervey also supports a later birthdate, reporting that Mrs. Howard was about forty when George II succeeded to the throne in June 1727, but his editor inserted that she was forty-six. See Lewis Melville, *Lady Suffolk and Her Circle* (Boston: Houghton Mifflin, 1924) and John, Lord Hervey, *Memoirs of the Reign of George II*, 3 Vols., ed. Romney Sedgwick, 1 (New York: AMS Press, 1970): 42.

10. See Anne Laurence's study of the varied lives English women lived in *Women in England 1500-1760* (New York: St. Martin's Press, 1994. Among the success stories noted by Laurence are the portrait painter Mary Beale, the great collagist Mary Delany, writers Elizabeth Carter and Mary Barber, and translator Mary Arundell.

11. Joyce Ellis, "On the Town: Women in Augustan England," *History*

Today 45 (December 1995): 20-27. Ellis recounts the class constrictions of women like Mrs. Howard, permitted to mix only with those of equal social standing; men could fraternize with those both above and below them in rank with impunity.

12. See Lawrence Stone, *The Family, Sex and Marriage in England 1500-1800* (New York: Harper and Row, 1977), 527-545. Stone's work has been widely censured for its methodology; see, for instance, Alan Macfarlane's criticism in *History and Theory* 18 (1979): 103-126, and Linda Pollock, *Forgotten Children* (New York: Cambridge University Press, 1983), another systematic demolition of Stone.

13. Charles Chenevix Trench, *George II* (London: Allen Lane, 1973), 19.

14. Spencer Cowper, ed., *Diary of Mary, Countess Cowper* (London: J. Murray, 1864), 25. Lady Cowper's journal covers October 1714 to October 1716 and April to May 1720.

15. Additional MSS 22627, f. 13. British Library.

16. *Ibid.*, ff. 30, 39. Henrietta later adopted and educated a niece, Dorothy Hobart, and a grandniece, naming them her beneficiaries after the death of her childless son in 1745. See Croker, *Letters*, 1: xvi.

17. Hervey, 1: 42, 85.

18. Quoted in Charles Carlton, *Royal Mistresses* (London: Routledge, 1990), 103. Pope described himself thusly: "In moderation placing all my glory, while Tories call me Whig, and Whigs a Tory."

19. Horace Walpole, *Reminiscences* (Oxford: Clarendon Press, 1926), 51, 57; and also his *Memoirs of King George II*, 3 Vols., ed. John Burke (New Haven CT: Yale, 1985) 1: 117.

20. *Ibid.*, 1: 51. Walter's father, Viscount Robert Molesworth, was an "Old Whig" whose writings are a part of the English liberal tradition. See the profile of him and his circle in Caroline Robbins, *The Eighteenth Century Commonwealthman* (New York: Atheneum, 1968), 88-133. The viscount would have seen eye-to-eye with Welwood on most political issues and that may account for their children's marriage.

21. Historical Manuscripts Commission, *Report on Manuscripts in Various Collections*, 7 (London: HMSO, 1914): 281.

22. For a complete discussion of the South Sea Company and its subsequent failure, see John Carswell, *The South Sea Bubble* (London: Cresset, 1960).

23. Add. MSS 22629, f. 8.

24. Croker, *Letters*, 1: 55.

25. Charles Bechdolt Realey, "*The London Journal* and Its Authors, 1720-23," *Bulletin of the University of Kansas Humanistic Studies* 5 (1935): 4-5. By September 1722 the paper was taken over by the government of Robert Walpole.

26. Quoted in Melville, 176-177.

27. Add. MSS 22627, ff. 14, 17-18.

28. Croker and Melville inaccurately date as 1727 the May correspondence involving Welwood. Since the doctor died on 1 April, 1727, the letters in question must have been written the previous year. See Croker, *Letters*, 1: 51; Melville, 166-167. Their errors are understandable because the folios in the Suffolk correspondence have been numbered out-of-sequence. Welwood's death date provides the key to an accurate chronology.

29. Add. MSS 22627, ff. 30-31.

30. *Ibid.*, ff. 25, 27.

31. Walpole, *Reminiscences*, 62-63. According to Lord Hervey, Caroline may have preferred Mrs. Howard to another rival, but she still called her the king's "trull." Hervey, 2: 187. See also Add. MSS 22627, f. 28.

32. Hervey, 2: 473.

33. Add. MSS 22627, f. 22. Hobart was later named first Earl of Buckinghamshire by George II.

34. *Ibid.*, f. 32.

35. *Ibid.*, ff. 30, 34.

36. She did discuss her health with Dr. Arbuthnot, who recommended for her ailments riding, bathing and "hiera picra," a laxative he had also prescribed for Queen Anne. See Croker, *Letters*, 1: 296.

37. Add MSS 22627, f. 35.

38. *Ibid.*; Hervey 2: 473-474.

39. Add MSS 22627, f. 36.

40. Quoted in Hervey, 2: 601. Besides, the king wasted no time in finding a replacement for Henrietta.

Epilogue

1. The references for wills in the Prerogative Court of Canterbury have recently been converted by the Public Record Office into a new system.

James Welwood's will, formerly P.C.C., Farrant, f. 101, is now PROB 11, 615.

2. Susan Dwyer Amussen, *An Ordered Society: Gender and Class in Early Modern England* (Oxford: Basil Blackwell, 1988), 92. See also Amy Louise Erickson, *Women and Property in Early Modern England* (London: Routledge, 1993), 157-159.

3. The author thanks Sara Heller Mendelson for this citation; for more on biases against females, see her *Mental World of Stuart Women* (Amherst MA: University of Massachusetts Press, 1987).

4. She died in March 1732. The will can be found in PROB 11/651, f. 237RH-239RH, Public Record Office.

5. Herbert Butterfield, *The Whig Interpretation of History* (New York: W. W. Norton, 1963), 12. Butterfield subsequently muted his criticism of Whig history when he acknowledged "it had a wonderful effect on English politics." Quoted in Joseph Hamburger, *Macaulay and the Whig Tradition* (Chicago: University of Chicago Press, 1976), 229 n.100.

6. J. Hamburger, 82-87; Timothy Lang, *Victorians and the Stuart Heritage* (Cambridge: Cambridge University Press, 1995), 84.

7. Macaulay relied on Welwood's *Memoirs* for the thoughtful evaluation of Charles II's death (1: 330), *Reflections* for analysis of the Grandval conspiracy (3: 483), and *Answer to the Late King James' Last Declaration*, which Macaulay identified as Welwood's work, for Jacobite activity (3: 440; 4: 12). Throughout Volume 3, the editions of *Mercurius* cited are: 1689 September 18 and 25, October 8, December 4 and 11; 1690 February 12, June 11, and September 5; for 1691, April 11.

8. G. M. Trevelyan, *England under the Stuarts*, rev. ed. (London: Methuen, 1925), 419-420.

9. *Ibid.*, 516. For a critique of Trevelyan, see *New York Review of Books* 40, no.13 (July 1993): 9-13.

10. Robert C. Braddock, "J. H. Plumb and the Whig Tradition," in *Recent Historians of Great Britain*, ed. Walter Arnstein (Ames IO: University of Iowa Press, 1990), 116. Incidentally, Whig and neo-Whig historians are frequently honored with knighthoods; revisionists and Marxists are not!

11. J. P. Kenyon, "The Revolution of 1688: Resistance and Contract," *Historical Perspectives: Studies in English Thought and Society in Honour of J. H. Plumb* (London: Europa Publications, 1974), 47. Other influential

Plumb-trained experts include J. J. Scarisbrick, Neil McKendrick, G. V. Bennett, A. Rupert Hall, Eric Stokes, and Linda Colley.

12. William Munk, *Roll of the Royal College of Physicians of London*, 2 Vols. (London: Longman, Green, and Roberts, 1861) 1: 483.

13. *Bulletin of the Institute of Historical Research* 9 (1931-32): 203-205; *Dictionary of National Biography Supplement: Corrections and Additions* (Boston: G. K. Hall, 1966), 204-205. I have penned the entry for Welwood in the *New Dictionary of National Biography*, forthcoming from Oxford University Press under the general editorship of H. C. G. Matthew.

14. A. W. Pollard and G. R. Redgrave, *Short-Title Catalogue of Books Printed in England, Scotland, Ireland, Wales, and British America and of All English Books Printed in Other Countries, 1475-1640.* (London: Bibliographic Society, 1969); Donald G. Wing, *Short-Title Catalogue...1641-1700* (New York: Index Committee of the Modern Language Association, 1972).

15. David C. Douglas, general editor, *English Historical Documents,1660-1714*, Vol. 4 ed. Andrew Browning (London: Routledge, 1966), 899-900, 902-903.

16. John Bernard Burke, *Burke's Genealogical and Heraldic History of the Landed Gentry*, 18th ed. (London: Burke's Peerage, Ltd., 1965-72), 944-945. Welwoods can also be found in *Burke's Genealogical and Heraldic History of the Peerage, Baronetage, and Knightage* (London: Burke's Peerage Ltd., 1818-1906).

Bibliography

The educated layman who approaches any topic in the seventeenth or eighteenth centuries might be amazed at the wealth of primary sources available in print. Nothing is more inspiring than reading works in the original format and language; happily for both professionals and non-professionals alike, microfilmed collections of many early English books and newspapers are readily available at major libraries and through inter-library loan. The Wing Collection is your key to the Augustan Age. All of James Welwood's publications and those of his contemporaries can be read and enjoyed as intended, sipping coffee and mulling over timeless problems. The advertisements alone at the end of each issue of *Mercurius Reformatus* or *The London Gazette* are marvelous time capsules from their age. One of the things that amazed me about this project is that no one had as yet brought Welwood to the attention of a wider audience, given the fecundity of his pen and the availability of his publications. Countless government records of the era, memoirs, and letters are printed and ready for perusal, again to the benefit of any reader. Some Whiggish histories written in the Augustan Age are deservedly regarded as old chestnuts, still valued because they are so necessary to an understanding of the period. For all its flaws, Bishop Gilbert Burnet's *History of His Own Time* illuminates the "glorious" revolutionary path he walked, a path also trod by Dr. Welwood; Daniel Defoe's tour around Britain is a snapshot of the island in the 1720s, when Welwood was in his dotage.

As for secondary sources, the possibilities are endless and the works so rich that any reader of history (not to mention a writer) must be humbled by the choices. Traditionally, history books and college courses treated the Tudor-Stuart epoch as a piece to be followed by a discrete survey of the Hanoverians (or at least the first four Georges). Although a strong case can be made for making new historical segments, the latest panorama of the seventeenth century follows the conventional dynastic pattern and traditional interpretations of the British past. Mark Kishlansky's *A Monarchy Transformed: Britain 1603-1714* (bibliographic information follows) offers a stylish, fluid narrative of the Stuart block, sprinkled with witty observations and unburdened by revisionist interruptions. Another satisfying overview of the convoluted seventeenth century in Britain can be found in Barry Coward's *The Stuart Age*, often used as a text in university courses, and the early Georgian years can be sorted out in Dorothy Thompson's *Eighteenth Century England*. Answering the need for a short, analytical guide on the origins of party politics after the Restoration in England, Tim Harris has recently hacked his way through the dense partisan conflict from Court-Country tensions to the Jacobites. The result is *Politics under the Later Stuarts*, must-reading for anyone trying to unravel the era's complexities. The books of J. R. Jones always merit consideration for their lively revisionism of the fractious period before the "Glorious Revolution," and his *Revolution of 1688 in England* sets the standard for discussion on James' and William's intentions. W. A. Speck's *Reluctant Revolutionaries* supports Jones' conclusions about the Stuarts and his harsh opinion of the Whigs. John Miller's readable explanation of the impact of popery on politics makes a national obsession unpleasantly clear. I found P. W. J. Riley's *King William and the Scottish Politicians* to be a clear and cogent appraisal of the period 1688-1702. Recent books by R. O. Bucholz on Augustan court life and Paul Monod on Jacobitism suggest that profitable avenues in Augustan political history are still to be explored. The third and fourth volumes of *The Cambridge Cultural History of Britain* stunningly encompass the arts in the seventeenth and eighteenth centuries, but I recommend Mary Ede's compact and compelling *Arts and Society in England under William and Mary* for clarifying the nexus between politics and creativity after the 1688 coup.

Scotland's tumultuous past is best generally surveyed by John

Duncan Mackie, although interesting spins on Scottish nationalism can be found in work by Colin Kidd, particularly provocative in light of recent devolutionary developments there. The bottomless traditions of revolt in Scotland are excavated in a volume of articles edited by Terry Brotherstone, and J. H. S. Burleigh successfully unravels Scottish church history, which so directly affected Welwood's presbyterian family. For the Scottish witch-craze of Welwood's youth and any other witchcraft topic, Brian Levack's scholarship is the acknowledged *sine qua non*, although I find Christina Larner's book marvelous for its treatment of women. Roger Howell, Jr. has put his stamp on the history of seventeenth-century Newcastle, and in so doing has demonstrated the folly of separating local from national issues at a time of intense political polarization. Augustan London, Welwood's place of longest residence, can be visited via Valerie Pearl's path-breaking article on change and stability in the capital; Beier and Finlay's *London 1500-1700* and M. Dorothy George's classic *London Life in the Eighteenth Century* provide good overviews of their respective eras. Also recommended is Peter Earle's *A City Full of People: Men and Women of London 1650-1750* for its expansive examination of life and labor in the capital during Welwood's generation.

There are many tomes on education in the seventeenth century, especially as it affected science and medicine. For Scotland, the sketch of St. Andrews by Ronald Cant is useful, as is the collection of articles on the Scottish Enlightenment edited by Campbell and Skinner. A reader seeking broad insight into the evolution of higher education in France might best profit from the work of Laurence Brockliss, while Charles Courey has done valuable research on French medical schools. No English-language tome on the University at Reims is presently available, perhaps an incentive for anyone seeking to grasp the importance of that institution beyond the borders of France.

James Welwood centered his long life around three nuclei: writing, medicine, and family. Fascinating work on publishing and the development of reading has appeared since the 1970s; *The Practice and Representation of Reading in England* is a good place to start, although controversy persists about the meaning and measurement of literacy. Recommended for probing into the realm of communications are John Sommerville's new book on Augustan Age journalism and anything by

Lois Schwoerer, doyenne of English revolutionary propaganda. R. B. Walker's article on the Williamite press and Michael Harris' chapter in *Newspaper History* on ownership and control of the press are worthwhile to general reader and specialist alike. Tangential reading about the distribution of news, coffee-houses, and bookshops can shed light on the nascent consumer culture of the Augustan Age.

To assay Welwood's medical world, start with the series of essays that constitute *The Medical Revolution of the Seventeenth Century*, edited by Roger French and Andrew Wear, where one will find the engaging and thoughtful scholarship that is the hallmark of historian Harold J. Cook. Additionally, he has written the definitive investigation of the Royal College of Physicians' decline and the most delightful "microhistory" I know of for Williamite England, *Trials of an Ordinary Doctor*, the story of an acquaintance of Welwood. In many ways, the design of my biography of Welwood pays homage to Professor Cook, while my dissection of Dr. Welwood's newspaper and *Memoirs* follows the estimable model constructed in Charles Firth's analysis of Macaulay's history of England.

Dr. Welwood's family was also vital to his happiness, and he provided well for them. Those wishing to understand more about what was required in a substantial household like Welwood's might investigate Lorna Weatherill's *Consumer Behavior and Material Culture in Britain, 1660-1760*. Lawrence Stone, always at the center of academic controversy, provides fascinating details about family life in his book on early modern England, but his scholarship should be accompanied by a critical riposte; Alan Macfarlane's review in *History and Theory* will do nicely. For insight on parent-child relations, see Linda Pollock's *Forgotten Children*. She demolishes the notion that people did not love each other until the eighteenth century. Amy Erickson's recent scholarship mines the relationship of women and property, something Welwood, as the father of daughters, needed to ponder. Another oft-quoted author, although for a slightly later period than Welwood's, is Linda Colley; *Britons*, her judgment of what created the national British identity, has significance for an expatriate Scot like Welwood and for his family.

Biographies abound for key figures on the Augustan scene. Starting at the top of the social pyramid, Stephen Baxter published his life of

William III in 1966; its exclusive emphasis on politics undermines and dates its utility. Tony Claydon assessed the religious aspect of William's appeal, and Edward Gregg has limned a sympathetic portrait of Queen Anne. A new scholarly biography of Queen Mary II is needed, but after enduring Whiggish criticism over the centuries, James II is finally making a comeback, thanks in part to John Miller. Library shelves groan under the weight of Louis XIV's biographies, however Andrew Lossky's new book gives a sharp focus to the reign of the Sun King. Politicians' lives available include Henry Horwitz's classic study of Nottingham, Welwood's erstwhile nemesis. Paula Backsheider recently produced a literary biography of Welwood's polemicist competitor, Daniel Defoe, but surprisingly no modern biographies exist for Bishop Burnet, William Bentinck, or Richard Baldwin. Any work by Geoffrey Holmes is worth consulting, combining as he does graceful writing with ingenious scholarship, but I particularly recommend *The Trial of Doctor Sacheverell* to get an appreciation for the deep religious and political divisions within Augustan society. Gavin de Beer wrote about Hans Sloane's connection to the British Museum, but the plethora of rival scientists and literati can be best sorted out in Joseph M. Levine's likeable, *Dr. Woodward's Shield*, also inestimable for its examination of the connection between scholarship and class; Levine has written another recommendable tome, *The Battle of the Books*, which explores the intellectual dispute over "the ancients versus the moderns" in educational circles. Finally, while Welwood remains underappreciated for his legacy to English historiography, Philip Hicks and J. P. Kenyon have produced informative books on the classical influences and the contemporary inspirations which shaped *The History Men*.

Primary and Manuscript Sources

Additional Manuscripts. British Library. London.

Anderton, William. *True Copy of the paper, delivered to the Sheriffs of London and Middlesex, by Mr. William Anderton.* London: n.s., 1693.

Annals of the Royal College of Physicians. Volumes 5-8. Library of the Royal College of Physicians. London.

Baston, Samuel. *Baston's Case Vindicated.* London: n.p., 1695.

Burnet, Gilbert. *History of His Own Time*. 2 Vols. London: Thomas Ward, 1724.

Calendar of State Papers, Domestic Series, for the Reign of William III. London: Mackie and Co., 1908-1937.

Calendar of State Papers, Domestic Series, for the Reign of William and Mary. London: Lyre and Spottiswood, 1895-1906.

Calendar of Treasury Books, 1660-1718. 5 (1691-95). London: His Majesty's Stationery Office, 1904.

Cowper, Spencer, ed. *Diary of Mary, Countess Cowper*. London: J. Murray, 1864.

Croker, John Wilson, ed. *Letters of the Countess of Suffolk and the Honorable George Berkeley*. 2 Volumes. London: J. Murray, 1824.

The Dilucidator: or Reflections upon Modern Transactions by Way of Letters from a Person at Amsterdam to His Friend in London. London: Randall Taylor, 1689.

Doebner, Richard, ed. *Memoirs of Mary, Queen of England*. London: David Nutt, 1886.

Hervey, John. *Memoirs of the Reign of George II*. 3 Vols. Edited by Romney Sedgwick. New York: AMS Press, 1970.

Historical Manuscripts Commission. *Report on Manuscripts in Various Collections*. Volume 7. London: H.M.S.O., 1914.

_____. *Report on the Manuscripts of the Late Allen George Finch*. Volume 2. London: H.M.S.O., 1922; Vol. 3, 1957; Vol. 4, 1965.

_____. *12th Report, Appendix, Part 7. The Manuscripts of S.H. Fleming*. Vol. 17, Part 2. London: HMSO, 1890.

_____. *Thirteenth Report, Appendix, Part 5. The Manuscripts of Sir William Fitzherbert and Others*. London: H.M.S.O., 1893.

The Historical Register. Vols. 12, 17. London: R. Nutt, 1727, 1732.

House of Commons Journal, November 1691.

Lansdowne Manuscripts. British Library. London.

Lucan. *Pharsalia*. Translation by Nicholas Rowe. Preface by James Welwood. London: J. Tonson, 1718.

March, John. *Sermons Preach'd on Several Occasions*. 2nd Edition. London: Robert Clavell, 1699.

A Modest Enquiry into the Causes of the Present Disasters. London: Richard Baldwin, 1690.

Register of the Privy Council of Scotland. Vols. 9-11. Edinburgh: Her Majesty's General Register House: 1877-1898.

Registered Copy Wills, Prerogative Court of Canterbury, Wills and Administrations. Farrant, f. 101 (now PROB11/615); PROB1 1/651, f.237RH-239RH. Public Record Office, Chancery Lane. London.

Reflections upon the Late Horrid Conspiracy Contrived by Some of the French Court to Murther His Majesty in Flanders. London: Richard Baldwin, 1692.

Reply to the Answer Doctor Welwood Has Made to King James' Declaration. London: 1693.

Rowe, Nicholas. *The Miscellaneous Works of Nicholas Rowe, Including a Character of Mr. Rowe by James Welwood*. London: W. Feales, 1733.

Sloane Manuscripts. British Library. London.

Walpole, Horace. *Memoirs of King George II*. 3 Vols. Edited by John Brooke. New Haven CT: Yale University Press, 1985.

_____. _. *Reminiscences*. Edited by Paget Toynbee. Oxford: Clarendon Press, 1926.

Welwood, Andrew. *Meditations Representing a Glimpse of Glory*. Boston: Rogers and Fowle, 1744.

Welwood, James. *Answer to the Late King James' Declaration to All His Pretended Subjects*. London: Dorman Newman, 1689.

_____. *Answer to the Late King James' Last Declaration, Dated at St. Germains*. London: Richard Baldwin, 1693.

_____. *Answer to the Vindication of the Letter from a Person of Quality in the North*. London: n.p., 1690.

_____. *Appendix to Mercurius Reformatus*. London: Richard Baldwin, 1692.

_____. *Compleat History of Europe for the Year 1705*. London: n.p., 1705.

_____. *An Exact Relation of the Wonderful Cure of Mary Maillard*. London: Richard Baldwin, 1694.

_____. *Memoirs of the Most Material Transactions in England for the Last Hundred Years*. 1st Edition. London: Tim Goodwin, 1700; 6th Edition. London: 1718.

_____. *Mercurius Reformatus*. London: 1689-1691.

_____. *Reasons Why the Parliament of Scotland Cannot Comply with the Late King James' Proclamation*. London: Dorman Newman, 1689.

_____. *Vindication of the Present Great Revolution in England*. London: R. Taylor, 1689.

____. *Weekly Remarks*. London: March 24, 1691-May 13, 1691.

Whitelocke, Bulstrode. *Memorials of the English Affairs*. Preface by James Welwood. London: E. Curll, 1709.

Xenophon. *The Minor Works of Xenophon: The Banquet of Xenophon*. Translated by James Welwood. London: J. Walker, 1813.

Secondary Sources

Allen, Phyllis, "Medical Education in Seventeenth-Century England," *Journal of the History of Medicine and Allied Sciences* 1 (1946): 115-143.

Backsheider, Paula. *Daniel Defoe*. Baltimore: Johns Hopkins University Press, 1989.

Barbour, James Samuel. *A History of William Paterson and the Darien Company*. Edinburgh: William Blackwood and Sons, 1907.

Bateson, F. W., ed. *The Cambridge Bibliography of English Literature*. Volume 2 1660-1800. Cambridge: Cambridge University Press, 1966.

Baxter, Stephen. *William III and the Defense of European Liberty*. New York: Harcourt Brace and World, 1966.

Baynes, John. *The Jacobite Rising of 1715*. London: Cassell, 1970.

Beddard, Robert. "Anti-Popery and the London Mob, 1688," *History Today* 38 (July 1988): 36-39.

Beik, William. "Louis XIV and the Cities." In *Edo and Paris*, edited by James McClain. Ithaca NY: Cornell University Press, 1994.

Beier, A. L. and R. Finlay, eds. *London 1500-1700*. 1986.

Beljame, Alexandre. *Men of Letters and the English Public in the Eighteenth Century 1660-1744*. London: Kegan Paul, Trench and Trubner, 1948.

Benedict, Philip, ed. *Cities and Social Change in Early Modern France*. London: Unwin Hyman, 1989.

Black, Jeremy. *The English Press in the Eighteenth Century*. Philadelphia: University of Pennsylvania Press, 1987.

Blagden, Cyprian. *The Stationers' Company*. Stanford, CA: Stanford University Press, 1960.

Boussinesq, Georges and Gustave Laurent. *Histoire de Reims*. 2nd ed. 2 vols. Reims: Matot-Braine, 1933.

Braddock, Robert C. "J. H. Plumb and the Whig Tradition." in *Recent Historians of Great Britain*, edited by Walter Arnstein. Ames IO: Iowa State University Press, 1990.

Brockliss, Laurence. *French Higher Education in the Seventeenth and Eighteenth Centuries*. Oxford: Clarendon Press, 1987.

Brown, Theodore M. "The College of Physicians and the Acceptance of Iatromechanism in England, 1665-1695," *Bulletin of the History of Medicine* 44 (1970): 12-30.

Bucholz, R.O. *The Augustan Court*. Stanford CA: Stanford University Press, 1993.

Buckroyd, Julia. *The Life of James Sharp, Archbishop of St. Andrews*. Edinburgh: John Donald, 1987.

Burleigh, J. H. S. *A Church History of Scotland*. London: Oxford University Press, 1960.

Burtt, Shelley. *Virtue Transformed: Political Argument in England, 1688-1740*. Cambridge: Cambridge University Press, 1992.

Butterfield, Herbert. *The Whig Interpretation of History*. New York: W. W. Norton, 1965.

Campbell, R. H. and Andrew Skinner, eds. *The Origins and Nature of the Scottish Enlightenment*. Edinburgh: John Donald, 1982.

Cant, Ronald G. *The University of St. Andrews*. Edinburgh: Scottish Academy Press, 1970.

Carlton, Charles. *Royal Mistresses*. London: Routledge, 1990.

Carr, Gregg. *Residence and Social Status: The Development of Seventeenth-Century London*. New York: Garland Press, 1990.

Carswell, John. *The Descent on England*. New York: John Day, 1969.

_____. *The South Sea Bubble*. London: Cresset, 1960.

Chalmers, Peter. *Historical and Statistical Account of Dunfermline*. 2 Vols. Edinburgh: William Blackwood and Sons, 1859.

Chenevix Trench, Charles. *George II*. London: Allen Lane, 1983.

Clark, George. *A History of the Royal College of Physicians*. Volume 1. Oxford: Clarendon Press, 1964.

Clark, Peter and Paul Slack. *English Towns in Transition 1500-1700*. London: Oxford University Press, 1976.

Claydon, Tony. *William III and the Godly Revolution*. Cambridge: Cambridge University Press, 1996.

Clifton, Robin. "James II's Two Rebellions," *History Today* 38 (1988): 23-29.

Clippingdale, Samuel D. Medical Court Roll. 2 Vols. Royal College of Surgeons Library. London.

Clive, John. *Not by Fact Alone: Essays on the Writing and Reading of History*. New York: Alfred A. Knopf, 1989.

Colbourn, H. Trevor. *The Lamp of Experience*. Chapel Hill NC: University of North Carolina Press, 1965.

Colley, Linda. *Britons*. New Haven CT: Yale University Press, 1992.

Comrie, John D. *History of Scottish Medicine*. 2 Vols. London: Bailliere, Tindall and Cox, 1932.

Cook, Harold J. *The Decline of the Old Medical Regime in Stuart London*. Ithaca NY: Cornell University Press, 1986.

_____. "Living in Revolutionary Times: Medical Change under William and Mary." in *Patronage and Institutions: Science, Technology, and Medicine at the European Court*, edited by Bruce T. Moran. Rochester NY: Boydell Press, 1991.

_____. "Practical Medicine in the British Armed Forces after the 'Glorious Revolution,'" *Medical History* 34 (1990): 1-26.

_____. *Trials of an Ordinary Doctor*. Baltimore MD: Johns Hopkins, 1994.

Coury, Charles. "The Teaching of Medicine in France from the Beginning of the Seventeenth Century." In *History of Medical Education*, edited by C. D. O'Malley. Los Angeles: University of California Press, 1970.

Craig, W. S. *History of the Royal College of Physicians of Edinburgh*. Oxford: Blackwell Scientific Publication, 1976.

Cressy, David. *Literacy and the Social Order: Reading and Writing in Tudor and Stuart England*. Cambridge: Cambridge University Press, 1980.

Cross, F. L., ed. *Oxford Dictionary of the Christian Church*, 3d ed. Oxford: Oxford University Press, 1997.

Cruickshanks, Eveline, ed. *By Force or By Default: The Revolution of 1688-1689*. Edinburgh: John Donald Publishers, 1989.

Cruickshanks, Eveline and Jeremy Black, (eds.). *The Jacobite Challenge*. Edinburgh: John Donald, 1988.

de Beer, G. R. *Sir Hans Sloane and the British Museum*. London: Oxford University Press, 1953.

Defoe, Daniel. *A Tour through the Whole Island of Great Britain*. 2 vols. London: Dent, 1962.

DeKrey, Gary S. *A Fractured Society*. Oxford: Clarendon Press, 1985.

____. "Political Radicalism in London after the Glorious Revolution," *Journal of Modern History* 55 (December 1983): 585-617.

Desportes, Pierre, ed. *Histoire de Reims*. Toulouse: Universe de la France et des Pays Francophone, 1983.

Dictionary of National Biography. 22 volumes. New York: Macmillan, 1908.

Dictionary of National Biography Supplement: Corrections and Additions. Boston: G. K. Hall, 1966.

Dill, Marshall, Jr. *Paris in Time*. New York: G. P. Putnam's Sons, 1975.

Durkan, John. "The French Connection in the Sixteenth and Early Seventeenth Centuries." In *Scotland and Europe*, edited by T.C. Smout. Edinburgh: John Donald, 1986.

Dwyer, John, Roger Mason and Alexander Murdoch. eds. *New Perspectives on the Politics and Culture of Early Modern Scotland*. Edinburgh: John Donald, 1979.

Earle, Peter. *A City Full of People: Men and Women of London, 1650-1750*. London: Metheun, 1994.

Ede, Mary. *Arts and Society in England under William and Mary*. London: Stainer and Bell, 1979.

Ellis, Aytoun. *The Penny Universities: A History of the Coffee-Houses*. London: Secker and Warburg, 1956.

Ellis, Frank. "The Background of the London Dispensary," *Journal of the History of Medicine* 20 (1965): 197-212.

Ellis, Joyce. "On the Town: Women in Augustan England," *History Today* 45 (December 1995): 20-27.

Erickson, Amy Louise, *Women and Property in Early Modern England*. London: Routledge, 1993.

Evans, Joan. *History of the Society of Antiquaries*. London: Oxford, 1956.

Feather, John. *A History of British Publishing*. London: Routledge, 1988.

Fenwick, Hubert. *The Auld Alliance*. Kineton, Warwickshire: Roundwood Press, 1971.

Ferris, Forrest G. and Forrest G. Ferris, Jr. *The Law of Extraordinary Legal Remedies*. St. Louis MO: Thomas, 1926.

Fiennes, Celia. *Through England on A Side-Saddle in the Time of William and Mary*. London: Field and Tuer, 1888.

Firth, Charles. *A Commentary on Macaulay's 'History of England'*. London: Frank Cass, 1964.

Ford, Boris, ed. *Cambridge Cultural History of Britain*. Vols 3-4. Cambridge: Cambridge University Press, 1992.

Frank, Jr., Robert G. "Science, Medicine and the Universities of Early Modern England," *History of Science* 11 (1973): 194-216; 239-269.

French, Roger and Andrew Wear. *The Medical Revolution of the Seventeenth Century*. Cambridge: Cambridge University Press, 1989.

Furdell, Elizabeth Lane. "Medical Personnel at the Court of Queen Anne," *The Historian* 68 (1986): 412-429.

George, M. Dorothy. *London Life in the Eighteenth Century*. 3rd ed. London: London School of Economics, 1951.

Goldie, Mark. "John Locke's Circle and James II," *Historical Journal* 35 (1992): 557-587.

_____. "The Revolution of 1689 and the Structure of Political Argument," *Bulletin of Research in the Humanities* 83 (1980): 473-564.

Gooch, Leo. *The Desperate Faction?: Jacobites of North East England*. Kingston upon Hull, Humberside: University of Hull Press, 1995.

Goubert, Pierre. *Louis XIV and Twenty Million Frenchmen*. New York: Vintage Books, 1966.

Gregg, Edward. *Queen Anne*. London: Routledge and Kegan Paul, 1980.

Hamburger, Joseph. *Macaulay and the Whig Tradition*. Chicago: University of Chicago Press, 1976.

Hamburger, Philip, "Seditious Libel," *Stanford Law Review* 37 (1985): 661-720.

Hamilton, Elizabeth. *William's Mary*. New York: Taplinger, 1972.

Harris, Michael. "The Structure, Ownership and Control of the Press, 1620-1780," in *Newspaper History*, edited by George Boyce, James Curran and Pauline Wingate. London: Constable, 1978.

Harris, Michael and Alan Lee, eds. *The Press in English Society from the Seventeenth to the Nineteenth Centuries*. Rutherford NJ: Fairleigh Dickinson University Press, 1986.

Harris, Tim. *Politics under the Later Stuarts: Party Conflict in a Divided Society*. London: Longman, 1993.

_____. *London Crowds in the Reign of Charles II*. Cambridge: Cambridge University Press, 1987.

Hatton, R. M. *George I, Elector and King*. Cambridge MA: Harvard University Press, 1978.

Henry, John. "The Scientific Revolution in England," in *The Scientific Revolution in National Context*. Edited by Roy Porter and Mikulas Teich. New York: Cambridge University Press, 1992.

Hicks, Philip. *Neoclassical History and English Culture: From Clarendon to Hume*. London: Macmillan, 1996.

Hoak, Dale and Mordechai Feingold, eds. *The World of William and Mary*. Stanford CA: Stanford University Press, 1996.

Holmes, Geoffrey. *Augustan England: Professions, State and Society 1680-1730*. London: George Allen and Unwin, 1982.

_____. *The Trial of Doctor Sacheverell*. London: Eyre Methuen, 1973.

Horsley, P.M. *Eighteenth-Century Newcastle*. Newcastle: Oriel Press, 1971.

Horwitz, Henry. *Parliament, Policy and Politics in the Reign of William III*. Manchester: Manchester University Press, 1977.

_____. *Revolution Politicks: The Career of Daniel Finch, Second Earl of Nottingham*. Cambridge: Cambridge University Press, 1968.

Howell, Roger, Jr. "Newcastle and the Nation: The Seventeenth Century Experience." In *The Tudor and Stuart Town*, edited by Jonathan Barry. London: Longman, 1990.

_____. *Newcastle upon Tyne and the Puritan Revolution*. Oxford: Clarendon Press, 1967.

Hudson, Geoffrey Lewis. "Negotiating for Blood Money: War Widows and the Courts in Seventeenth-Century England." In *Women, Crime and the Courts in Early Modern England*, edited by W.A. Maguire. Chapel Hill NC: University of North Carolina Press, 1995.

Humphreys, A. R. *The Augustan World*. New York: Harper, 1963.

Imbert-Terry, Henry M. "Some Memorialists of the Period of the Restoration." In *Essays by Divers Hands: Transactions of the Royal Society of Literature of the United Kingdom*, edited by William R. Inge. New Series, Volume 2. London: Humphrey Milford, 1922.

Insh, George Pratt. *The Company of Scotland Trading to Africa and the Indies*. New York: C. Scribner's Sons, 1932.

Jacquinet, Andre. *Le Centre Universitaire Medical de Reims: 1550-1967*. Reims: Coulon, 1967.

Johnson, Odai. "Pope-burning Pageants: Performing the Exclusion Crisis," *Theatre Survey* 37 (1997): 34-58.

Jones, Clyve, ed. *Britain in the First Age of Party 1680-1750*. London: Hambledon Press, 1987.

Jones, J. R. *The First Whigs*. London: Oxford University Press, 1970.

____. *The Revolution of 1688 in England*. New York: Norton, 1973.

Jones, J. R., ed. *Liberty Secured? Britain before and after 1688*. Stanford CA: Stanford University Press, 1992.

Kearney, Hugh. *Scholars and Gentlemen: Universities and Society in Pre-Industrial Britain 1500-1700*. Ithaca NY: Cornell University Press, 1970.

Kenyon, John Philips. *History Men: The Historical Profession in England since the Renaissance*. Pittsburgh PA: University of Pittsburgh Press, 1983.

____. *The Popish Plot*. New York: Penguin, 1974.

____. *Robert Spencer, Earl of Sunderland*. Westport CT: Greenwood Press, 1958.

Kidd, Colin. *Subverting Scotland's Past: Scottish-Whig Historians and the Creation of an Anglo-British Identity*. Cambridge: Cambridge University Press, 1993.

Kiernan, V.J. "A Banner with a Strange Device: The Later Covenanters." In *Covenant, Charter and Party: Traditions of Revolt and Protest in Modern Scottish History*, edited by Terry Brotherstone. Aberdeen: Aberdeen University Press, 1989.

Kishlansky, Mark. *A Monarchy Transformed: Britain 1603-1714*. New York: Alan Lane/Penguin Press, 1997.

Lang, Andrew. *Sir George Mackenzie, King's Advocate*. London: Longman, Green and Company, 1909.

Lang, Timothy. *Victorians and the Stuart Heritage*. Cambridge: Cambridge University Press, 1995.

Larner, Christina. *Enemies of God*. Baltimore MD: Johns Hopkins University Press, 1981.

Laurence, Anne. *Women in England 1500-1760*. New York: St. Martin's, 1994.

Levack, Brian. *The Formation of the British State: England, Scotland, and the Union*. Oxford: Clarendon Press, 1987.

____. "The Great Scottish Witch Hunt of 1661-1662," *Journal of British Studies* 20 (1980): 90-108.

____. *The Witch-Hunt in Early Modern Europe*. 2nd Ed. New York: Longman, 1995.

Levine, Joseph M. *The Battle of the Books: History and Literature in the Augustan Age*. Ithaca: Cornell University Press, 1991.

_____. *Doctor Woodward's Shield: History, Science, and Satire in Augustan England*. Ithaca NY: Cornell University Press, 1977.

_____. *Humanism and History: Origins of Modern English Historiography*. Ithaca NY: Cornell University Press, 1987.

Lillywhite, Bryant. *London Coffee Houses*. London: George Allen and Unwin, 1963.

Lister, Martin. *A Journey to Paris in the Year 1698*. Edited by Raymond Phineas Stearns. Urbana IL: University of Illinois Press, 1967.

Lossky, Andrew. *Louis XIV and the French Monarchy*. New Brunswick NJ: Rutgers University Press, 1994.

Macaulay, Thomas Babington. *History of England*. 4 Vols. New York: Dutton, 1968.

Macfarlane, Alan. "Review Essay", *History and Theory* 18 (1979): 103-126.

Mackie, John Duncan. *History of Scotland*. New York: Dorsett, 1985.

Macleod, Walter, ed. *Journal of the Hon. John Erskine of Carnock, 1683-87*. Edinburgh: University Press, 1893.

Maguire, W. A., ed. *Kings in Conflict*. Belfast: Blackstaff Press, 1990.

Matthews, Leslie G. "Italian Charlatans in England," *Pharmaceutical Historian* 9 (1979): 2-5.

_____. *The Royal Apothecaries*. London: Wellcome Institute, 1967.

McCoy, F. N. *Robert Baillie and the Second Scots Reformation*. Berkeley: University of California Press, 1974.

McCusker, J. J. *Money and Exchange in Europe and America, 1600-1715*. Chapel Hill: University of North Carolina Press, 1978.

McDowall, *History of the Burgh of Dumfries*. Yorkshire: E.P. Publishers, 1972.

McMahon, Marie P. *The Radical Whigs, John Trenchard and Thomas Gordon*. Lanham MD: University Press of America, 1990.

Melville, Lewis. *Lady Suffolk and Her Circle*. Boston: Houghton Mifflin, 1924.

Mendelson, Sara Heller. *The Mental World of Stuart Women*. Amherst MA: University of Massachusetts Press, 1987.

Miller, John. *Bourbon and Stuart: Kings and Kingship in France and England*. New York: Franklin and Watts, 1987.

____. *James II: A Study in Kingship*. East Sussex, UK: Wayland Publishing, 1978.

____. *Popery and Politics in England 1660-1688*. Cambridge: Cambridge University Press, 1973.

Monod, Paul Kleber. *Jacobitism and the English People, 1688-1788*. Cambridge: Cambridge University Press, 1989.

Morrill, John. "The Later Stuarts: A Glorious Restoration?," *History Today* 38 (July 1988): 8-17.

Munk, William. *Roll of the Royal College of Physicians*. 2 Volumes. London: Longman, Green, and Roberts, 1861.

Nutton, Vivian. ed. *Medicine at the Courts of Europe 1500-1837*. London: Routledge, 1990.

Okie, Laird. *Augustan Historical Writing*. Lanham, MD: University Press of America, 1991.

Olson, Alison. "Coffee House Lobbying," *History Today* 41 (Jan. 1991): 35-42.

Pearl, Valerie. "Change and Stability in Seventeenth-Century London." In *The Tudor and Stuart Town*, edited by Jonathan Barry. London: Longman, 1990.

Pelzer, John and Linda Pelzer. "The Coffee Houses of Augustan London," *History Today* 32 (Oct. 1982): 40-48.

Phillipson, Nicholas. "The Scottish Enlightenment," in *The Enlightenment in National Context*. Edited by Roy Porter and Mikulas Teich. Cambridge: Cambridge University Press, 1981.

Piggott, Stuart. *Ancient Britons and the Antiquarian Imagination*. London: Thames and Hudson, 1989.

Plant, Marjorie. *The English Book Trade*. 3d ed. London: George Allen and Unwin, 1974.

Plomer, Henry. *Dictionary of the Printers and Booksellers Who Were at Work in England, Scotland and Ireland from 1688-1725*. Oxford: The Bibliographic Society, 1968.

Plumb, J. H. *The Growth of Political Stability 1675-1725*. New York: Macmillan, 1967.

Pollock, Linda. *Forgotten Children: Parent-Child Relations in England, 1500-1800*. New York: Cambridge University Press, 1983.

Porter, Dorothy and Roy Porter, eds. *Doctors, Politics and Society: Historical Essays*. Amsterdam: Rodopi, 1993.

Porter, Roy. *London: A Social History*. Cambridge MA: Harvard University Press, 1995.

Poynter, F. N. L., ed. *The Evolution of Medical Education in Britain*. London: Pitman Medical Publishing Company, 1966.

Pyarali, Rattansi. "Paracelsus and the Puritan Revolution," *Ambix* 11 (1963):24-32; 12 (1964): 1-23.

Raven, James, Helen Small, and Naomi Tadmore, eds. *The Practice and Representation of Reading in England*. Cambridge: Cambridge University Press, 1996.

Realey, Charles Bechdolt. "The London Journal and Its Authors," *Bulletin of the University of Kansas Humanistic Studies* 5, no. 3 (1935).

Riley, P. W. J. *King William and the Scottish Politicians*. Edinburgh: John Donald Publishers, 1979.

_____. *The Union of England and Scotland*. Manchester: Manchester University Press, 1978.

Robbins, Caroline. *The Eighteenth Century Commonwealthman*. New York: Atheneum, 1968.

Robinson, Edward. *The Early English Coffee House*. Christchurch, Dorset: Dolphin Press, 1972.

Sachse, William L. "The Mob and the Revolution of 1688," *Journal of British Studies* 4 (1964): 23-40.

Sainty, J.C. and R.O. Bucholz. *Officials of the Royal Household 1660-1837*, Part I: Department of the Lord Chamberlain and Associated Offices. London: University of London, 1997.

Schwoerer, Lois G. "Propaganda in the Revolution of 1688-89," *American Historical Review* 82 (1977): 843-874.

Scott, Hew. *Fasti Ecclesiae Scoticanae: The Succession of Ministers in the Parish Churches of Scotland*. 3 Volumes. Edinburgh: William Paterson, 1867.

Sharpe, Kevin. "Religion, Rhetoric, and Revolution in Seventeenth Century England," *Huntington Library Quarterly* 57 (1994): 255-300.

Sibbald, Robert. *History, Ancient and Modern, of the Sheriffdoms of Fife and Kinross*. London: n.p., 1804.

Smith, R. W. Innes. *English-Speaking Students of Medicine at the University of Leyden*. Edinburgh: Oliver and Boyd, 1932.

Smout, T. C. *Scottish Trade on the Eve of Union*. Edinburgh, Oliver and Boyd, 1963.

Sommerville, C. John. *The News Revolution in England*. New York: Oxford University Press, 1996.

____. *The Secularization of Early Modern England*. Oxford: Oxford University Press, 1992.

Speck, William A. *Reluctant Revolutionaries*. Oxford: Oxford University Press, 1988.

Staley, Vernon. "The Commemoration of King Charles the Martyr." In *Liturgical Studies*. London: Longmans, Green, 1907.

Statt, Daniel. *Foreigners and Englishmen*. Newark, DE: University of Delaware Press, 1995.

Stephan, Deborah. "Laurence Echard: Whig Historian," *Historical Journal* 32 (1989): 843-867.

Stone, Lawrence. *The Family, Sex and Marriage in England 1500-1800*. New York: Harper and Row, 1977.

Stewart, Byron S. "The Cult of the Royal Martyr," *Church History* 38 (1969): 175-187.

Sulloway, Frank. *Born to Rebel: Birth Order, Family Dynamics, and Creative Lives*. New York: Pantheon, 1996.

Sundstrom, Roy. *Sidney Godolphin*. Newark DE: University of Delaware Press, 1992.

Szechi, Daniel. "The Jacobite Revolution Settlement, 1689-1696," *English Historical Review* 108 (1993): 610-628.

Traskey, J. P. *Milton Abbey*. Tisbury, Wiltshire: Compton Press, 1978.

Treadwell, Michael. "Lists of Master Printers: The Size of the London Printing Trade, 1637-1723." In *Aspects of Printing*, edited by Robin Myers and Michael Harris. Gosport, Hampshire: Oxford Polytechnic Press, 1987.

Trevelyan, George M. *England under the Stuarts*. London: Methuen, 1904.

Trevor-Roper, Hugh. *The European Witch-Craze*. New York: Harper and Row, 1969.

____. *Religion, the Reformation and Social Change*. London: Macmillan, 1972.

Turchetti, Mario. "Religious Concord and Political Tolerance in Sixteenth- and Seventeenth-Century France," *Sixteenth Century Journal* 22 (1991): 15-26.

van der Zee, Henri and Barbara. *William and Mary*. New York: Alfred A. Knopf, 1973.

Veitch, Andrew. *Richard Cameron: Lion of the Covenant*. London: Pickering and Inglish, 1948.

Walker, Patrick. *Six Saints of the Covenant*. London: Hodder and Stoughton, 1901.

Walker, R. B. "The Newspaper Press in the Reign of William III," *Historical Journal* 17 (1974): 691-709.

Walsh, Elizabeth., et al. *Yesterday's News: Seventeenth Century English Broadsides and Newsbooks*. Washington DC: Folger Library, 1996.

Weatherill, Lorna. *Consumer Behavior and Material Culture in Britain, 1660-1760*. London: Routledge, 1988.

Webster, Charles, *The Great Instauration: Science, Medicine and Reform in England, 1626-1660*. New York: Holmes and Meier, 1976.

Weinreb, Ben and Christopher Hibbert, eds. *The London Encyclopedia*. Bethesda, MD: Adler and Adler, 1986.

Williamson, Arthur. *Scottish National Consciousness in the Age of James VI*. Edinburgh: John Donald, 1979.

Wilson, Charles. "1688 and the Historians," *History Today* 38 (July 1988): 3-7.

Wilson, Kathleen. "Inventing Revolution: 1688 and Eighteenth-Century Popular Politics," *Journal of British Studies* 28 (1989): 349-387.

Wodrow, Robert. *The History of the Sufferings of the Church of Scotland from the Restoration to the Revolution*. 4 Volumes. Glasgow: Blackie and Sons, 1836.

Wood, Paul. "The Scientific Revolution in Scotland," in *The Scientific Revolution in National Context*. Edited by Roy Porter and Mikulas Teich. New York: Cambridge University Press, 1992.

Woolf, D. R. *The Idea of History in Early Stuart England*. Toronto: University of Toronto Press, 1990.

Yonge, James. *The Journal of James Yonge*. Edited by F.N.L. Poynter. Hamden CT: Archon Books, 1963.

Young, Douglas. *St. Andrews: Town and Gown, Royal and Ancient*. London: Cassell, 1969.

Young, Elizabeth and Wayland Young. *London's Churches*. Topsfield, MA: Salem House, 1986.

Zook, Melinda. "Early Whig Ideology, Ancient Constitutionalism, and the Reverend Samuel Johnson," *Journal of British Studies* 32 (1993): 139-166.

Index